Famine Pots

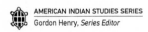

Famine Pots

The Choctaw–Irish Gift Exchange, 1847–Present

EDITED BY LeAnne Howe and Padraig Kirwan

MICHIGAN STATE UNIVERSITY PRESS | *East Lansing*

♾ The paper used in this publication meets the minimum requirements of
ANSI/NISO Z39.48-1992 (R 1997) (Permanence of Paper).

Michigan State University Press
East Lansing, Michigan 48823-5245

LIBRARY OF CONGRESS CATALOGING-IN-PUBLICATION DATA
Names: Howe, LeAnne, editor. | Kirwan, Padraig, editor.
Title: Famine pots : the Choctaw-Irish gift exchange, 1847–present / edited by LeAnne Howe and Padraig Kirwan.
Other titles: American Indian studies series.
Description: East Lansing : Michigan State University Press, [2020] |
Series: American Indian studies series | Includes bibliographical references and index.
Identifiers: LCCN 2019043638 | ISBN 978-1-61186-369-7 (paperback) | ISBN 978-1-60917-643-3 (PDF)
| ISBN 978-1-62895-404-3 (ePub) | ISBN 978-1-62896-405-9 (Kindle)
Subjects: LCSH: Choctaw Indians—History—19th century. | Food relief—United States—History—
19th century. | Food relief—Ireland—History—19th century. | Ireland—History—Famine, 1845-1852.
Classification: LCC E99.C8 F36 2020 | DDC 976.004/97387—dc23
LC record available at https://lccn.loc.gov/2019043638

Book design by Charlie Sharp, Sharp Designs, East Lansing, Michigan
Cover design by Erin Kirk
Front cover: Photograph of a famine pot taken at the National Famine Museum
at Strokestown Park. Copyright © 2019 Eunan Sweeny. *Back cover:* "Choctaw Food:
Remembering the Land, Rekindling Ancient Knowledge," 2019, by Ian Thompson, Choctaw Print.

Michigan State University Press is a member of the Green Press Initiative and is committed to developing
and encouraging ecologically responsible publishing practices. For more information about the Green
Press Initiative and the use of recycled paper in book publishing, please visit www.greenpressinitiative.org.

Visit Michigan State University Press at *www.msupress.org*

For Jim, and for Marion.

• • •

Hatak okla hut okchaya bilia hoh-illi-bila.
Maireann croí éadrom i bhfad.

Contents

Acknowledgments

Many people were important in our research for *Famine Pots: The Choctaw–Irish Gift Exchange, 1847–Present*. We thank and acknowledge the following people and organizations for their support: the University of Georgia's Willson Center for the Arts and Humanities; Nicholas Allen, director of the Willson Center; and Winnie Smith, program coordinator at the Willson Center. Our thanks to other UGA professors who helped make the 2015 event a success: Jace Weaver, John Lowe, Channette Romero, and Magdalena Zurawski. Our thanks to Ian Thompson for the use of his "Choctaw Corn Soup." We are grateful to Chadwick Allen, associate vice provost, professor of English at University of Washington, for suggesting *Famine Pots* as a title to show that both nations, the Irish and the Choctaws, experienced terrible hardships involving famines.

We greatly appreciated the assistance provided by Deirdre Nally, Office of the President, Áras an Uachtaráin, and wish to thank her for liaising with us regarding President Michael D. Higgins's foreword, which appears at the front of this collection. We also thank the former consulate general of Ireland, Paul Gleeson of the Irish Consulate in Atlanta, for his presentation at our 2015 UGA event. We wish him well in his new post as Ireland's ambassador to Chile. Tracy McKaughan, special assistant to the chief at Choctaw Nation of Oklahoma, provided us with assistance along the way, and we would like to express our gratitude for her help.

The Department of English and Comparative Literature, Goldsmiths, hosted a lecture in 2016 that focused on the gift, and we would like to thank Professor Lucia Boldrini, who was then head of department, for her support and encouragement around that time.

The London Irish Centre continues to be a site of hospitality, one that welcomes people and new conversations; our special thanks to Gary Dunne for helping to organize a public lecture about the Choctaw-Irish connection in 2016.

Our thanks to the musical genius of director Stephen Gardner and singer Ellen Demos, and all the musicians who performed the libretto of *Singing Still* at the National Famine Museum at Strokestown Park, Ireland, on May 22, 2019. We thank Mark McGowan, University of Toronto; Christine Kinealy, Ireland's Great Hunger Institute at Quinnipiac University; and John O'Driscoll and Martin Fagan at the National Famine Museum at Strokestown Park, for their generous and wide-ranging discussions at the Strokestown Park event in May 2019. Many thanks also to photographer Eunan Sweeney and to Martin Fagan, archivist at Strokestown House, for providing the image that appears on the front cover of this book. Alex Pentek, the artist responsible for the stunning sculpture *Kindred Spirits*—which is installed in Bailic Park, Midleton, Ireland—generously took the time to speak to us about the conception of his work and his sense of the installation's meaning; we are most grateful to him for that.

We would be remiss not to thank the friendship and Irish hospitality of the following: Caroilin Callery of the Irish Heritage Trust and the National Famine Museum; Jason King, Irish Heritage Trust and the National Famine Museum; and the 2019 Famine Walkers who traced the National Famine Way along rural Roscommon roads and through Counties Longford, Westmeath, Meath, and Kildare before arriving in Dublin.

We wish to extend our sincerest thanks to the team at Michigan State University Press, especially Professor Gordon Henry, editor of the American Indian Studies Series, and Julie Loehr, senior acquisitions editor, and all the wonderful editorial staff. Without their vision and support, this book would not have been possible.

As editors, we took a winding road through three nations to grasp the enormity of the 1847 gift and the lasting friendships it has left us. We would like to express our profound thanks to Gary Batton, chief of the Choctaw Nation, and to Michael D. Higgins, the president of Ireland, for their insights and belief in the people.

Here we recognize the spirits of the Choctaw people and the Irish people and their guidance upon which we relied to complete our journey. There are still roads ahead; may we remember to be generous.

A Word from the President of Ireland

Michael D. Higgins

During the year 1847, the people of Ireland were the beneficiaries of an extraordinary act of solidarity, generosity, and empathy. It came in the form of a $172 donation to the Irish Famine Relief Fund from the Choctaw Nation, a Native American tribe living in the South Central United States. The Choctaw Nation had, just sixteen years earlier, suffered their forced removal from Mississippi to what is now known as Southern Oklahoma—a cruel and harrowing experience during which many, including a significant number of young children, died from disease, starvation, and extreme cold.

There are no better words to convey both the harsh experience of dislocation and the kind and generous spirit of the Choctaw Nation than those written in a "Letter to the American People" by George W. Harkins, a mixed-heritage Choctaw leader, who wrote in 1831, on the eve of the first wave of displacement:

> We go forth sorrowful, knowing that wrong has been done. Will you extend to us your sympathizing regards until all traces of disagreeable oppositions are obliterated, and we again shall have confidence in the professions of our white brethren. Here is the land of our progenitors, and here are their bones; they left them as a

sacred deposit, and we have been compelled to venerate its trust; it is dear to us, yet we cannot stay.... Let me again ask you to regard us with feelings of kindness.

Those are profoundly moving words from an impoverished people willing, even at a time of despair, to reach out to another impoverished people. The money which the survivors of that traumatic event managed to gather together was badly needed for food and clothes and proper shelter for themselves. The Choctaw Nation, however, decided to give their money to an Ireland in the throes of famine, a gesture of commonality that is as remarkable as it is moving.

Historians and researchers differ as to the exact amount the Choctaw people gathered, whether it was $170 or $710—both sums being, in any case, extremely sizable, and equivalent to thousands of dollars today. The specific amount sent by the Choctaw is not, however, what matters. People gave what they could give. What really matters is the act of giving, and the truly extraordinary nature of the gesture of solidarity extended by the Choctaw people to another people living thousands of miles away.

That profound act of kindness and charity would become the foundation on which a great friendship between our two nations would be built and strengthened—a friendship which continues today and was recently marked by the unveiling in County Cork of a beautiful sculpture commemorating the generosity of the Choctaw Nation. Today, as we stand at a critical and greatly challenging moment in world history, that simple gesture of solidarity by the Choctaw Nation speaks profoundly to modern-day Ireland as to how we should embrace our responsibilities as global citizens.

This contemporary moment calls on us to make a fresh commitment to the universality of human rights and to the common humanity of all. Ireland has a lengthy history of humanitarian engagement, strongly influenced by our experiences of famine and of emigration. Our humanitarian action is therefore shaped in many ways by a tragic history, but it is rooted in values that remain relevant in a contemporary world—solidarity, community, democracy, justice, freedom, and respect for human rights and equality. They are values which must continue to guide us as we navigate our future direction as citizens of an interconnected world.

No humanitarian crisis, no incidents of mass displacement, happens in isolation. Such crises call for a profound understanding of—and empathy across—our shared humanity. The present crisis of displacement cannot be viewed as a regional concern, outside of our responsibility as global citizens.

To choose short-term and short-sighted responses based on a narrow sense of national self-interest would be, for humanity in general and our shared future, nothing short of disastrous. It is undeniably a global issue which is directly and primarily concerned with the protection of human rights.

A shared humanity is what connected the Choctaw and the Irish people across the Atlantic Ocean. That bond of humanity is what we have in common, what we share with other peoples in the world, and what encourages us, today again, to reach out to countries who suffer from extreme poverty and hunger, and those who must leave their homeland and seek refuge from persecution or war.

The act of generosity by the Choctaw Nation was a remarkable one. It was a gesture of compassion for strangers, a gesture of solidarity with a land they did not know, and a reaching out across oceans and borders to a people who were suffering and in great need.

As we stand at this critical moment in world history, facing not only a series of tests and choices that will determine the fate of millions of our fellow global citizens now, but also tests and choices that will define the future of our planet, let us meet these challenges with such a generous vision as will allow us to see beyond our own immediate needs and to recognize the human dignity of those who suffer in countries across the world. The language of justice and humanity, spoken so eloquently by the Choctaw Nation many years ago, still echoes across the decades that separate us from that moment of extraordinary generosity. It is a language we must listen to carefully as we seek to play our part in an increasingly complex and interconnected world.

The most vulnerable people on our fragile planet require us to stand in solidarity with them and to speak in unity for a better and more secure world. They deserve no less.

Irish President Michael D. Higgins and his wife Sabina, pictured with Chief Batton, seated right front, and representatives of the Choctaw Nation, and Padraig Kirwan, standing far right, at Áras an Uachtaráin on June 20, 2017.

A Word from the Chief of the Choctaw Nation of Oklahoma

Gary Batton

Astory of a selfless act to a nation four thousand miles away has always been close to my heart. *Famine Pots: The Choctaw–Irish Gift Exchange, 1847–Present* is a collection of essays inspired by the gift of hope sent to Ireland by the Choctaw Nation and the bond that still exists between the two nations. The contributors—four Choctaw and four Irish—not only cover the historical facts of the donation; they also describe what it means to them.

The donation was relatively small. It was dollars and change gathered by a group of Choctaw people who had been reduced by thousands as they were displaced from their homeland a few years before they heard of the Great Famine. They related to the loss of lives as few others could—they related to the loss of family. The amount sent from the Choctaw Nation to Ireland in 1847 was the difference between life and death for many.

Hunger, disease, and death influenced the paths of the Choctaw and the Irish. They traveled under horrible weather conditions, with barely any food and no one to help. The Trail of Tears had to still be strong in the memories of the Choctaw people when they made the donation. They knew too well what the Great Famine was causing. It is beyond my imagination to grasp how terrible the conditions were—so terrible that the donation is legendary in Ireland.

Famine Pots: The Choctaw–Irish Gift Exchange, 1847–Present is a gift to us as well. It carries on the link between our nations—nations that have shared a similar history of tragedy, perseverance, and strength. We have a kindred spirit of caring for others, and I hope and believe we can make a positive difference in our people and in the world.

Introduction

The remarkable story of the gift sent by the Choctaw to the Irish in 1847 is one that is often told and remembered by people in both nations. *Famine Pots* came to life in the bid to honor that extraordinary gift, and to provide some context and consideration; it has long been our intention to examine what might be called the deep ecology of the relationship between the Choctaw and the Irish. We hope that this book initiates conversations and considerations, not least because we believe that this connection deserves further, sustained attention. We also know that there are many ways in which our stories, and even our ways of telling stories, are connected. Indeed, one has only to compare the tales told by contemporary Choctaw storytellers such as Tim Tingle and the late Greg Rodgers on one hand, and those narrated by the Irish *seanchaidh* Sean Henry and Eddie Lenihan on the other to see some distinct connections and similarities in both style and purpose. Intensely interested in the power of verbal art and in storytelling as a dynamic form, these performers continue the folk traditions found in both communities, and place modern audiences in contact with past contexts, historic events, personal and communal memories. It would appear to be no accident, then, that many of the stories told by Tingle and Henry, respectively, focus on the Trail of Tears and the Great Famine and do so as a means of recollecting, framing, and even embodying past histories and contemporary relationships to place, community, and language. Tingle argues in a 2011 TeachingBooks interview that those stories are very often about "dealing with loss and maintaining a positive, healthy outlook." In 1980 Henry recalled his time listening to tellers such as Farrell Lavelle from Achill, and, thereafter, weaving together stories of his grandmother's life and accounts of the famine as well as the Irish Rebellion in 1798.[1]

In thinking about the meandering and vital nature of stories, one of us has previously written about searching for the "unending connections [between] past, present and future" that occur within Choctaw storytelling.[2] The rhetorical space that is shaped by this type of connectedness essentially becomes the means through which "Native people created narratives that were histories and stories with the power to transform."[3] Chickasaw scholar Jodi Byrd has suggested that this is a metaphoric cosmos or worldview, one that "locates itself initially within the particularities of Chickasaw and Choctaw structures of relationality and governance, and from there it looks out toward a region, a hemisphere, to a world."[4] We believe that those "structures of relationality" simultaneously underpinned the Choctaw's recognition of the Irish in 1847 and created a context in which stories might be shared and a rhetorical space might be enlarged. We are also minded to believe that Henry's comment on story's function and form reveals the extent to which Irish storytellers often seek to work in a communally informed and textured way. The idea of looking beyond the self and telling shared stories is, if one thinks about it, common to both the Choctaw and the Irish. It is no accident, then, that the gift was sent, nor that it has lived on in the minds and the mouths of both communities.

The storied and emplotted spaces explored by Choctaw storytellers such as Tingle and Philip Carroll Morgan put us very much in mind of Seamus Heaney's "Bogland." That poem not only offers one of the most arresting, disruptive, and dexterous challenges to the notion of untamed, uncivilized land, but also shows that "the Irish land was never empty; it is saturated with layer upon layer of human history." Heaney's landscape, according to Marjorie Howes and Kevin O'Neill, "is embodied by the soft, shifting, ill-defined contours of the bog itself, a history whose uncertainties, present implications, and potential dangers are infinite."[5] Most important, however, is the reality that the landscape—and the poet's relationship with it—reflects not only the "disparate kinds of visual imagination, historical awareness, and political tradition" found in Ireland, but also a realization that the bog, the epitome of Irish homelands in many respects, might contain "Atlantic

seepage" and is "bottomless."[6] By summoning up a vision of the ancestors—"pio-
neers" moving "inwards and downwards," in Heaney's words—and by placing them
in their natural relationship with the bog, before then introducing the loaded image
of the Atlantic waters, the poem establishes a profoundly embodied sense of the
local before moving to the international. That sense of connectedness between a
specific landscape, story, and ancestry (in this case Irish) on one hand, and the wider
world on the other is surely a large part of what Byrd finds most momentous about
Howe's sense of "tribalography." Heaney, like the Choctaw ancestors, looked towards
"a region, [and] a hemisphere, to a world." This is hardly surprising; the very best
artists from our communities have a very particular notion of the manner in which
the local represents the universal. By the same token, there is more than an echo
of the beliefs that the Choctaw have about their relationship to the storytellers of
the past to be found in Eddie Lenihan's avowal that when he's telling a story, it's the
voice of those who have gone before: "their [sic] dead—but they're not dead! While
I'm telling their stories they're still alive. And it was the same from way before."[7]
The associative and connective strengths found within the stories told within our
communities ultimately become palimpsestic, with the remembering of local and
familial traditions informing the lived realities of today.[8]

Such narratological layering is, of course, informed by and reflective of the
prehistorical spiritual and landscape traditions of both the Choctaw and the
Irish. The tribe was among a number of ancient mound-building civilizations in
southeastern North America, and built mounds that continue to be revered sites.
Nanih Waiya, located in present-day Winston County, Mississippi, is the mound
that the tribe holds most sacred.[9] Although its exact age is unknown, the large
structure—which is forty feet high and has a base of approximately one acre in
size—probably dates from around 500 BC, and is central to the tribe's origin. In
one of the two creation stories told, the tribe—as well as the Cherokee, the Creek
(Muscogee), the Chickasaw, and the Seminole—emerged from Nanih Waiya, or the
"leaning hill." In another version of the story, the Choctaw are said to have traveled
from the American West, carrying the bones of the ancestors with them to their
new home. Once there, they interred the remains at Nanih Waiya, a site that had
spiritual, political, and ceremonial importance. It is hard not to be struck by the
similarities between the Choctaw site and the megalithic structures found in Brú
na Bóinne in Ireland, especially Newgrange, Knowth, and Dowth. Thought to date
from 3,200 BC, the largest of these Neolithic structures is, of course, to be found in
Newgrange. Thirty-nine feet high and also covering an acre of ground at its base, the

passage tomb at Newgrange consists of layers of stone and earth, and excavations there have proven without doubt that it was a burial chamber. The archaeologist Michael J. O'Kelly has gone so far as to suggest that the people who worshipped at Newgrange were part of a "cult of the dead."[10] Long since associated with Irish mythology, particularly the story cycles of Tuatha De Danann, which tell of the divine race that populated Ireland, the mounds found at Brú na Bóinne resonate not only with the physical structures found in Mississippi and Oklahoma, but with the palpable links between place and narrative too. Although the tales told in Choctaw country and Ireland are radically different, there is, perhaps, much about the way that the inhabitants of these storied landscapes think about their worlds, ancestors, and histories that can be compared. Recognition of those similarities, however fleeting and cursory, may have helped to shape the exchanges that have taken place between the tribe and the Irish to date.

Most crucial, perhaps, is the fact that those forms of exchange have endured. In May 1995 Mary Robinson became the first president of any country to visit the Choctaw Nation. While visiting the tribal complex in Durant, Oklahoma, President Robinson met with Chief Hollis Roberts and spoke about the nature and significance of the gift, telling those assembled:

> This gesture by the Choctaw people, coming at a time when Ireland was facing the greatest calamity in its history, was and is extraordinarily special. For Irish people in the generations since the Famine, this wonderful donation, and the enormous generosity of the Choctaw people, has been an important part of our folk memory. This gift, so much from those who could afford so little, has given the Choctaw people a unique and cherished place in Irish history, and in the imagination and hearts of our people.

Shortly afterwards, in 1996, she reminded those assembled at a White House state dinner in her honor that "we must ... [have] a sense of history," adding that the gift from the Choctaw "has never been forgotten in Ireland." Robinson's successor, President Mary McAleese, paid tribute to the gift on numerous occasions during her presidency. In 2002, while addressing the crowd at the official dedication of the Irish Hunger Memorial in New York, President McAleese noted that Ireland is "a first world nation with a third world memory." Whether consciously or unconsciously quoting Irish scholar Luke Gibbons, who made that very point in his 1998 essay "Ireland and the Colonization of Theory," the president's comment emanates from a similar impulse—the impulse to understand the present, and to map new futures, by charting the waters of our shared histories. On September 10, 2011, President McAleese recalled the circumstances surrounding the gift itself while speaking at National Famine Memorial Day, acknowledging "the Choctaw tribe of native American Indians who, in 1847, donated the equivalent of more than $100,000."[11] This story of the gift has inspired more than spoken references to transatlantic connection; in 2013, the town council in Midleton, County Cork, voted unanimously to launch a competition that would lead to its commissioning of a large public sculpture that would call to mind, honor, and recognize the tribe's generosity. That competition led to Alex Pentek's creation of *Kindred Spirits*, a public sculpture consisting of nine stainless-steel feathers that are twenty feet tall and arranged in a circle. The piece itself establishes various fields of interaction, and the feathers can be viewed from any number of perspectives, including: either inside or outside of the circle that they collectively create; with the estuary in the background (facing north); with land in the background (facing south). That north/south axis alone is capable, therefore, of summoning up either the long history of migration from Cobh (which the estuary runs past as it reaches the Irish Sea), on one hand, or the manner in which the donation arrived on Irish shores and was then distributed inland, throughout several parishes and locations, on the other hand. Ideally, it will be seen from both of those vantage points, as the majority of those visiting Bailic Park will move around, between, and through the individual feathers. By availing himself of the opportunity to mimic the natural curvature of eagle feathers, and placing them in a circle, Pentek appears to allude to the shape of a food bowl; to Choctaw traditions, especially the tribe's belief in feeding and giving; to the circular nature of the connection between the discrete geographical spaces; and, finally, the strength that is inherent in the structure's steel parts, and the delicateness of the feather. "I wanted to try and create a fusion," he told one of the editors in 2016, one "that would somehow visually symbolize the history of the famine and the Choctaw donation—the humanity and tenderness in such a terrible time, amidst the horror of what was going on Ireland, but also [what had happened] thirteen years previous during the Trail of Tears." As an artist, he says, some of the most exciting ideas arise out of the notion of "blurred boundaries and interconnectedness."[12]

Questioning Affinities

But it is not all plain sailing, of course. What has sometimes been forgotten in Ireland, at least to some extent, are the more disquieting images of Irishness in America: the unsettling truths that trouble what can, at times, be an overly easy affinity, and that disrupt exaggeratedly tidy alliances. Accordingly, historian Kevin Kenny has referred to the need to consider "earthier, more conflict ridden narrative[s]" about the "past."[13] As well as reflecting on the form of profound empathy that is apparent in an act such as the Choctaw gift, Irish authors, artists, and scholars are also pondering darker moments in our shared history too. Sebastian Barry's novel *Days without End*, for instance, considers the cruel acts that often grew out of the Irish immigrants' role in the settling of the United States. Set against the backdrop of some of the most calamitous events in nineteenth-century Irish and American history—the Great Famine, the Civil War, and Indian Removal—that novel is narrated by a "hunger knower" who fled the famine in Ireland only to find himself locked in war with the Oglala, and even taking "a strange pleasure from [an] attack" on one of the tribe's villages.[14] The inspiration for at least some of the moments found in Barry's fiction is surely the lives and times of figures such as General Philip Henry Sheridan (1831–88). Although we cannot be sure whether Sheridan was Irish or Irish American (he may have been born at the ancestral home in Killenkere, County Cavan; on board the boat that carried his Irish parents to the United States; or in Albany sometime afterwards), he rose to the rank of major general while fighting for the Union during the American Civil War. Having been promoted to lieutenant general and given control of the Military Division of the Missouri in 1869, Sheridan spent his later career waging vicious campaigns in the Plains throughout the 1870s. In his book *Phil Sheridan and His Army*, Paul Andrew Hutton recalls that Sheridan is reported to have spoken those enduring words: "The only good Indians I ever saw were dead" during a meeting with Comanche leader Toch-a-way at Fort Cobb in 1869.[15] Regardless of whether or not the story is apocryphal, Little Phil's hatred for indigenous peoples is well documented and certain. As a result, we must remember that moments of great generosity can be followed by moments of horror and avariciousness. Peter O'Neill's essay in this collection is a salient reminder of the fact that we must know the full story of our shared history. *All* settlers must acknowledge the debts that have been accrued; each of us is obliged to remember the need for reparations for all that was taken by force.

There are also amazingly complex moments of recognition that followed the gift. We might consider Éamon de Valera's visit to America in 1919, when he was graciously hosted by the Anishinaabeg at the Lac Courte Oreilles reservation. His apparent affinity with the tribe appears to reflect on the nuances of the experiences that they have lived through at the hands of colonial forces. De Valera's stirring address (which is quoted at length in the chapter by Padraig Kirwan) subsequently builds on the powerful sense of political and cultural solidarity that the gift symbolizes; his words drew on an easy and enduring connection between the Irish and the Anishinaabe. At the same time, however, Dev's speech possibly occluded some of the complications within that relationship; the murky dimensions of Irish American involvement in post-Revolution American nation-building go unmentioned. On many levels, then, the speech and the circumstances surrounding it are testimony to the intricate nature of the gift and its various meanings. On one hand, this visit to the Lac Courte Oreilles reservation could appear as an act of political theater that played to the gallery of international opinion in 1919; the War of Independence was raging in Ireland at that moment, and de Valera and others sought the recognition of Woodrow Wilson and other world leaders. Having failed to secure a meeting with Wilson, the Irishman subsequently turned to those who had so often been out of sight and out of favor with more powerful political forces within the United States. On the other hand, one might regard de Valera's move as instinctive and genuine, even if it was somewhat contrived and opportunistic; enough of a bond existed for him to make the trip. Most importantly, perhaps, the Anishinaabeg's reception of this somewhat desperate (if not comical) Irishman is proof not only of their generosity but of their decision to exercise their sovereign right to practice the fine art of diplomacy and welcome the leader of a foreign state (albeit it a state that was politically unrecognized by Wilson and others) to their tribal lands.

So, while the complications of the relationship between indigenous communities and the Irish (especially those who emigrated to the United States) should in no way diminish or tarnish the proud memory of the gift, or the enduring and deep friendship between the Choctaw and the Irish, they should be acknowledged as being part of the tapestry of stories that conjoin our people. Today, as in 1847, it is vital that we go beyond the glances that may reflect an instantaneous or undemanding, fleeting moment of recognition. As my fellow contributor Eamonn Wall—a fellow voyager on this journey of ours—has written, we must resist the "all too easy connections between Irish history and [Native American] history, between Wounded Knee and Vinegar Hill [the site where the United Irishmen were finally vanquished by English soldiers]." "It is true that they overlap," Wall argues, before concluding: "they are not the same and can never be honestly compared."[16] We must explore the overlap and the depths, but remember the limitations with doing so.

Just as it is important to acknowledge some of the more violent moments in the shared histories of the Irish and countless Native American tribes, it is also imperative that we recognize the problems associated with vain attempts by Irish people to connect with, reify, or—worse—appropriate aspects of indigenous spirituality, culture, or identity. Sadly, this still happens today; various New Age projects in Ireland, which describe themselves as sustainable living communities, have sought to provide a response to the deteriorating environmental conditions of the planet by "playing Indian" in both the Dublin and Wicklow Mountains, and elsewhere. One such community, not far from where one of the editors grew up, promises to lead newcomers in the "Way of the Goddess" via a number of shamanistic practices, including participation in sweat lodges. That community may believe that it is exploring the links between our cultures, but the fact remains that their bid to re-create ceremonies and spiritual practices that are not theirs is heartbreaking and deeply distressing to us. It is deceitful and dishonorable. This gift across borders and between nations must remind us too of the need to respect the cultural values, the spiritual beliefs, and the traditions of all communities. The appropriation of any of these amounts to nothing other than a disrespecting of the ancestors' generosity and legacy.

What *can* we do, we might ask, and what overlapping territory *is* there to be explored? What, in short, is the work that this project might do, and what are its prospects as well as its boundaries? Well, to our mind, the possible avenues for research are as exciting as they are plentiful. Borrowing from Wai Chee Dimock's account of "deep time," we might continue the study of what Sandra Manning and Andrew Taylor call a transatlantic "circuit of influence."[17] Jace Weaver's *Red Atlantic* and Peter O'Neill's coedited volume *The Black and Green Atlantic* have done this very well—thereby situating Irish and Choctaw presences within "far-flung temporal and spatial coordinates."[18] The existing scholarship has, in this regard, begun the task of examining the Choctaw and the Irish as "active agents," to borrow a term from Weaver.[19] It has also begun to explore the "differential positioning within emerging state formations of divergent kinds," as David Lloyd would have it.[20] As well as continuing the vital work of recontextualizing Native and Irish situatedness—in the Americas, Ireland, and globally—and as well as searching out what Michael Malouf describes as the cross-cultural political solidarities within overlapping diasporas, this project might also speak to who we are when we are at home.[21] As Jacki Thompson Rand's work on the politics of international aid has recently shown, our journeys abroad and our actions there radically shape our notion of who we are at home. As well as interpreting transatlanticism as a heuristic that affords us a clearer sense of patterns of movement and exchange, we might read the moment of contact—*or* the sending of the gift—as not only being crucial to cross-cultural synergy, but also being central to the definition of nationhood, cultural ideologies, Irishness, and indigenousness. We might focus on variously nuanced forms of acceptance: acceptance in the sense of *recognizing* another community's status within a territory and acknowledging its continuance even in the face of stark adversity; acceptance in terms of *reception* and being welcomed; acceptance in terms of the *approval* of honorable acts of selflessness and solidarity—acts that are emblematized by the $710; acceptance in terms of taking *receipt* of the $710. It is crucial to note too that the *Arkansas Intelligencer* reported $710 as being the actual amount that the Choctaw people collected and sent to Ireland (April 3, 1847). It has since been questioned whether the amount was $710 or $170. Here we must remind readers that the history of American Indians and their money has a long history of accounting discrepancies by the federal government, Indian traders, and land speculators. Reports of the amount sent to Ireland vary, and the contributors to this book have used three different figures as a result: $710, $170, and $174. The editors would prefer to use the $710 figure mentioned in the *Arkansas Intelligencer*. However, by referring to all three amounts we are consciously raising three points: we are acknowledging the discrepancy in the public and historical record; we are reminding readers that stories about the Choctaw and the Irish poor often included inaccuracies; and most importantly, we are underlining the simple fact that acts of giving and acceptance are the most important elements of this story. The dollar amount is not the key detail here. What is vital, however, are the various forms of recognition that now exist between the Choctaw and the Irish; these populations have a shared and common currency in more ways than one. Of course, this book is but one small part of it.

Accordingly, it is our hope that this book might allow us to focus on the potential for empathy and dialogue between culturally distinct but historically comparable communities; the importance of sharing and collective well-being; and the interstices between academic history, popular history, oral narrative, and historical fiction. Such a focus can, we believe, reveal moments of connection and reciprocity as well as the value and wider significance of such moments. We are intrigued by the possibility that the gift speaks to the conceptualization, realities, and recognition of distinct, discrete sovereignties; that it invites reflection on processes of cultural formation within Choctaw and Irish society alike, and throws some light, perhaps, on an abiding concern with spiritual and social identity(s); that it may facilitate a fuller understanding of the historical complexities that surrounded migration and movement in the colonial world; and, finally, that it may lead to a more fruitful consideration of the ways in which Irish studies, Native American studies, and Atlantic studies might be fruitfully drawn together through the very kind of conversation that this book hopes to both initiate and form a part of. It is possible to think of the gift in various contexts: the significance of the gift and its place within various precolonial, colonial, and (in the Irish context) postcolonial discourses; the scholarly means though which a deeper appreciation of the gift might become possible; potential avenues for investigation beyond this publication. We find ourselves simultaneously energized and challenged by the task of locating and examining what we refer to above as the "deep ecology" of the Choctaw donation to the people of Ireland. In the final event, the gift of $710 has profound consequences regarding the possible recognition of dynamic forms of Native-to-non-Native and nation-to-nation recognition; the vital role(s) that tribal peoples played—and continue to play—in shaping the global village; and the opportunities that arise out of processes of civic, cultural, and political engagement.

Each of the essays in this book is engaged with these questions and topics. Rather than provide a purely scholarly interpretation of both the circumstances surrounding the gift and the narratives that retell the powerful story of that gift, this collection aims to blend strictly academic commentary with more creative pieces that offer a response to the Choctaw/Irish relationship. Our ambition has been to provide readers with not only some of the particulars that we have discovered during our research, but also a sense of the oral history, the shared narrative, and the sense of personal and collective exhilaration that we have experienced while working on this book. Our contributions as editors, when taken together, are offered in the spirit of combining the investigation of historical sources with a slightly more imaginative speculation on the meaning of the gift. The ambition was to reveal new facts but also unfurl our growing sense of the gift's numerous relevancies. In short, as well as pondering what we already know, and adding to a specific field of knowledge, our chapters seek to prompt more questions, memories, and ideas from our readers and colleagues.

The opening chapter, "Recognition, Resilience, and Relief," provides an interpretation of the ways in which the gift demonstrates that the tribe was not only acknowledging the Irish and their plight, but was also relating to them. Here, Padraig Kirwan hopes to show that the recognition revealed in this moment came to be associated with the deep senses of empathy, connection, and appreciation as well as the form of political and cultural autonomy that was inherent in the sovereignty of both the Choctaw and the Irish. By closely examining the newspapers of the day, and by considering the analogies and synergies that the two communities often made and generated between them, he argues that the gift has become a powerful placeholder for both communities' pride in their own sense of charity, internationalism, resilience, and spirit.

Writer and Choctaw scholar Phillip Carroll Morgan shows in "Love Can Build a Bridge" how being "cooperative and forward-thinking" may have saved the Choctaws from annihilation from the U.S. government's Gatling guns that were used out west on American Indian tribes. Yet, forced removal nevertheless left the tribe crippled as a nation until 153 years later when they ratified a new constitution on June 9, 1984. Morgan explains, "In plain language, the Choctaws were promised that they could remain a self-governing people, with all the rights accruing to the citizens of their old and respected society." Of course this did not happen, and many Choctaws simply did not survive. "Precise record keeping," writes Morgan, "during this most chaotic transition period, which spanned two harsh winters and a cholera epidemic, was impossible, but the total population of the Choctaw Nation in 1830 is accurately estimated at 25,000. The (conservative) estimate of 2,500 Choctaws who died during the exodus from Mississippi means that at least one Choctaw of every ten died during the fall of 1831 through the winter of 1832–33. This figure does not include the six hundred men, women, and children who died in the epidemic after the Arkansas River flooded in 1833, during the Choctaws' second summer in Indian Territory."

Christine Kinealy's contribution, "An Ocean of Benevolence," provides much-needed and extremely welcome insight into the charitable efforts that were being made in the United States in 1846 and thereafter. Her work dexterously maps out the differentiated landscapes upon which news of the Irish Famine traveled; Kinealy helps us to gain an understanding of the involvement of protagonists such as the Quakers and the General Relief Committee of New York, thereby framing the Choctaw gift in a thoroughly useful way. In many respects, this chapter reminds us not only of the amounts dispersed, but far more importantly, of the motivations and the means that were behind each act of giving. It is impossible not to be haunted by the fact that the poorest often gave the most, as Kinealy reminds us.

Choctaw storyteller Tim Tingle, in "I Should Have Known," writes about his personal relationships with the Irish as an invited storyteller to Ireland. He writes of the many similarities between Irish and Choctaw peoples and their ways of surviving heartbreak and happiness. He says, "The strength and power of belief, of never allowing tragedy to rule your vision, is both Irish and Choctaw, and feeds families and individuals with a taste of hope. We also share an eerie understanding of life's arc—the expectation of tragedy. My grandmother warned us 'to see the world through Choctaw eyes only sometimes, when you are surrounded by family and friends.' Though the Trail of Tears and the Irish Famine are often ignored in our teachings, to avoid the pain they carry, we know that we are meant to endure sorrow, and we use whatever tools we can to light those tiny, flickering flames of joy."

In "Ima, Give," LeAnne Howe's essay makes clear that "giving" is a Choctaw cultural lifeway, one that was practiced with the French in the eighteenth century when rainfall and flooding wiped out the French settlement. She cites other modern examples of Choctaw giving such as the 2018 event when the Choctaw Nation came to the aid of another nation, the Standing Rock Sioux Tribe in North Dakota. The people of Standing Rock were protesting the Dakota Access Pipeline across waterways near the reservation. Tribal members from the Choctaw Nation brought firewood, sleeping bags, generators, propane heaters, tents, thousands of gallons of water, and other supplies to them in North Dakota.

In his consideration of Irish and Native American literary traditions and contemporary writing practice, Eamonn Wall seeks out some of the connections between the two. In particular, he examines some of the more significant ways in which writers from both communities meditate on, and write about, their relationship with place and with identity. In focusing on the work of the late Choctaw-Cherokee-Irish scholar Louis Owens, this chapter searches out the numerous—and, at times, nearly numinous—territories in which we explore and come to know what Owens once referred to as "our larger selves." Wall teases out the complexities of belonging via his treatment of indigenous and Irish literatures, and suggests that the analogous histories of the Choctaw and the Irish create moments of rich dialogue as well as moments of "negotiation, accommodation, and trade."

Jacki Thompson Rand's essay, "Reconciliation," considers the nineteenth-century newspaper accounts of the Choctaw donation to the Irish and international aid. She suggests the bias of these historical reports creates the impression that colonized Indians would give charity to the very same people that brutalized them. (After all, President Andrew Jackson's family had recently emigrated from Ireland.) Rand writes, "Subsequent Irish expressions of gratitude found in print and commemorative practice intimate a kind of political solidarity between two oppressed peoples upon whom colonial powers inflicted terrible traumas leading to land and population losses." This essay prompts us to acknowledge, and honor, the price that Choctaw diplomacy and charitableness came at. Rand also reminds us, affectingly and powerfully, of the opportunity for reconciliation and true understanding that the memory of gift brings to us all.

Peter O'Neill's "Famine Irish Catholics" also challenges readers with a sometimes thorny, but always necessary consideration of the vicissitudes and vagaries of the relationship between America's indigenous communities and the Irish—vicissitudes and vagaries that we may often shy away from if we refuse to consider the part that certain Irish immigrants played in nineteenth-century settlement. Like Rand's chapter, O'Neill's contribution unambiguously states that some of those fleeing *an Gorta Mór* (the Great Famine) became, over time, violent settlers. He recalls the fact that former subjugated Irish Catholics subsequently adopted vicious behavior during the process of what scholars describe as U.S. nation-building. Specifically, O'Neill offers a deft study of the sermons of Father James Chrysostom Bouchard, SJ, a Catholic priest of Lenni Lenape ancestry and hailing from the tribal homelands on the East Coast. In doing so, he suggests that leaders from indigenous and Irish communities sometimes found solidarity through anti-immigrant rhetoric and riots; ultimately, and somewhat controversially, he argues that neither group was impervious to the solidification of racial hierarchies in the nineteenth century, nor did the better angels always prevail.

Each of these interventions and contributions are interpolated—or, more properly, enriched—by the poetry of LeAnne Howe and the Irish poet Doireann Ní Ghríofa. In 2016 LeAnne and Doireann entered into a long and sustained conversation about the connections that exist between the Choctaw and the Irish. While considering various aspects of those links, these two poets have turned to the dynamic nature of language, and have pondered the enduring nature of ancestral voices and languages. The poems offered in this book form a part of the ongoing conversation between the Choctaw and the Irish, and comprise, in Ní Ghríofa's words, "a call and response." It is surely worth quoting her description of this collaboration at some length, since it is a salient reminder of the work that this collection aims to do:

Over many months, we wrote poetry that became a collaborative pamphlet in "call and response" mode. It is, in many ways, a conversation across the Atlantic, across cultures, and across time. In other ways, it is a song. As LeAnne says, these are "poems dedicated to our ancestors, the Irish and the Choctaws who lived and died through the hunger years, suffering at the hands of colonialism." The poems themselves are trilingual, allowing English to form a bridge between our own native languages.[22]

We hope, along with Doireann and Phillip Carroll Morgan, that we can help to build that bridge.

Finally, there are numerous photographs of pots dispersed throughout the prose herein. Several of these images are of pots that have been found in Ireland and are often colloquially known as famine pots. Designed to hold sufficient food to cater for a large number of people at one time, these pots were often provided and stocked by charitable foundations and groups. They were often all that stood between life and death. They have a somewhat controversial place in history too; many commentators have accused religious missionaries of providing soup in return for promises of conversion. Others point out that these pots were sometimes placed at the workhouses that tenant farmers were herded towards in some famine-stricken parts of Ireland. One of the pots included was pictured at the famine cemetery at Bodyke, County Clare (courtesy of Mark McGowan and John McManus). Its position at a mass grave speaks volumes. However we interpret the story of these pots, the fact remains that their very existence reminds us of strife and endurance, hunger and charity, death and survival, want and plenty. They are a powerful emblem of the Great Famine. Meanwhile, the Choctaw bowls and pots that are pictured contain foods that might be deemed traditional staples of the tribes—*tofulla* or corn soup. Like the nourishment provided in the famine pots, *tofulla* was often made of simple, homegrown ingredients. The recipes for *tofulla, pashofa,* and *banaha* usually come out whenever certain occasions are imminent: family gatherings, birthdays, and reunions. *Pashofa*, in particular, is a dish that Choctaws *and* Chickasaws cooked in huge outdoor pots and then shared among those gathered. Also this special food is traditionally served when a healing *pashofa* dance takes place. Yet, those traditional foods have not always been associated with times of celebration; there have been moments in Choctaw history when one pot fed many who were on the brink of starvation and death too. Just as the Irish relied on the potato in the nineteenth century, the Choctaw were heavily dependent on corn as part of their staple diet. A drought in Indian Country in 1860 and an ensuing poor corn harvest in 1861 meant that many of the people within the Choctaw Nation went hungry.[23]

These pots, some of which are historical artifacts and some of which remain in use today, have a symbolic as well as a material significance. It is no coincidence that the artist Alex Pentek describes his enlivening sculpture *Kindred Spirits* as an arrangement of feathers that take the shape of a bowl or pot (it also resembles a cupped hand, possibly suggesting a hand of friendship). As we wrote our contributions for *Famine Pots*, we thought, more often than not, of the sustenance that these pots provided for our ancestors, and may continue to provide for us. We thought of the act of giving, of sharing meager rations, and of the moments when our people have relied on the help of others. We also thought of the moments that our people have been in a position to provide help to others. And we were called upon to remember the want and the privations felt by the Choctaw and the Irish, as only we could.

In any event, we hope that this book honors and endorses collective moments of recognition and acts of sharing, charity, and compassion.

NOTES

1. *Western Journal* (June 27, 1980): 25. It is important to note too, as Declan Kiberd has, that the "'seanchaí' told his story as if he himself had witnessed it" ("Story-Telling: The Gaelic Tradition," in *The Irish Short Story*, ed. Terence Brown and Patrick Rafroidi [Gerrards Cross, UK: Colin Smythe 1979], 15).

2. LeAnne Howe, "The Story of America: A Tribalography," in *Clearing a Path: Theorizing the Past in Native American Studies*, ed. Nancy Shoemaker (New York: Routledge, 2002), 29–48, 47.

3. LeAnne Howe, "Tribalography: The Power of Native Stories," *Journal of Dramatic Theory and Criticism* 14, no. 1 (Fall 1999): 117–26, 118.

4. Jodi Byrd, "Tribal 2.0: Digital Natives, Political Players, and the Power of Stories," *Studies in American Indian Literatures* 26, no. 2 (2014): 55–64, 56.

5. Marjorie Howes and Kevin O'Neill, "Introduction: Toward a History of the Irish Landscape," in *Éire/Land*, ed. Vera Kreilkamp (Chicago: University of Chicago Press, 2015), 13–26, 13.

6. Ibid., 15; Seamus Heaney, *Door into the Dark* (London: Faber and Faber, 1969), 56.

7. John S. Gentile, "Stories of the Otherworld: An Interview with Eddie Lenihan," *Storytelling, Self, Society* 5, no. 3 (2009): 152–75, 158.

8. Lenihan is keen to point out that "a person who knows a small area . . . can go back 300, 400 or 500 years," and recalls being astounded when a storyteller, in "2000 or 2002," pointed to an empty field and told him the name of the young girl who had babysat in a long-since vanished house that had stood there during the famine years. Interestingly, and standing in contrast to the type of knowledge that Lenihan describes, nontraditional storytellers (very often not from Ireland) have sought to assume or create an Irish or Celtic identity for themselves. In his essay "Celticity and Storyteller Identity: The Use and Misuse of Ethnicity to Develop a Storyteller's Sense of Self," Patrick Ryan has pointed out some of the ways in which these contemporary storytellers often perform a form of Celtic identity and imply "that everything 'Celtic' is also 'indigenous' or 'aboriginal'" (*Folklore* 117, no. 3 [December 2006]: 317). In considering the similarities between both the Choctaw and the Irish storytelling traditions, it is wise to in no way suggest that they are somehow intertwined, or amount to the same thing. At the same time, and somewhat ironically, it is possibly worth pointing out that a general propensity to treat identity and tradition in a reasonably superficial way has affected artists from both communities. Writers and storytellers from both cultures have been also disserved by those who choose to play at being Native or Irish, for either financial gain or perceived cultural esteem.

9. Several other mounds, such as Spiro Mounds in Oklahoma, are of great importance to the tribe too.

10. Michael J. O'Kelly, *Newgrange* (London: Thames and Hudson, 1982), 112.

11. *Irish Times*, September 12, 2011.

12. Alex Pentek, personal interview.

13. Kevin Kenny, "Taking Care of Irish Culture," *American Quarterly* 49, no. 4 (1997): 806–24, 809.

14. Sebastian Barry, *Days without End* (New York: Viking, 2017), 44, 32.

15. Paul Andrew Hutton, *Phil Sheridan and His Army* (Lincoln: University of Nebraska Press, 1985), 180.

16. Eamonn Wall, *From the Sin-é Café to the Black Hills* (Madison: University of Wisconsin Press, 1999), 123.

17. Wai Chee Dimock, "Deep Time: American Literature and World History," *American Literary History* 13, no. 4 (Winter 2001): 755–75, 759; Susan Manning and Andrew Taylor, eds., *Transatlantic Literary Studies: A Reader* (Edinburgh: Edinburgh University Press, 2007), 7.

18. Jace Weaver, *The Red Atlantic: American Indigenes and the Making of the Modern World, 1000–1927* (Chapel Hill: University of North Carolina Press, 2014); Peter D. O'Neill and David Lloyd, eds., *The Black and Green Atlantic: Cross-Currents of the African and Irish*

Diasporas (London: Palgrave Macmillan, 2009).

19. Weaver, *The Red Atlantic*, xi.

20. O'Neill and Lloyd, *The Black and Green Atlantic*, 3.

21. Ibid., 149.

22. This quotation appears on Doireann's website, and can be accessed at https://doireannnighriofa.wordpress.com/2017/07/11/singing-still-a-libretto-for-the-1847-choctaw-gift-to-the-irish-for-famine-relief.

23. Kevin Z. Sweeney, *Prelude to the Dust Bowl: Drought in the Nineteenth-Century Southern Plains* (Norman: University of Oklahoma Press, 2016), 98.

Famine Pots

Homeland

LeAnne Howe

n the beginning, some say the Choctaw people came up out of the mound at Nanih Waiya singing

Issa hal-a-li haa- toko Ik-sa illok isha shkee
Issa hal-a-li haa- toko Ik-sa illok isha shkee
Issa hal-a-li haa- toko Ik-sa illok isha shkee
Issa hal-a-li haa- toko Ik-sa illok isha shkee

Because you are holding onto me I am not dead yet.

NOTE

George Aaron Bardwell's spelling and translation of the line used here appears in *A Choctaw Reference Grammar* (Lincoln: University of Nebraska Press, 2006), 320. For an older spelling, see *Choctaw Hymns* (Ringold, OK: Native American Bible Academy, 1997), 93. I suggest the Choctaw phrase *Issa hal-a-li haa- toko Ik-sa illok isha shkee* may be a stanza from a mound song, an expressive artifact lying dormant in a nineteenth-century Choctaw hymn titled "Evening Song 93."

Recognition, Resilience, and Relief

The Meaning of Gift

Padraig Kirwan

> The manner of giving is worth more than the gift.
>
> —Pierre Corneille

I n the winter of 1847, as the people of Ireland were being struck by a devastating famine, members of the Choctaw Nation met in a small town in Indian Territory called Skullyville.[1] There, members of the tribe discussed the experiences of the Irish poor, and it was proposed that they would gather together what monies they could spare in the wake of their recent removal from their tribal homelands east of the Mississippi River. Ultimately, they collected $710, a sum roughly equivalent to $20,440 today.[2] Reports of this amount have been corroborated by several commentators, including Anelise Hanson Shrout and Mike Ward.[3] It is not possible to know what source(s) Ward is quoting, but he is possibly citing Carolyn Thomas Foreman's entry in the *Chronicles of Oklahoma*, in which Foreman writes:

> In 1847 a meeting was held at Skullyville where a collection of $710 was taken up for the relief of victims of the Potato Famine in Ireland. Agent William Armstrong

presided and contributions were made by traders, agency officials and missionaries, but the Indians gave the largest part of the money.[4]

He might also be referring to Angie Debo's famous historical work *The Rise and Fall of the Choctaw Republic.*[5] It is worth noting that a donation of $170 is often referred to (a figure approximately equivalent to $4,895 today). This smaller amount is the one mentioned by Irish historian Christine Kinealy in her work *Charity and the Great Hunger in Ireland: The Kindness of Strangers.*[6] It is also mentioned numerous times online and elsewhere: in an online article written for *Irish America*, Kinealy states that $174 was sent by the Choctaw, rather than $170; the *Irish Examiner* newspaper, meanwhile, has made reference to $179.[7] The disparity between $170 and $710 is hugely significant; it raises the question of whether or not a transcription error occurred, or, worse still, some of the monies were siphoned off during transit. The discrepancy certainly warrants further investigation. For now, it is fair to say that the amount in question was surely sizable. More importantly, the act of giving, and the form of international recognition that the gift symbolized, was of the greatest significance. Here I will refer to the $710 amount.

Rather than use what money they had to buy badly needed resources in the new territory—land, food, housing, and so on—the tribe made the altogether remarkable decision to send a goodly portion of their money to those who were starving and destitute in Ireland. Although the international dimension of this charitable aid is itself notable, it is the fact that the Choctaw themselves had endured displacement, poverty, and untold hardship that makes this donation particularly marvelous. Removed from their ancestral lands by state and governmental policies that supported and enabled not only white settlers' land claims in Georgia and Mississippi but also further and sustained encroachments into land west of the Mississippi River, the Choctaw tribe had suffered great losses in the early decades of the nineteenth century. Indeed, it "is difficult," as Hanson Shrout has recently noted, "to imagine a people less well-positioned to act philanthropically." The Choctaw—and the Cherokee, who also sent vitally important aid—"were unlikely donors" primarily because "both tribes had been forcibly removed from their lands in the Southeast only a decade earlier . . . [and] they had limited financial and emotional resources to share with distant sufferers."[8] This essay—much like the book that it appears in—aims to consider the broader contextual frameworks that informed this particularly affecting instance of generosity. It will examine a number of parallels within the cultural landscapes inhabited by the Irish and

Choctaw during the Great Irish Famine (1845–49). Accordingly, beyond presenting the Choctaw gift as something of a placeholder for intense acts of international, political, and cultural discernment in the nineteenth century, as Hanson Shrout so elegantly does, this essay will speak to various co-temporal (albeit not conterminous) points of connection between both communities in several sequential eras, including precolonial and twentieth-century ones. It will do so because it is surely worth considering whether those correlations may have influenced the Choctaw donors' decision to send aid in the first place, and whether they continue to shape or inform contemporary understandings of the gift's significance, be it in Ireland, in the Choctaw Nation, or further afield. Before considering wider cultural and political points of that particular connection, historically or in more recent times, it is, of course, constructive to momentarily reexamine the events in Ireland that both led to the 1847 donation and made it necessary.

Frightful Sufferings

In the years from 1845 to 1849, the worst famine that was to befall any Europe country in the nineteenth century hit the population of Ireland. The blight that decimated the potato crop in 1845 was a calamity of huge proportions, and the "Great Irish Famine killed at least 1 million people and led more than that number to emigrate."[9] It is perhaps ironic that the type of transatlantic exchange and movement that would, in time, facilitate and frame the remarkable connection between the Choctaw and the Irish was partly responsible for nineteenth-century Ireland's reliance on the potato. Although "potatoes were not seen by Europeans before 1532 when Pizarro first ascended the Andes of northern Peru at Cajamarca," the humble spud provided the Irish with a stable, nutritious, and relatively cheap crop; it traveled well from the high Andes to the damp Irish soil.[10] Potatoes also become a standard field crop throughout much of Europe during the eighteenth century, as John Reader has noted.[11] The potato was especially needed in Ireland during the nineteenth century, however. "By the 1830s," Kevin Whelan has reminded us, "three million 'potato people' relied on the tuber for more than 90 per cent of their calorie intake."[12] Broadly speaking, a number of factors led to that rather startling reliance on one single crop. These included both an increase in the number of tenant farmers existing at subsistence level during their bid to simultaneously pay their rent to the landlord and export cereals to England, and an increased rate of poverty among a growing population. The late J. E. Pomfret, writing in an earlier time (1930), once "thought it pointless to distinguish between 'farmer' or tenant and 'cottier,' as most landholders were miserably poor peasants."[13]

However one chooses to refer to my ancestors, it is undoubted that it was a grim moment of historical happenstance that served to deepen their connection with the American continent: the phytophthora strain of potato blight made its way across an ever-shrinking world and arrived in Ireland in 1845.[14] On one hand, Ireland was a part of a global network of trade and travel. On the other hand, it was seen as a world apart. That confluence precipitated both a shortage of food *and* some rather troubling responses to the ensuing famine. Although well-connected to the wider world in terms of commerce, enterprise, literature, and religion—sometimes tragically so, when one thinks of the blight that made its way across the Atlantic— the Irish were often viewed as a disparate and distinct people. Indeed, they were a race apart despite their country's geopolitical positionality and its proximity to the United Kingdom. Making the plight of these "poor peasants" all the more shocking is the fact that Ireland was not just next door to an increasingly wealthy and dominant Great Britain during the Victorian era, but that it was, of course, part of that same Union. Yet, so reviled were the Irish in some quarters that even those who fled the starving nation were sources of scorn and ignominy; reflecting (and perhaps forming) some of the racialized thinking of the day, Friedrich Engels cast aspersions on those who had left the island: "The worst dwellings are good enough for them; their clothing causes them little trouble, so long as it holds together by a single thread; shoes they know not," he wrote in *The Condition of the Working Class in England*. He went on to comment on that "race's" proclivity for the potato too (both boiled and distilled): "their food consists of potatoes and potatoes only; whatever they earn beyond these needs they spend upon drink."[15] Even if Engels's allegation regarding alcohol is somewhat mean-spirited, his comment on the spud is well-founded; Whelan's point above underlines the fact that during the first decades of the nineteenth century, more than a third of Ireland's population had become wholly reliant on a crop that had been brought to Europe by the conquistadors and then possibly passed along by the Spanish (in a poem written in 1750, titled "Cáth Bearna Chroise Brighde" [The Battle of the Gap of St. Bridget's Cross], Seán O'Neachtain referred to the potato as "An Spaineach Geal," which translates as "the kind-hearted Spaniard"). The sudden loss of this vital food source, along with the degree of governmental and administrative intransigence that followed, meant that a huge swath of the nation encountered untold hardship.

The story of *an Gorta Mór* is an appalling tale of death and depopulation, and it is an event that historians have sought to understand ever since. The bid to reach such understanding means that there have been numerous debates about the sources of that inequality, the political and social structures of Irish society during the nineteenth century. The legacy of English colonial practice in Ireland and British responses to the news of famine during that period has also come under increased scrutiny. Some commentators have argued, along rather Malthusian lines, that the Irish population had grown rapidly in the decades leading up to 1845, and was therefore likely to undergo a sharp reduction in numbers.[16] Others have provided altogether more sophisticated—and convincing—analyses of the complex connection between rising poverty levels, landlessness, inequality, and the blight that struck the potato in 1845 and 1846.[17] There now seems to be some consensus that a deadly mixture of "providentialism, stadialism and neoclassical economics" ultimately came to inform what has been described as the British state's "catastrophic failure" to tackle the causes of the Famine.[18] Regardless of how one seeks to parse historical events and political machinations, the simple fact remains that the population of Ireland declined from over 8 million people in 1846 to 6.6 million in 1851. Contemporary eyewitness accounts of the suffering are utterly shocking. Many readers will have encountered the testimony of William Forster, an English Quaker who visited Ireland in 1846 in order to survey the country's need for famine relief. Forster's agonized portrayal of children who "were like skeletons, their features sharpened with hunger and their limbs wasted, so that there was little left but bones" is known to many.[19] His account invites comparison with the depth of suffering outlined in another well-known piece—a letter that appeared in the *Times* on Christmas Eve, 1846. Penned by Nicholas Cummins, a justice of the peace from County Cork, that correspondence recounted the author's sense of complete dismay and mounting shock during a visit to the same town that Forster had gone to: Skibbereen. Cummins wrote of "scenes that . . . no tongue or pen can convey the slightest idea of," before attempting to convey to the reader a sense of the death and destruction that he had encountered:

In the first [cabin], six famished and ghastly skeletons, to all appearance dead, were huddled in a corner. . . . I approached in horror, and found by a low moaning they were alive. It is impossible to go through the detail. Suffice it to say, that in a few minutes I was surrounded by at least 200 of such phantoms, such frightful spectres as no words can describe. By far the greater number were delirious either from famine or from fever. Their demonic yells are still ringing in my ears, and their horrible images are fixed on my brain.[20]

Reporting on behalf of the *Illustrated London News*, the Irish artist James Mahony gave his own report of the unfathomable suffering that was being experienced in that town—and elsewhere—during the year that ultimately became known as "Black 47." On his travels Mahony witnessed, among other abominations, a "hut . . . surrounded by a rampart of human bones." "In this horrible den," he found "in the midst of a mass of human putrefaction, six individuals, males and females . . . were huddled together, as closely as were the dead in the graves around."[21] Ultimately, an amalgamation of events that would be deleterious and dangerous for any nation came to pass; famine, emigration, and delayed marriage almost certainly accounted for a halving of the Irish population between 1845 and 1911. The single detail that surpasses the dreadfulness of those facts is, perhaps, the stance taken by some members of the British civil service and members of Parliament during the crisis itself. As incoming assistant secretary to the Treasury in 1846, Sir Charles Trevelyan infamously adopted a laissez-faire approach that was dangerously allied with a zealous, evangelical Protestantism. "The great evil with which we have to contend is not the physical evil of the famine," he opined in December 1846, "but the moral evil of the selfish, perverse and turbulent character of the [Irish] people."[22]

Trevelyan was not the only man disdainful of what he saw as a rather dissolute reliance on government funding and support. In January 1846 the Duke of Cambridge supposed that "rotten potatoes and sea-weed, or even grass, properly mixed, afforded a very wholesome and nutritious food," before adding that "All knew that Irishmen could live upon anything and there was plenty grass in the field though the potato crop should fail."[23] Fortunately, not all commentators were quite as ruthless. Many international observers commented, impartially, on the worst of the privations, and both the consequences of the blight and the plight of the Irish people came to their attention.[24] Just as importantly, several reporters had actually warned of an imminent danger of famine a full decade earlier. In his diaries, Alexis de Tocqueville, the French sociologist and political theorist, foreshadowed the terrible sights that would be later seen by Forster, Cummins, and Mahony. In a letter to his mother in August 1835, de Tocqueville described his journey to Castlebar, in the west of Ireland. After traveling from "cabin to cabin," he wrote, solemnly, "[I found] a collection of misery such as I did not imagine existed in this world."[25]

In the context of this volume's greater project—the consideration of the connections between the Irish and the Choctaw—it is remarkable that de Tocqueville's assessment of the desolation that he found in Ireland was made in view of the deprivations that he had recently seen in America. There, by all accounts, the scarcity and hardship suffered by several tribes was similarly shocking.[26] In 1831, just four years before his trip to Ireland, de Tocqueville had witnessed very similar levels of anguish and distress when he observed "the frightful sufferings" that were the result of the "forced migrations" of the Choctaw in Memphis. What lay behind this mass movement of people was, according to Clara Sue Kidwell, the expansionist policy adopted by the U.S. government during the early years of the nineteenth century. To her mind, the "defeat of the British in the War of 1812" relieved "the threat of invasion [of the United States] by a foreign power" and "opened up new economic opportunities for trade along the Mississippi River."[27] The period between 1812 and 1831 subsequently saw a consolidation of, and increase in, governmental and state practices that hinged, by and large, upon the implementation of Thomas Jefferson's model of yeomanry and agrarianism. That model necessitated the removal of several tribes and the "freeing" of land; it is a long time since historian Russell Thornton reminded readers that "as many as 100,000 American Indians were removed from eastern homelands to locations west of the Mississippi River during the first half of the 19th century." "Most of this number," Thornton continues, "were members of five tribes: Cherokee, Chickasaw, Choctaw, Creek, and Seminole," and "most of the relocations occurred in the decade following passage of the United States Indian Removal Act of 1830."[28] It was against this backdrop that groups within the Choctaw tribe entered into successive treaties with the government. Agreements such as the Treaty of Doak's Stand (1821) and the Treaty of Dancing Rabbit Creek (1830) redrew land boundaries and radically rearranged all aspects of life for tribal communities, both for the hunters who lived west of the Mississippi River and for those farming east of it.[29] For instance, under the terms of the 1821 treaty, the tribe relinquished approximately six million acres on the western edge of the Choctaw Nation in exchange for approximately thirteen million acres in Arkansas Territory. Meanwhile, under the terms of the Treaty of Dancing Rabbit Creek, which was "formally acknowledged by only a small number of Choctaws," it was agreed that the tribe would "cede to the United States . . . [the] entire country they own and possess, east of the Mississippi River; and they agree to move beyond the Mississippi River, early as practicable."[30] What followed, then, was a period of unprecedented suffering in the history of the tribe, beginning with what one Choctaw chief—most likely Nitakechi—described as a "trail of tears and death."[31] So, although the treaties were, on the face of it, intended to guarantee the tribe's future, especially by shoring up land rights and territorial dominion, they were largely the result of governmental and military pressure.

Such was the extent of the Choctaw's misery that de Tocqueville feared, on some level, that he would be accused of "coloring the picture too highly" if he gave a full and frank report of it.[32] Indeed, even though he often adopted the loathsome parlance of the day and referred to the Choctaw as "savages" (showing some of the same racism that Engels had shown towards the Irish), the Frenchman seemed to be genuinely disturbed by the tribe's suffering; he was conscious of language's inability to fully capture or reflect the depth of the terrible torments he saw. Consequently, he professed to being concerned that he had been "witness of sufferings that [he had] not the power to portray."[33] Nevertheless, like Nicholas Cummins, he attempted to convey at least some sense of that anguish, writing:

> It was . . . the middle of winter, and the cold was unusually severe; the snow had frozen hard upon the ground, and the river was drifting huge masses of ice. The Indians had their families with them, and they brought in their train the wounded and the sick, with children newly born and old men upon the verge of death. They possessed neither tents nor wagons, but only their arms and some provisions. I saw them embark to pass the mighty river, and never will that solemn spectacle fade from my remembrance.[34]

The snow and freezing temperatures caused multiple deaths and appalling hardship in 1831, and it is estimated that six thousand Choctaw people died overall during removal—15 percent of the tribe's total population.[35] Decades later the historian H. B. Cushman would recall witnessing a similar "scene of despairing woe" in 1832 in Hebron, Mississippi. An outbreak of cholera also stalked the tribe that same year, and deaths were a daily occurrence. The journal of one S. T. Cross, who accompanied one group in his official capacity as "Assistant Agent Choctaw removal," recorded no less than eighteen deaths in the seventeen days between November 12 and November 29.[36] Cross escorted a group numbering (by his estimation) approximately "one thousand two hundred," and traveled to a designated meeting point—Ecore de Fabre—by way of the Ouachita River. Upon arrival at this juncture on the tribe's journey, he found that there was no transportation to bring the "emigrants" across the waterway, nor were there any agents on the far side to commence the next leg of the passage. In a letter written to General George Gibson, commissary general of subsistence, Cross subsequently recalled the haphazard and poorly thought-out circumstances in which the removals had taken place (February 9, 1832). Although there was undoubtedly a degree of infighting within military and governmental ranks—either because of a propensity to place blame elsewhere or to assume the worst of far-off, unsupervised officials—it is patently the case that the removal of the tribe's people was as chaotic as it was brutal.

A brief comparison of the accounts provided by William Forster, John Mahony Cushman, Cross, and others surely reveals the extent to which the horrors experienced in Mayo were, in many respects, analogous to those in Mississippi. Yet, it is the temporal and contextual framing provided by de Tocqueville's commentary that possibly provides the starkest analogy of all; these events were taking place within 48 months of each other, and were being witnessed by an international community of independent and mobile eyewitnesses. In this regard, it is possible to argue that the French diplomat's itinerary and recollections rather uniquely tie the stories about the Irish and the Choctaw together in the nineteenth century. Beyond this particular point of connection, there are countless other, no less complicated or affecting correlations. As we now know, an echo of the disastrous administrative bungling and the poor planning—if one can say that there was planning at all—that S. T. Cross sketches out in his letter to Washington can be heard in tales of catastrophic governmental blundering during the Irish Famine. In closing the soup kitchens after just six months, failing to prohibit the exportation of grain from Ireland, doing little to stem the tide of mass evictions, and paying miniscule wages to those working on public-works schemes (all in 1846–47), the British government essentially withdrew basic humanitarian aid from Ireland at the time when it was most needed.

It should also be noted that the closing of the soup kitchens was itself part and parcel of the complex paternalistic relationship that the British sought to cultivate with Ireland and other colonies.[37] On many levels, the imperialist rhetoric of benevolence often played a part in the justification of British colonial expansionism throughout the eighteenth and nineteenth centuries. The Irish, it was reckoned, were simply hopeless. In Britain a debate raged about which deficiency was the greater cause of the Irish people's misery; in response to the *Times*'s suggestion that the "Celtic stock" of Ireland's population would be much improved if alloyed with "Saxon enterprise, steadiness and industry," the writers at the *Protestant Magazine* felt compelled to argue that the Irish must be freed from much worse: "the shackles of Popery . . . and the iron bondage of superstition."[38] Regardless of which claim could have been said to prevail—be it genetic or spiritual deficiency that was worst—the inference was that the starving poor in Ireland were hungry either because of their indolence or because of their deference to a brutal, pious master. Neither condition suggested that the Irish were themselves capable of improving their lot. Deemed incapable of self-government, the colonies were, in the minds of many, in need of foreign rule and (in some cases) a degree of humanitarian aid. However, even the question of aid was not straightforward; if Ireland was given such charitable assistance, many nineteenth-century commentators argued, the people would continue to rely on the home nation and therefore fail to cultivate more-civilized cultural and material conditions. By opening soup kitchens for just six short months, the British government possibly only succeeded in highlighting the imperialist inclination towards interventionism *and* condescension. The provision of public relief efforts had other deleterious effects too; even those who recognized the humanity of the Irish and sought to view Irish affairs with a degree of fairness and noninterference were driven to recognize that the Irish Poor Law Act of 1838 had detrimentally affected the nation's economy. One such businessman was Vere Foster, a member of the Anglo-Irish gentry and founder of the Irish Pioneer Emigration Fund. For his part, he "did not think that there was an innate backwardness and primitiveness to Irish Catholics," but he *did* believe that the Poor Law Act had "created an artificial and poorly run market for Irish labor."[39] In Foster's case there was a genuine concern for both the health of the Irish economy and the condition of the people of Ireland. For many other landlords and politicians, Patrick Brantlinger explains, the joint forces of profitability and politicking meant that the good intentions associated with nineteenth-century philanthropy were quickly jettisoned once the Irish labor market had been damaged. Then (as now, some might argue) "the principles of political economy . . . overruled humanitarian intentions."[40] Hence, it is possible to argue that economic imperatives steadily and irrevocably diminished the British government's capacity for compassion and charity. We might also consider a more troubling possibility, however. That is that the rhetoric of benevolence—popular in the pre-famine years—was possibly adopted by countless British politicians and landowners who wished to appear compassionate outwardly, but who were concerned with what they deemed to be the realpolitik of Ireland. In that reading, the rhetoric of benevolence is simply a means of masking self-interest, and any ensuing altruism quickly disappears in response to difficult market conditions.[41]

We might find another crucial point of connection between British and American imperialism here, insofar as the expansion of both empire and nation relied heavily on nineteenth-century understandings of the doctrine of liberalism and the belief that all civilized individuals have the capacity for reason and self-government within a commercial society. The expansionist vision of President Andrew Jackson meant that he viewed capitalist development in much the same way that British philosophers and political economists such as John Stuart Mill saw market capitalism—as an enlightened and rational response both to the savage native's innate love of freedom, and to the types of obedience and enslavement found in less-developed, barbarous, and feudal societies. For Mill, only commercial society could produce "the material and cultural conditions that [would] enable individuals to realize their potential for freedom and self-government."[42] It is not difficult to see how, from a British perspective, mid-nineteenth-century Ireland—which lacked "Saxon enterprise, steadiness and industry" or was inhibited by "the shackles of Popery . . . and the iron bondage of superstition"—could be said to have much to gain from a rapidly accelerating and expanding commercial society. This was a form of benign imperialism—an imperialism that was not geared towards "political domination and economic exploitation," but was instead "a paternalistic practice of government that exports 'civilization' (e.g. modernization) in order to foster the improvement of native peoples."[43] Notably, that beguiling admixture of paternalism and commercialization is what drove American expansion in the nineteenth century too. According to Michael Paul Rogin, it was by removing the Choctaw and other tribes that Jackson effectively "liberated land from communal use and thrust it into the [contemporary] market."[44] Moreover, he did so after the fashion in which "European imperialism [had earlier] carried out primitive accumulation against" the indigenous population in several of the colonies. Whatever the base intention—paternalism or materialism—men like Jackson and directors of the British East India Company (Mill's employers) can be seen to have exploited market forces in order to establish colonial or imperial power. God featured too, of course. The providentialism that commonly informed the British relationship to Ireland appears to mirror, directly, the U.S. government's attitude toward the tribes. It is not difficult to see a great deal of similarity between Trevelyan's description of the famine as "a direct stroke of an all-wise and all-merciful Providence" and what Kidwell describes as the American government's "colonial evangelical impulse toward Indians."[45] Where Trevelyan viewed the famine as a "great opportunity" and an "effectual remedy" to the "social evil found in Ireland," Andrew Jackson, then president of the United States, described the 1830 Indian Removal Act as "generous," explaining that the tribes would "gradually ... through the influence of good counsels ... cast off their savage habits and become an interesting, civilized, and Christian community."[46] Those words clearly recall nineteenth-century religious and economic moralism. They also recall a pronouncement made in the *Times*, England's paper of record, in 1799, which stated: "Nothing can tend to humanize the barbarous Irish as a habitual intercourse with [Britain] ... and the opportunities of observing the civilized manners of those who are from [there.]"[47] Although not entirely transposable, attitudes towards the Irish and the Choctaw (and tribal communities in general) were certainly very alike.

Transatlantic Exchanges

Thus, it is not altogether surprising to learn that British and American processes of expansion and colonization often mirrored one another. Much has been written about this phenomenon. Yet, as Anelise Shrout has pointed out, less has been written about the extent to which members of various communities in Ireland and Indian Territory would have known about one another during the nineteenth century. Shrout's dexterously argued and cogent scholarship does an excellent job of glossing "the treatment of the Irish famine and famine philanthropy in the Indian press."[48] From an Irish perspective, even a cursory glance at the newspapers of the day will reveal a great deal of interest in, and coverage of, the tribes' lifestyles, political organization, and dealings with the U.S. government. Even if we take just one newspaper, Belfast's *News Letter*—the oldest English-language newspaper in Europe—we will find repeated references not only to American political life and culture, but also to indigenous issues. On February 28, 1804, the paper printed details of the Louisiana Purchase, including section 9 of the bill, which commented on President Jefferson's decision to force tribes residing east of the Mississippi to accept lands west of the river in exchange for territories ceded. That same organ, the title of which reflected the fact that the editors literally received packets of letters that contained news from far-off lands, also reported on the drawing of boundaries in the United States, noting, "The whole country eastward of the Mississippi is now cleared of its original proprietors, and an ample field is thereby open for the vast plans of colonization which are now projected by the American Government" (February 6, 1818).

In December of that same year, the *News Letter* reprinted President James Monroe's State of the Union address, in which he referred to ongoing "negotiations" with several of the tribes, including the Choctaw, and spoke of "cessions already made . . . [and which] have been obtained on conditions very satisfactory to the Indians" (December 29, 1818). The April 10, 1821, edition carries news of another of Monroe's speeches—although this time relegating the tribes to little more than a footnote—and the February 1, 1833, edition of the newspaper reprinted a report titled "Stewart's America," which gave an account of the "400,000 persons" deemed to be indigenous and living in Indian Territory. The latter gave an especially glowing account of lifestyle and practices of the Cherokee, who were described as "the most civilized of" the tribes.

To my mind, there are two particularly arresting details about the *News Letter*'s coverage of international and American affairs. Firstly, the regular appearance of detailed reports reflects the extent to which news from Indian Country frequently reached an Irish readership in the early years of the nineteenth century. Secondly, and perhaps more importantly, I would argue that the manner in which the news was presented and framed possibly comments on the complex political and cultural contexts that existed within Ireland and America at the time. In particular, it is worth noting that the paper's reporting of Indian Removal was largely uncritical of the U.S. government's stance. Moreover, it remained so during a period when the organ's editorial line changed fundamentally; while under the ownership of Frances Joy and his family, the *News Letter* had "welcomed the American and French revolutions" (and could therefore be said to support antigovernment, anti-British forces in Ireland), but it subsequently "became a [pro-government] bulwark of the unionist cause" after it was sold to a Scottish consortium in 1795.[49] In effect, a crucial shift from revolutionary republicanism to conservative unionism did little to affect what can only be described as a rather pragmatic assessment of the dislocation of America's "original proprietors."

This seems to raise some crucial points and questions. Evidently, above all else, tribal communities were presented as yielding, quite necessarily, to what were sold as vital and positive forces of change: namely, those heralded by the foundation of a new American republic. What might be less obvious, however, is why, exactly, an increasingly unionist *News Letter* might choose to continue uncritical coverage of the governmental policies adopted by the new republic—a country that Great Britain had so recently fought a war with. On some level, this esteem or regard of the nascent country might be read as an act of political expediency. Simply put, both the United States government and the unionists in Ireland were more concerned with the application of civilizing force and issues such as prosperity, enterprise, and religious values than they were with the plight of either the Choctaw or the disenfranchised Roman Catholics in Ireland. An implicit forbearance with American political and military expansionism may also reflect a shared appreciation of the economic and spiritual merits of colonization. Indeed, a certain degree of homogeneity appears to have existed within conservative political forces in Britain, America, and Northern Ireland; leaders within all three constituencies appeared to be devoted to finding the means through which to manage and suppress what they regarded as disruptive and disturbing portions of the populace. This last point seems to be borne out by the fact that the April 10, 1821, edition of the *News Letter* carried not only extensive coverage of Robert Peel's vociferous argument against the Catholic Emancipation Act, which he gave in Westminster, but also reprinted portions of U.S. President James Monroe's second inaugural address. Just as Peel believed that the move to allow Catholics to hold public office "would not produce tranquility" in Ireland, Monroe was keen to ameliorate "all future annoyance from powerful Indian tribes."[50] The reporting journalist also suggested that Monroe had made clear his intention to make some "improvements in the *system* hitherto pursued towards the Indian tribes" (emphasis added). A contemporary reader may well find a good deal of paternalism and self-interest in Peel's desire that the British government and the Anglican minority retain control in Ireland, and Monroe's bid to establish "civil government over" the tribes. Meanwhile, the February 1, 1833, edition of the *News Letter* features a bitingly acerbic satire of the Irish emancipationist Daniel O'Connell, which describes him as "Ireland's Mimber." The boisterous and somewhat bawdy ode establishes a kind of wild voraciousness that is then immediately associated with the men of the Roman Catholic Church and a shared love—or, rather, *lust*—for money. Notably, an in-depth treatment of the increased sophistication and progressiveness of one of the so-called "Five Civilized Tribes," the Cherokee, appears on that same page. Whether it is intentional or not, the account of the tribe's printing presses, judiciary, government, and civic orderliness looms over a highly unflattering account of O'Connell's "sweating" and "roaring" accomplices in Parliament. In short, the paper appears to condone and celebrate very particular forms of social enlightenment and progressiveness.

Biases of a slightly different, but no less difficult, nature are evident in the *Freeman's Journal*, a daily, four-page newspaper that was founded in Dublin in 1763. Although moderately nationalist at its inception, the *Journal* became closely allied with government forces in Dublin Castle, mainly as a result of the maneuverings of Francis Higgins, who acquired ownership in 1783. The newspaper became "a mouthpiece of rule from London, receiving subsidies for the publication of proclamations" under Higgins, who was colloquially known as "Sham Squire" and was an infamous informer and supporter of the British.[51] Containing very little Irish news, the *Journal* focused extensively on British and international affairs, and often carried reports from America. Most of these were unflattering to the tribes, and several were concerned with the Choctaw, the Chickasaw, and the Creek. On April 1, 1788, it covered the tale of a young man from the east of England who had infiltrated the Choctaw and Chickasaw tribes, and supplied "the savages . . . with warlike stores."[52] In 1791 information about the treaties being drawn up between the Cherokee and government ended with reference to "savage barbarity" and "deprivations on the frontier."[53] That pattern continued: on December 2, 1818, several columns were given over to a description of a group described as a "remnant of the hostile Creeks"; just under two months later, a full page was dedicated to a Department of State report of U.S.-Spanish relations following the War of 1812 and the Creek War of 1813–14.[54] In terms of editorial bias and an imperial or colonial rhetoric of benevolence, it seems extremely telling that an 1820 account of the admission of the state of Alabama into the union—an account that outlines the fact that "select committees were appointed on the subjects of improving the Indian tribes in the arts of civilized life"—appears alongside a notice for the eighth annual general meeting of the Society for Promoting the Education of the Poor of Ireland (other staples that appeared in the *Journal* too, of course: advertisements for the latest fashions, news of a planned quadrille ball, a long story about the Duke of Kent).[55] These column inches, abutting one another as they do, possibly speak volumes about the extent to which the British and U.S. governments viewed segments of the Irish and Native American populations as rowdy, primitive, and in need of governance.

Officially speaking, the majority of newspapers neither expressly condoned nor condemned the actions of either government; instead, the majority, patriot and unionist alike, adopted what Vincent Morley describes as a rather "staid" approach, and tended to cover international correspondence and official communiqués impartially.[56] That fact notwithstanding, it seems reasonable to presume that readers would have been tempted—and were sometimes very nearly invited—to make certain comparisons and deductions. Indeed, editors not only abridged original documents in many instances—thereby placing a particular emphasis on certain concerns that appeared within longer, very detailed parliamentary debates or presidential statements—but they also arranged the resulting articles in an altogether striking manner. Those with a vested interest in maintaining the Union between Great Britain and Ireland, or holding lands had one reading of the newspapers. Meanwhile, Irish nationalists had another. For instance, on February 5, 1803, the editor of *Finn's Leinster Journal* reprinted Thomas Jefferson's second annual message, which referred to the need to fund both "regular troops" and "militia" in order to preserve military order, and the need to continue with Choctaw removal.[57] Meanwhile, on the opposite page, a report from the General Sessions (the local courts in Ireland) noted that the chairman had sought more rigorous enforcement of the law in "every barony," and stated that this should be achieved through the holding of weekly sessions in each area. In the opening lines of that report, the author praised the chairman's condemnation of lawlessness.[58] On the face of it, the position of the second article appears to invite a comparison between the "tranquility" sought in the Rathkeale court and the "law [and] order" that Jefferson finds as a virtue in the new American republic. However, evaluation of the coverage of both speeches reveals a potentially complicated relationship between the state of affairs in both jurisdictions. On one level, it could be suggested that in these articles the Indians and the Irish were viewed as "unruly." On another level, however, Irish patriots may have found some grist for the mill by comparing the United States' civic values of the new republic and its government to those found in Britain and the colonies. That is, rather than focusing on Jefferson and the chairman, as well as their shared concern for harmony and peacefulness, nationalists in Ireland might have cited these two columns as proof of the fact that self-rule and republicanism was politically and legally superior (as well as preferable) to colonial rule; America was becoming more peaceful now that the tribes were given jurisdiction over their own lands (albeit lands that were not their original homelands), whereas Ireland continued to be unruly. And yet, whatever echo of popular sovereignty that the patriots might have found audible in the president's report on this new American liberty was, very possibly, drowned out by his description of the land newly acquired from the Choctaw Nation as "an outpost of the United States."[59] On the deepest level, Jefferson's description of a "distant land" that had been depopulated of its original inhabitants, and which he wished to populate with a "very respectable population," was not just an unsavory reminder of the earlier plantation of Northern Ireland, but it also created a contemporary, equally unsettling correspondence in which the U.S. government gave the impression of adopting the approach that Westminster and

Dublin Castle had taken for years. In effect, Jefferson was, quite simply, speaking of lands "beyond the pale."

It seems crucial, then, that the editorial commentary that frames and interpolates the speech delivered at the General Sessions may have implicitly connected the lot of the disenfranchised Catholic majority in Ireland with Jefferson's apparent "aloof distaste" for those whom he disregarded as citizens: the slaves and the indigenous population.[60] In what is a subtly sarcastic and disingenuous description, the journalist depicts the chairman's speech as "most excellent . . . temperate, judicious and enlightened." In equally telling fashion he adds a rider to the phrase "the learned Chairman bespeaks": "and we hope truly." He quickly goes on to finesse his point somewhat, adding, rather acerbically, that "neither respect for the Law and its natural consequence, general tranquility can be the boast of this country" until such time as "the wild and vulgar predilection for Military authority be abandoned, and the Constable's Staff put in place of the bayonet."[61] It is implied that those who have taken power after the dissolution of the Irish parliament (1800) are the ones figured here as being "wild and vulgar," not the general populace. It now seems more decisive that Jefferson's reliance on "militia" and "regular troops" arose largely out of his need to suppress the slave population and remove the tribes; the unemancipated Catholics of Ireland would surely have noticed a troubling correspondence in the application of military authority and the subjugation of the poor and the helpless—especially after the editorial had parsed the stories mentioned above and thereby provided a particular context in which to read them. Ultimately, then, the reader is helped to decipher what, or more specifically *who*, is the source of the "headlong and undiscriminating prejudice" that the inhabitants of County Limerick are subjected to; martial law, it is suggested, is a poor substitute for self-governance and the proper administration of justice. We see here the need for a form of readerly interpretation or decoding that is very similar to that outlined by Shrout. In her essay she quotes James Scott, who refers to the need to decipher these messages and "hidden transcripts."[62] Subtext is all important. Hence, even though the positioning of these articles might initially appear to suggest that in terms of law and order the United States and Great Britain are alike—benignly rational—it might also have served to remind readers that they are ultimately divergent in terms of the patriotic ideal. More importantly, in the Irish context a conterminous and considered reading of both pieces may well have jarred the reader's sensibilities even more; ultimately, both articles actually gesture towards the government's subjugation of a native population by armed force. Whatever doubts might exist in our minds about this being the central concern, both for the paper's publishers and the readership alike, are possibly assuaged by the forcefulness of the editorial line.

The robustness of such commentary continued on into the early decades of the nineteenth century, and the *Kerry Evening Post* carried a hard-hitting account of tribal mortality in April 1838. Significantly, it ran that report alongside news from the parliamentary debate on the Irish Poor Law. A column outlining the contents of a letter sent by a correspondent named Major Pilcher to one General William Clark, superintendent of Indian Affairs, described the "literal depopulat[ion]" that had occurred as a result of numerous outbreaks of smallpox amongst the Mandan, the Assiniboine, the Cree, the A'aninin, and the Sáhniš ("Dreadful Mortality amongst the North-West American Indians").[63] While explaining that the areas affected had become "one great graveyard" as a result of the epidemic, Pilcher provided a truly heartbreaking account of the fates of those who survived (an estimated one in fifty): "Most of ... [them] committed suicide, despairing, I suppose at the loss of friends, and the changes wrought by the disease in their persons—some by shooting, others by stabbing, and some by throwing themselves from the high precipices along the Missouri." Harrowing in the extreme, the *Post*'s short piece might be said to have chimed with the dreadful scenes witnessed by de Tocqueville in Ireland in 1835 more easily than it did with long, dry reports on parliamentary debate. With that, many Irish parliamentarians, a majority of whom were mindful of the decimation unfolding around the island, may well have connected the loss of life, disease, and relocation in America with the fate of the Roman Catholics in Ireland.[64] For that reason, it seems worth noting that the newspaper's account of the deliberation on the subject of the Poor Relief (Ireland) Bill in Westminster included the opinion of one N. Roche, who pointed out that "employing the paupers would tend to keept [*sic*] down those who were struggling to keep out of the workhouse."[65] Virginia Crossman points out that the "act introduced a nationwide system of poor relief based on the workhouse and financed by a local property tax."[66] This meant that the poor were put in fear of being effectively incarcerated in the workhouses that one reformer, Laura Stephens, described as "the great gloomy pile of grey stone buildings, surrounded with high walls" found in many towns in Ireland. This cultivated a system that "encourage[d] landlords to evict their smallest tenants," thereby ameliorating the economic damage caused by "falling rent rolls, and the [landlords'] liability ... to pay the poor rates on holdings worth less than £4 per annum."[67] Roche, like many others, saw the act as producing a perfect storm, wherein the government's apparent charity would, in effect, not only enable and encourage the removal of the Irish poor from the land, but also create a context in which that removal could be recast as a benevolent act. From there, the death and depopulation described by Pilcher would not be far away. Crucially, Roche's comment does *not* appear in the minutes of the debate held in Westminster, meaning, therefore, that the newspaper went to some great lengths to include this criticism of the bill in its communiqué.[68] That additional insight would have had the effect of balancing the opinions provided by champions of Poor Relief, including that of another Irish MP—W. S. O'Brien—whose input is also recorded in the *Post*'s pages.[69] The story of the Mandan, the Assiniboine, the Cree, the A'aninin, and the Sáhniš could be read as premonitory when read alongside the report from London. In the end, there is no looking beyond the fact that countless stories of the various afflictions and torments that affected the Choctaw and several other tribes reached Ireland's shores on a regular basis during the first half of the nineteenth century. Those stories undoubtedly reverberated in the minds of Irish readers, just as accounts of the Famine in Ireland would have a resounding effect on the Choctaw just a few years later.

Courtesies of a Small and Trivial Character

In her book *Charity and the Great Hunger in Ireland*, our fellow contributor Christine Kinealy explores the unprecedented global response to the Irish Famine of 1845–52. Charitable donations, she explains, came from all corners of the world. Calcutta, as it was known then, was one of the first places where money was collected to be sent to Ireland, and 29,633 rupees had been collected there by January 10, 1846.[70] At the same time, a committee had been established in Boston in the United States, and it quickly gathered together $750. Lionel de Rothschild, a London-based Jewish banker, formed the British Relief Association in January 1847, and it was to Rothschild's fund that Queen Victoria donated £2,000 (a donation that did not spare her the indignity of becoming colloquially known as "The Famine Queen," a moniker assigned to her after the apocryphal rumor that she donated £5 to help the starving Irish was widely disseminated). One thousand Roman crowns were donated by Pope Pius IX, and the president of the United States, James Polk, donated $50—an amount that the Morgan Friedman inflation calculator estimates to be approximately $1,307 today, when adjusted for inflation.[71] More arresting, perhaps, is the fact that "subscriptions to Ireland came from some of the poorest and most invisible groups in society . . . [including] former slaves in the Caribbean, who had only achieved full freedom in 1838." Donations were also received from Barbados, Jamaica, St. Kitts, and elsewhere. It is also profoundly affecting that paupers in an orphanage in New York scraped together $2 for the poor of Ireland, and that prisoners serving time in Sing Sing Prison in America—as well as convicts on board a prison ship at Woolwich in London—also donated money.[72] The significance of the latter donation deepens when one considers that all of those aboard that sorrowful ship would themselves be dead within twelve months of making their contribution. These facts, and many more, are outlined in Kinealy's chapter.

What is particularly useful about her methodical research is that it reminds us not only that there were many sources from which this global generosity emanated, but also that there were various motivations behind the benevolence shown to the Irish. For instance, whereas the relief committee in Boston was heavily invested in the fight for Ireland's independence, the charitable souls in India were spurred into action by the notion that it was their "fellow subjects 'at home'" who were in dire need of financial assistance.[73] So, as well as detailing the manner in which money poured into Ireland in greater and lesser amounts, her historical detective work reveals a broader picture of the specific contextual framework in which the global response to the famine unfolded at the time. The Choctaw gift, meanwhile, can surely be situated within the complex eddy of benevolent giving in the nineteenth century and the various agendas that often "politicized philanthropy."[74] The tribe's concern for the people of Ireland may well be viewed in terms of diplomacy and perhaps even some deliberateness; the $710 gathered in Skullyville became, in many respects, emblematic of the Nation's continued autonomy, strength, and robustness primarily because it was a sign of Choctaw endurance and moral strength.

As Shrout, Laura Wittstock, and others have noted, this particular charitable donation also focused attention on the extent to which the Irish and the Choctaw had a collective or shared experience of colonization, albeit in discrete and alternate realms. It is crucial, then, that we recognize not only the fact that the "Indian Territory press also used philanthropic acts . . . to make tacit comparisons between British misgovernment and American policy," but also that certain protagonists within the Irish press had invited comparison between the two groups even before then, albeit in less explicit terms.[75] This fact is borne out not only in the reporting on tribal concerns in the years running up to the Famine (as mentioned above), but also in the widespread coverage that the gift itself received in 1847; seven of the country's most popular papers gave an account of the tribe's amazing generosity.[76]

Although the news of the donation was carried by newspapers in all four corners of Ireland, several communiqués also took the opportunity to tease out some of the broader significances of the contribution to famine relief. The most pointed of these was, perhaps, the *Pilot*'s description of the circumstances in which the Choctaw—and others—made their endowment. The journalist in question did his damndest to highlight not just the openhandedness of donors, but also the particular conditions in which they chose to perform a profound act of kindness. "The contributions still go on. Some of them are remarkable," he writes, before singling out the people of Tampico and Monterey in Mexico (key sites in the run-up to the Mexican-American War) and the Choctaw. The latter, he notes, have cemented a special bond with the Irish: "'Lo! The poor Indian'—he stretches his red hand in honest kindness to his poor Celtic brother across the sea." Finally, he also remarks that Washington bankers Corcoran and Riggs gave $5,000, a figure that, he argues, put Queen Victoria to shame since she had given "but twice as much." In what can only be described as a coup de grâce, he concludes: "All power to the princely bankers for their generosity which casts into the shade the offering of the Queen of rich England" (which is possibly one of the last public compliments paid to bankers!). That same report was carried the following day, June 19, 1847, in the *Dublin Weekly Register*. Only a few short weeks later, the *Freeman's Journal* printed a letter by Myndert Van Schaick, the New York businessman who led the General Relief Committee, which signaled out the Choctaw's contribution: "They have given their cheerful hand in this good cause though they are separated from you by miles of land and an Ocean's breadth" (July 3, 1847).

A significant part of the gift is, then, not the donation itself, but rather the recognition of, as well as the opportunities to speak both to and about, cotemporal (albeit not conterminous) experiences of colonial rule. Thus, the package that was sent by the Choctaw was accompanied by something that was possibly more important—crucial acknowledgments of the warp and weft of historical similarities. In that context, it is not only striking that a paper such as the *Armagh Guardian* should report both on the state of the Choctaw's nation-to-nation negotiations with the U.S. government in 1846 *and* the tribe's recognition of events in the international arena in 1847. Even more telling than the appearance of these reasonably brief references to Choctaw politics and charity is the *Wexford Independent*'s reprinting of a speech by Choctaw headman Colonel Samuel Cobb under the title "Indian Eloquence," also in 1846. Appearing directly under a ballad that calls for "true [Irish] patriots to free / The land of their birth from accursed tyranny," Cobb's address reminds the

U.S. government that "when you took our country you promised us land," but that twelve years later, the tribe had "received no land" (October 21, 1846).[77] A similar bid to reflect on the displacement and relocation that the Choctaw and other tribes had endured is also apparent in the *Galway Vindicator, and Connaught Advertiser*'s reprinting of an extract taken from David B. Edwards's *The History of Texas*.[78] There, in a column titled "Choctaw Tradition," Edward recounts a "traditional story" told to him by a "Choctaw warrior," and which ends with the pronouncement that "the Choctaws had *never* spilt the blood of a white man!" (August 7, 1847). Clearly a retelling of one version of the Choctaw and Chickasaw origin story, the tale recalled the tribes' premonition that settlers, or "children from the far East," would arrive in their country bringing with them the "avaricious" and "ravenous appetite of the wolverine when it has seized the harmless argali of the mountains." The allusion would not have been lost on the people of Galway. Hence, if it can be argued that the Choctaw viewed the donation as part of a clear process of self-definition in Indian Country (and I think it can be), then it is surely possible to argue that Irish stories that told of the receipt of the gift were informed by a very similar instinct and spirit. Referenced and recalled time and again, the $710 created a point of enduring and lasting contact between communities that were far distant, but who saw themselves as being related through the concomitantly chaotic experiences that colonization and imperial subjugation brought them.

It became something of a placeholder for an intense act of political and cultural discernment during the twentieth century too. Indeed, it seems likely that this point of connection, among others, would have been on the mind of Éamon de Valera, leader of the first Dáil (the Irish Parliament), when he left Ireland bound for the United States in October 1919.[79] As noted in the introduction to this collection, his visit to the United States, which took place during the early phases of the Irish War of Independence, was driven partly by a need for political recognition of the new Irish nation, and partly by a need to launch an appeal for funds to secure the future of de Valera's parliamentary party; where better to go than to the country that so many donations had come from in the past, and to which so many Irish emigrants had fled during the famine years. In strictly financial terms de Valera's "efforts proved successful," according to the University College Dublin Archives, and he "raised a significant amount of money for the Irish cause."[80] However, in political terms, the "long fellow," as he was colloquially known, failed "to receive recognition from President Woodrow Wilson, who viewed the Irish question as a matter for Anglo-Irish, rather than international, relations." In truth, Wilson felt that political discord in Ireland had effectively derailed his bid to lead the League of Nations; although he had refused to raise the issue of Ireland's freedom at the 1919 Paris Peace Convention, the distraction caused by the "Irish had [nevertheless] wrecked his whole program for adoption of the work at Paris."[81] Ironically, or perhaps deceivingly, Wilson had made a great deal out of his Tyrone ancestry during his 1912 presidential campaign, thereby courting votes from the Irish American community. He also invited the Irish suffragette, nationalist, and pacifist Hannah Sheehy-Skeffington to the White House in 1918, spurring her to note that she was "the first Irish exile and the first Sinn Féiner to enter the White House, and the first to wear there the badge of the Irish Republic." De Valera was right to expect more of a welcome, it seems. Nevertheless, when that welcome wasn't forthcoming, it was fitting and appropriate that it was the enduring strength of the connection between the Irish and tribal communities that proved to be deep-seated; when the promise of a conventional political connection failed—mainly because Ireland was little more than a nuisance to a world leader set on extending and expanding the United States' influence internationally—de Valera turned to other friends and allies. That he should do so is possibly as telling as it is compelling. It seems highly likely that de Valera would have known about the Choctaw gift, and was keenly aware of the esteem that existed between tribal communities and the Irish. Knowledge of that relationship may well have led him to accept the invitation issued by the Anishinaabeg at Lac Courte Oreilles, who offered to host the Irish leader in the wake of Wilson's snub. On October 25, 1919, the *Irish World and American Industrial Liberator* reported that the Irish political leader had been adopted by the tribe. Chief Billy Boy and Joe Kingfisher, another one of the tribal leaders, addressed de Valera directly during a ceremony that, according to the correspondent, "took place in an open field in the reservation in the presence of more than 3,000 Indians and white people." "You come to us as a representative of one oppressed nation to another," Kingfisher noted. At that point,

> Mr. De Valera rose and walked to the center of the ring . . . accepted the head dress of a Chippewa chieftain with gravity as the tom toms sounded louder and louder . . . [and] began talking in Gaelic. "I speak to you in Gaelic," he said, reverting to English, "because I want to show you that though I am white I am not of the English race. We, like you, are a people who have suffered and I feel for you with a sympathy that comes only from one who can understand as we Irishmen can. You say you are not free. Neither are we free and I sympathize with you because we are making a

Éamon de Valera wearing a headdress presented to him by the Lac Courte Oreilles Tribe, one of six bands of the Lake Superior Band of Chippewa Indians who entered into treaties with the United States in 1837, 1842, and 1854.

similar fight. As a boy I read and understood of your slavery and longed to become one of you." Mr. De Valera then told the [listeners] how Ireland had been oppressed by England for 750 years. "I call upon you, the truest of all Americans," he said, "to help us win our struggle for freedom." The Indians listened to his impassioned address with owllike gravity, but when Ira Isham, the tribe interpreter, translated Mr. De Valera's words into Chippewa they cheered him wildly."[82]

Journalistic license, some dreadful stereotypes on the author's part, and the Irishman's account of his childhood "longing" aside, it is possible to see that the encounter concurrently arises out of, relies on, *and* produces a complex transatlantic narrative of recognition and acceptance.

Establishing not only the facts of an earlier, jurisdictional autonomy—both in Ireland and the Americas—the leader of the Dáil (who was, incidentally, born in New York and raised in Limerick) deconstructs racial codes that had, by the nineteenth and twentieth centuries, come to inform conventional narratives of conquest and colonization. Here, "whiteness" no longer corresponds with, emblematizes, or indeed bestows any form of political power or agency. Instead, it is a very different form of common currency—the costs endured by an oppressed people—that are called to mind, remembered, and exchanged. It is hardly surprising that this should be the case, since, as Edward T. O'Donnell has speculated, the original gift had possibly been sent in recognition of political and cultural analogies. The tribe's "sympathy [most likely] stemmed from their recognition of the similarities between the experiences of the Irish and Choctaw," O'Donnell argues.[83] For that reason, it is no great struggle to see—or understand—why both populations might have sought to underline the story of the gift for political reasons, and as a means of challenging colonial rule. So, if "Irish sufferers were deliberately selected as recipients of aid" by the Choctaw, as Shrout explains, then it is surely the case that Irish patriots and nationalists retold the story of the gift in a deliberate and purposeful manner. Crucially, they also spread stories of Choctaw removal and resistance.[84] There is far more than that sense of political activism to the story, however. As the authors of this book are keen to demonstrate, the two communities in question recognized in one another a shared sense of humanity and revealed a great eagerness to lend a helping hand. They saw in one another's relationship to the land, sense of story, memory of the ancestors, and connectedness to a world beyond their nations, forms of appreciation, spirituality, and generosity that resonated deeply with them.

The sense of having shared in the experience of having a specific type of encounter, albeit not actual events themselves, endures in both Ireland and the Choctaw Nation today. There is in Ireland, in terms of cultural memory, contemporary discourse, and global political relations, a propensity to recall two donations above all others: those made by Queen Victoria and the Choctaw. Of course, it certainly is not all that difficult to see how or why these two particular gifts might appear to crystallize vital strands of the historical narratives that rehearse various accounts of Ireland's relationship with its nearest neighbor; as well as bringing to mind the suffering experienced during the Famine itself, a comparative assessment of the Queen's donation and that made by the tribe brings a number of previously disparate political and cultural agents into contact with one another. Here, the oppressor's rather benign benevolence stands radically opposed to the altogether more affecting munificence of a recently discouraged and migratory minority group—old enemies and new friends. This standpoint is, in O'Donnell's opinion, also reflected in the views of "contemporary Choctaw" who "note that both groups were victims of conquest that led to loss of property, forced migration and exile, mass starvation, and cultural suppression (most notably language)."[85] The memory of that form of "cultural suppression" lives on within both communities, and, I would add, results in there being far more to the story than questions of politics alone; although the donation may have initially served as a means to acquire "moral and political capital" by engaging in a form of "politicized philanthropy," it has come to symbolize something much bigger than a mere tool in the political armory of the Choctaw.[86] By realizing the connection between experiences including the loss of land, life, and language in our two cultures, the $710 doesn't just offer us a means to consider, comprehend, and bear witness to the horrors of our collective past; it also underlines the similarities that existed *prior* to colonization, *and* the enduring nature of both communities as well as the cross-cultural connection(s) between them. So, beneath that essential story of subjugation and sympathy—which has been co-opted by various groups in a number of ways—there are possibly far more complicated and compelling stories to be told about both the historical circumstances surrounding the Choctaw donation itself, and the complete range of energies that are framed not only by the gift itself, but also by perceptions of its meaning and import.

NOTES

1. Skullyville is in current-day Oklahoma, which was admitted as the forty-sixth state of the Union in 1907. Oklahoma is an amalgamation of Indian Territory and Oklahoma Territory. Skullyville was an altogether apt place to gather and collect money on many levels; Muriel H. Wright notes that "The word iskvlli means a 'small piece of money or coin,' in [the] Choctaw" language, and that "the name 'Skullyville' was given the village that grew up around" the Indian agency founded in 1832. This was mainly because the name was "a corruption and a combination of the word iskvlli and the English suffix ville, literally meaning 'money town'" ("Organization of Counties in the Choctaw and Chickasaw Nations," *Chronicles of Oklahoma* 8, no. 3 [September 1930]: 318). Wright also notes that the Choctaw "themselves probably spoke of the agency as 'Iskvlli ai ilhpita,' meaning 'the place where money is donated or presented'" (*Chronicles*, 319). It is entirely fitting that the donation was gathered at this complex site; as a result, Skullyville was associated not only with Choctaw trading but also with the receipt of monies from the United States government after the tribe had been forcibly removed from Mississippi and into Indian Territory. Moreover, the town's genesis and development reflects the continuation of reciprocal obligations on one hand, but also the tribe's dislocation and

experiences at the hands of the United States government on the other. That members of the tribe should gather there to think of Ireland's starving poor, and decide to send a donation to people thousands of miles away is illustrative of both their awareness of their history as powerful negotiators, traders, and politicians, and the extent to which national and international events had shaped their lives through their contact with the market economy, missionaries, and various government agents. The Choctaw sensed that they were a proud people who had often helped others in the past, but that their recent history meant that they also shared a common bond with the poor, the landless, the dispossessed, and the dying in Ireland.

2. The comparison is between 1850 and 2016, and the source is the Federal Reserve Bank of Minneapolis's "Consumer Price Index (estimate) 1850–," https://minneapolisfed.org/community/teaching-aids/cpi-calculator-information/consumer-price-index-1800.

3. Anelise Hanson Shrout, "'Voice of Benevolence from the Western Wilderness': The Politics of Native Philanthropy in the Trans-Mississippi West," *Journal of the Early Republic* 35, no. 4 (2015): 553–78, 563; Mike Ward, "Irish Repay Choctaw Famine Gift: March Traces Trail of Tears in Trek for Somalian Relief," https://sites.uwm.edu/michael/choctaw-homepage/irish-repay-choctaw-famine-gift-march-traces-trail-of-tears-in-trek-for-somalian-relief.

4. Carolyn Thomas Foreman, "Organization of Counties in the Choctaw and Chickasaw Nations," *Chronicles of Oklahoma* 8, no. 3 (1930): 318.

5. Angela Debo, *The Rise and Fall of the Choctaw Republic* (Norman: University of Oklahoma University Press, 1934), 59.

6. Christine Kinealy, *Charity and the Great Hunger in Ireland: The Kindness of Strangers* (London: Bloomsbury, 2013), 104.

7. "International Relief Efforts during the Famine," *Irish America* (August/September 2009); "Choctaw Leader Speaks of Unique Famine Bond," *Irish Examiner*, May 14, 2009.

8. Shrout, "Voice of Benevolence," 558, 554. I will concern myself with the Choctaw gift in this essay, primarily because this is the donation that is most often mentioned in Ireland. There is certainly much work to be done on the circumstances surrounding the Cherokee gift, however, and I am sure that that research will be carried out in the very near future.

9. Timothy W. Guinnane, "The Great Irish Famine and Population: The Long View," *American Economic Review* 84, no. 2 (1994): 303; Cormac O'Grada, *Black '47 and Beyond: The Great Irish Famine in History, Economy, and Memory* (Princeton, NJ: Princeton University Press, 2000), 110; David Dickson, "Famine and Economic Change in Eighteenth-Century Ireland," in *The Oxford Handbook of Modern Irish History*, ed. Alvin Jackson (Oxford: Oxford University Press, 2014), 432.

10. J. G. Hawkes and J. Francisco-Ortega, "The Early History of the Potato in Europe," *Euphytica* 70 (1993): 1.

11. John Reader, *Potato: A History of the Propitious Esculent* (New Haven, CT: Yale University Press, 2008), 115.

12. Kevin Whelan, "The Long Shadow of the Great Hunger," *Irish Times*, September 1, 2012.

13. R. A. Houston, *Peasant Petitions: Social Relations and Economic Life on Landed Estates, 1600–1850* (London: Palgrave Macmillan, 2014), 3.

14. D. Andrivon, "The Origin of Phytophthora Infestans Populations Present in Europe in the 1840s: A Critical Review of Historical and Scientific Evidence," *Plant Pathology* 45 (1996): 1027–35.

15. Friedrich Engels, *The Condition of the Working-Class in England in 1844* (New York: Cosimo Classics, 2009), 91.

16. Mary Daly, who taught me as an undergraduate at University College Dublin in the 1990s, was one such historian. For a synopsis of the general opinion of Daly and others, see Patrick Brantlinger's essay "The Famine," *Victorian Literature and Culture* 32, no. 1 (2004): 193–207.

17. Thomas Malthus was simply of the opinion "that land in Ireland is infinitely more peopled than in England." It was Malthus's conviction, as a result, that "to give full effect to the natural resources of the country, a great part of the population should be swept from the soil." See Patrick Brantlinger's *Dark Vanishings: Discourse on the Extinction of Primitive Races, 1800–1930* (Ithaca, NY: Cornell University Press, 2003). Readers wishing to explore the various arguments surrounding the ideologically bound perspectives that shaped, and even governed, responses to the famine in Ireland would do well to start with Christophe Gillissen's useful survey of the field, "Charles Trevelyan, John Mitchel and the Historiography of the Great Famine," *Revue Française de Civilisation Brittanique* 19, no. 2 (2014).

18. Whelan, "The Long Shadow of the Great Hunger."

19. Anthony Trollope, the English novelist, drew on Forster's accounts of his time in Ireland when writing his final novel, *The Landleaguers* (London: Trollope Society, repr. ., 1905), xi.

20. Christine Kinealy, "The British Relief Association and the Great Famine in Ireland," *Revue Française de Civilisation Britannique* 19, no. 2 (2014): 49.

21. *Illustrated London News*, February 13, 1847.

22. Brantlinger, "The Famine," 198. Prior to the formation of a new Whig government in 1846—and Trevelyan's subsequent appointment—the Conservative British prime minister, Sir Robert Peel, had made several practical and successful attempts to alleviate the hunger of the Irish people. It is crucial, therefore, to differentiate between the

approaches taken to the Irish crisis. Most notable among Peel's initiatives was the repeal of the Corn Laws in 1846 and his decision to buy Indian corn in the United States and ship it to Ireland that same year. Together, these moves temporarily staved off widespread famine. The repeal of the Corn Laws, which had kept bread prices artificially high, led to Peel's political demise; he succeeded in pushing through the controversial repeal with minority support from his own party and the help of Opposition (i.e., Whig) members of Parliament and free traders, but never fully recovered his power thereafter.

23. Robert Kee, *The Green Flag: A History of Irish Nationalism* (1972; London: Penguin/ Weidenfeld and Nicolson, 2000), 247. The Duke of Cambridge's comments are recorded in Chrysostom P. Donahoe, *Popular Life of Daniel O'Connell: Including the Funeral Oration of Padre Ventura at Rome, Father Burke's Sermon at Glasnevin, and Wendell Phillip's Centennial Oration* (Boston: T.B. Noonan, 1875); and Mary Francis Cusack's *Life of Daniel O'Connell, the Liberator: His Times—Political, Social, and Religious* (New York: D. & J. Sadlier, 1875). Adolphus Frederic, the Duke of Cambridge (February 24, 1774—July 8, 1850), was the tenth child and seventh son of George III and Queen Charlotte. The website for the Parliament notes, with some understatement, that the "new government led by Lord John Russell did not handle the famine effectively," http://www.parliament.uk/about/living-heritage/evolutionofparliament/legislativescrutiny/parliamentandireland/overview/the-great-famine.

24. It should also be noted that several international visitors and social reformers shared at least some of the concerns voiced by Trevelyan. The abolitionist and black leader Frederick Douglass wrote to William Lloyd Garrison in August 1845 and informed his collaborator that "an Irish hut is pre-eminent" in terms of "human misery, ignorance, degradation, filth and wretchedness" (*The Liberator*, March 27, 1846, reprinted in *Life and Writings of Frederick Douglass*, vol. 1, ed. Philip Foner [New York: International Publishers, 1950], 138). Rather than suggest that the conditions that he witnessed were in any way linked to what Peter Gray describes as the complete absence of a "national statutory provision for poor relief," or questioning where, exactly, the "problem of poverty" had come from, Douglass argued that "The immediate, and . . . [possibly] the main cause of the extreme poverty and beggary in Ireland, is intemperance" (Gray, "The Irish Poor Law and the Great Famine," paper presented at IEHC [2006] in Helsinki; *The Liberator*, March 27, 1846). Although Douglass's reasoning steered clear of the "'orthodox' view of Irish poverty"—that there was "an imbalance between population numbers and the country's productive capacity"—it was, nevertheless, politically and ideologically driven; this rather subjective perception of the root causes of Irish suffering was, on the face of it, consistent with the views of members of the temperance movement and the

religious reformers who were a key part of the abolitionist movement that Douglass
cared so deeply about.

25. *Alexis de Tocqueville's Journey in Ireland, July–August, 1835*, ed. Emmet J. Larkin
(Washington, DC: Catholic University of America Press, 1990), 14.

26. The irony of referring to de Tocqueville's writing in order to substantiate the suffering
of the Irish—and to suggest that the French traveler was sympathetic to the plight of
a colonized people—is not lost on me. Jack W. P. Veugelers has pointed out that de
Tocqueville "never abandoned his opinion that France must consolidate its hold over
Algeria for reasons of strategy and international reputation," and ultimately "accepted
and even praised their manner of waging war against the Algerian people" even though
he "deplored the pre-eminence of military men over the political affairs of the young
colony" ("Tocqueville on the Conquest and Colonization of Algeria," *Journal of Classical
Sociology* 10, no. 4 [2010]: 339–55, abstract).

27. Clara Sue Kidwell, *Choctaws and Missionaries in Mississippi, 1818–1918* (Norman:
Oklahoma University Press, 1995), 26.

28. Russell Thornton, "Cherokee Population Losses during the Trail of Tears: A New
Perspective and a New Estimate," *Ethnohistory* 31, no. 4 (1984): 289–300, 289.

29. Kidwell, *Choctaws and Missionaries in Mississippi*, 141.

30. Treaty with the Choctaw, Sept. 27, 1830, 7 Stat., 333, Proclamation, Feb. 24, 1831, http://
digital.library.okstate.edu/kappler/Vol2/treaties/cho0310.htm#fna. The circumstances
behind the signing of the earlier treaties are complex and multifaceted, insofar as
various forces are at play, both within the tribe and externally. Furthermore, the
machinations of both state and government policies are further complicated by often
strained relationships between the various Choctaw chiefs, including Pushmataha,
Puckshanubbee, Mushulatubbee, Nitakechi, David Folsom, John Garland, and
Greenwood Leflore. At various points in time, each of these men held their own view on
the possibility—and probability—of the tribe's moving to the west of the Mississippi.
Kidwell argues that the "Treaty of Dancing Rabbit Creek epitomizes the changing nature
of tribal identity and individual political power in the Choctaw Nation. The [U.S.]
government had gotten its first major cession (Doak's Stand) by exploiting the division
in the tribe between the hunters who constituted a virtually separate nation west of the
Mississippi and those who remained in Mississippi and were becoming settled farmers.
By 1830, the tribe was arbitrarily stripped of its political autonomy in Mississippi, and the
division the government could exploit was . . . based . . . on the disputes over leadership
and who would profit most from the inevitable removal" (Kidwell, *Choctaws and
Missionaries in Mississippi*, 141).

31. Nitakechi is reported to have made this remark to a reporter writing for the *Arkansas Gazette*. Sandra Faiman-Silva mentions this quotation in her book *Choctaws at the Crossroads: The Political Economy of Class and Culture in the Oklahoma Timber Region* (Lincoln: University of Nebraska Press, 2000). Faiman-Silva cites Betty Jeanne Ward Poulin's entry in the *Poor's Manual of Industrials* (1910–15) as one of her sources. James L. Nolan Jr. repeats the phrase in his recent work *What They Saw in America: Alexis de Tocqueville, Max Weber, G. K. Chesterton, and Sayyid Qutb* (Cambridge: Cambridge University Press, 2016). Thornton, meanwhile, attributes the phrase to the Cherokee, explaining that "the removal of the Cherokee during the late 1830s was so arduous that they subsequently named it *Nunna daul Tsuny* (Trail Where We Cried); it has become known in English as the 'Trail of Tears'"; Thornton, "Cherokee Population Losses," 289.

32. Alexis de Tocqueville, *Democracy in America*, trans. Henry Reeve Esq., 3rd ed. (New York: George Adlard, 1839), 338.

33. Ibid.

34. Ibid.

35. Virginia R. Allen, "Medical Practices and Health in the Choctaw Nation, 1831–1885," *Chronicles of Oklahoma* 48 (1970): 124–43. Quoted in Thornton, "Cherokee Population Losses," 293.

36. "Journal of Occurrences," *Journal of S. T. Cross—Choctaw Removal, 1832*, http://ualrexhibits.org/trailoftears/eyewitness-accounts/journal-of-st-cross-choctaw-removal-1832. Sadly, little needs to be said about the troubling euphemism "occurrences" here.

37. One might also suggest that the need for soup kitchens—the provision of which was both brief and necessary—was itself the result of the paternalistic, authoritarian, and hierarchically arranged structure of colonial power. That structure might also be said to have stifled agricultural development in Ireland and made the population reliant on Britain, thereby necessitating the provision of charity.

38. *Protestant Magazine* 11 (October 1849), quoted in Denis G. Paz, *Popular Anti-Catholicism in Mid-Victorian England* (Stanford, CA: Stanford University Press, 1992), 154.

39. Andrew Urban, *Brokering Servitude: Migration and the Politics of Domestic Labor during the Long Nineteenth Century* (New York: New York University Press, 2018), 42.

40. Patrick Brantlinger, "A Short History of (Imperial) Benevolence," in *Burden or Benefit? Imperial Benevolence and Its Legacies*, ed. Helen Gilbert and Chris Tiffin (Bloomington: Indiana University Press, 2008), 14.

41. It is important to note that the Irish people were not wholly reliant or entirely dependent upon or simply waiting expectantly for help from the British government. It should also be acknowledged that Irish MPs took their seats in Parliament, and therefore played

some role in deciding government policy. Nevertheless, it is still the case that the inaction of the House of Commons in Westminster stymied any proper response to both the events that led to the Great Famine and the death and loss that followed. For further consideration of the colonial power's responsibilities and the response of the colonized to same, see Pat Noxolo, Parvati Raghuram, and Claire Madge's essay "Unsettling Responsibility: Postcolonial Interventions," *Transactions of the Institute of British Geographers* 37 (2012): 418–29.

42. Margaret Kohn and Kavita Reddy, "Colonialism," in *Stanford Encyclopedia of Philosophy*, ed. Edward N. Zalta (Fall 2017 edition), https://plato.stanford.edu/archives/fall2017/entries/colonialism.

43. Ibid.

44. Michael Paul Rogin, *Fathers and Children: Andrew Jackson and the Subjugation of the American Indian* (1975; London: Transaction Publishers, 2009), 167.

45. Kidwell, *Choctaws and Missionaries in Mississippi*, 24.

46. C. R. Trevelyan, *The Irish Crisis* (London: Longman, Brown, Green and Longmans, 1848), 201; Andrew Jackson's Message to Congress "On Indian Removal" (1830), in "A Century of Lawmaking for a New Nation: U.S. Congressional Documents and Debates, 1774–1875," Register of Debates, 21st Congress, 2nd Session, x, https://memory.loc.gov/cgi-bin/ampage?collId=llrd&fileName=010/llrd010.db&recNum=439.

47. Jackson, Message to Congress "On Indian Removal, " ix; *Times*, April 12, 1799. Quoted in Michael de Nie, *The Eternal Paddy: Irish Identity and the British Press, 1798–1882* (Madison: University of Wisconsin Press, 2004).

48. Shrout, "Voice of Benevolence," 554.

49. Bill Rolston, *The Media and Northern Ireland: Covering the Troubles* (London: Palgrave Macmillan, 1991), 156.

50. Stanislaus Murray Hamilton, ed., *The Writings of James Monroe*, vol. 6, *1817–1823* (New York: G.P. Putnam's Sons, 1903), 168.

51. *Freeman's Journal*, British Newspaper Archive, http://www.britishnewspaperarchive.co.uk/titles/freemans-journal.

52. "Extract of a Letter from Kingston, Jan. 19," *Freeman's Journal*, April 1, 1788.

53. *American News*, October 20, 1791. The fact that it was "not known . . . what nation the Indians who [had] committed these depredations belong[ed]" to—or if there were indeed Natives at all—did little to dissuade the journalist from placing the news alongside the story about the Cherokee.

54. "America—Lord Selkirk—The Indians"; "American Intelligence," *Freeman's Journal*, December 2, 1818.

55. According to Nigel Johnston, project archivist with the Crowley Project at the National Archives of Ireland, "The Kildare Place Society was founded in 1811 with an ethos of providing non-denominational education to the poor of Ireland. It provided for shared teaching to pupils of all religious beliefs of regular literary subjects, while promoting daily reading of the Bible unaccompanied by verbal elucidation." As such, the society appears to have been more interested in altruism than in paternalism. However, even though "the society [had] received broad support from the Catholic hierarchy," from the time of its origin, that backing "was slowly eroded as suspicions were aroused about its use of funds to support Protestant missionary agencies, and of failure to honor the agreement respecting reading of scripture in classrooms without remark." Johnston points out that in "1819, Daniel O'Connell raised objections about the religious impartiality of the society, and subsequently withdrew his support"; "Historical Commentary for 1818," Registered Papers of the Office of Chief Secretary of Ireland, http://www.csorp.nationalarchives.ie.

56. Vincent Morley, *Irish Opinion and the American Revolution, 1760–1783* (Cambridge: Cambridge University Press, 2002), 97.

57. "Congress, Wednesday, Dec 15," *Finn's Leinster Journal*, February 5, 1803.

58. "Sessions Notice, for 1803," in ibid.

59. "Congress, Wednesday, Dec 15."

60. David Brion Davis, *The Problem of Slavery in the Age of Revolution, 1770–1823* (Oxford: Oxford University Press, 1999), 195.

61. Vincent Morley describes *FLJ* as being part of "the patriot press," in *Irish Opinion and the American Revolution*, 98. It is worth noting, as Juliet Shields does in her work *Nation and Migration: The Making of British Atlantic Literature, 1765–1835* (Oxford: Oxford University Press, 2016), that the War of Independence had the effect of bringing "together Anglo-Irish Protestants and Irish Catholics in nonsectarian volunteer corps" (156). These were "armed bodies of citizens that operated independently of government control." In essence, "the American Revolution encouraged the Irish to reflect on Britain's colonial rule of Ireland," and even though "the Irish Parliament voted in support of Britain's war against the colonies, many among the Protestant Ascendancy, Ireland's ruling class, feared that the British Parliament might extend the economic restrictions it had placed on the American colonies to Ireland"; Shields, *Nation and Migration*, 156.

62. Shrout, "Voice of Benevolence," 567.

63. The A'aninin and the Sáhniš are referred to as Gros Ventures and Ricara, respectively, in the newspaper. I am using the names currently used by these communities today.

64. Again, I am attempting to read between the lines here. Cronin's research is based on the

newspaper's approach to reporting marches in support of Daniel O'Connell, and hinges on her assessment that the editors were unimpressed with the Liberator's rhetoric and the motives of his supporters; "'Of One Mind'? O'Connellite Crowds in the 1830s and 1840s," in *Crowds in Ireland, c.1720–1920*, ed. P. Jupp and E. Magennis (Basingstoke, UK: Palgrave Macmillan, 2000), 149. The Kerry Library website also describes the *Post* as a paper that was "written primarily for the Protestant Ascendancy"; see "Kerry 1916 from the Archives," http://www.kerrylibrary.ie/uploads/2/5/1/5/25158039/introduction.pdf. I would argue that it is likely that the comparison between sections of the Irish population and the Choctaw would not have been lost on many readers even if the newspaper did have a particular ideological bent.

65. It seems most likely that the 'N. Roche' quoted by the *Post* was Edmond Burke Roche—the MP who was elected to the House of Commons in 1837 for Cork—rather than William Roche, who was the first Catholic MP and who represented Limerick around the same time. Around the time that N. Roche spoke in Parliament, George Nicholls, the English Poor Law commissioner, was sent to Ireland by the secretary of state for the Home Department, Lord John Russell. Nicholls's task was to "arrive at a practical conclusion with respect of any measures to be introduced into parliament in 1837 for the benefit of the poor in Ireland."

66. Virginia Crossman, "The Poor Law in Ireland, 1838–1948," https://archives.history.ac.uk/history-in-focus/welfare/articles/crossmanv.html.

67. Ibid.

68. UK Parliament, "Minutes," HC Deb, April 11, 1838, vol. 42, c545, http://hansard.millbanksystems.com/commons/1838/apr/11/minutes.

69. O'Brien was in favor of the bill, and disliked Daniel O'Connell's style of leadership and protest, but he was, nevertheless, a resolute critic of the British imperialism, and once drew up a list of "grievances affecting the English Empire." He was also an advocate for equality in Ireland and wrote openly about his empathy for Roman Catholics: "From my boyhood I have entertained a passionate affection for Ireland. A child of its most ancient race, I have never read the history of their past wrongs, I have never witnessed the miseries and indignities which its people still suffer without a deep sentiment of indignation. Though myself a Protestant I have felt as acutely as any Roman Catholic—more acutely than many—the injustice to which the Roman Catholics of this country have been habitually subjected" ("Smith O'Brien, William [1803–1864]", The History of Parliament, Institute of Historical Research, https://www.historyofparliamentonline.org/volume/1820-1832/member/smith-obrien-william-1803-1864.

70. Kinealy, *Charity and the Great Hunger in Ireland*, 44.

71. Christine Kinealy, "Irish Famine Sparked International Fundraising," IrishCentral, https://www.irishcentral.com/roots/irish-famine-sparked-international-fundraising-237694651.

72. Ibid.

73. Kinealy, *Charity and the Great Hunger in Ireland*, 41.

74. Shrout, "Voice of Benevolence," 565.

75. Ibid., 564.

76. *Freeman's Journal*, June 14, 1847; *Dublin Weekly Nation*, June 19, 1847; *Dublin Evening Post*, June 15, 1847; *Mayo Constitution*, June 22, 1847; *Southern Reporter and Cork Commercial Courier*, June 12, 1847; *Drogheda Argus and Leinster Journal*, July 10, 1847.

77. The extract was taken from the memoir of Thomas Loraine McKenney, who is cited as T. L. M'Kenny in the newspaper. McKenney was as given to making pronouncements about the possibility of civilizing the indigenous population as many of his peers were, but he also held the opinion that "the Indian was, in his intellectual and moral structure, [the] equal" of the American (Stuart Ferguson, "Portraits of Native-American Leaders," *Wall Street Journal*, March 5, 2006). A full version of Cobb's speech can be found in *Memoirs, Official and Personal: With Sketches of Travels among the Northern and Southern Indians: Embracing a War Excursion, and Descriptions of Scenes along the Western Borders*, vol. 1, 2nd ed. (New York: Paine and Burgess, 1846), https://archive.org/details/memoirsofficialp00mcke_0.

78. David B. Edwards, *The History of Texas; or, The Emigrant's, Farmer's, and Politician's Guide to the Character, Climate, Soil, and Productions of That Country: Geographically Arranged from Personal Observation and Experience* (1836; Austin: Texas State Historical Association, 1990).

79. That de Valera was profoundly interested in the human aspect of the Irish Famine is undoubted. Haunted by the stories of tragedy, loss, and hunger that he heard as a boy, he would later, when Taoiseach, commission the first in-depth study of the tragedy in the 1940s. According to O'Grada, he was dissatisfied with the final edition of the book, *Studies in the History of the Great Irish Famine*, primarily because it was essentially an "administrative history of the period," and said little about the human toll; "Making History in Ireland in the 1940s and 1950s: The Saga of the Great Famine," in *Interpreting Irish History: The Debate on Historical Revisionism, 1938–1994*, ed. Ciaran Brady (Dublin: Irish Academic Press, 1994), quoted in "Erasures: Colm Tóibín on the Great Irish Famine," *London Review of Books* 20, no. 15 (July 30, 1998), https://www.lrb.co.uk/v20/n15/colm-Tóibín/erasures.

80. History Hub, School of History and Archives, University College, http://www.historyhub.ie.

81. See the chapter "Woodrow Wilson: The Denial of Exile," in Robert Schmuhl, *Ireland's Exiled Children: America and the Easter Rising* (Oxford: Oxford University Press, 2016), 75–118.

82. *Irish World and American Industrial Liberator*, October 25, 1919, http://historyhub.ie/ eamon-de-valera-chief. The *Chicago Sunday Tribune*, and several other newspapers, carried the story on October 19, 1919.

83. Edward T. O'Donnell, "Hibernian Chronicle 154 Years Ago: The Choctaw Send Aid," *IrishEcho*, https://www.irishecho.com/2011/02/hibernian-chronicle-154-years-ago-the- choctaw-send-aid-2.

84. Shrout, "Voice of Benevolence," 564.

85. Ibid., 564.

86. Ibid., 554 and 565.

An Glaoch/Singing, Still

Doireann Ní Ghríofa and LeAnne Howe

An Glaoch

Doireann Ní Ghríofa

Éist. Éist.
An gcloiseann tú é?

Éiríonn guth ón gcré.
Cór.

Listen.
Can you hear it?

From the land, a voice lifts.
It becomes a chorus.

Because you are holding onto me, I am not dead yet.
As long as you speak of us, you will not forget.
Glaoim

Glaoim ort
Glaoim orthu
Glaoim siar
Glaoim

I call
I call you
I call them
I call back
I call west

I call
Druidim mo bhéal.
I quieten. I wait.

Silence.
Tost.

Then,
Ansin,
ón dtost,
cloisim guth.

Éist.
Listen.
From silence,
a voice lifts.

Singing, Still

LeAnne Howe

Issa hal-a-li haa- toko Ik-sa illok isha shkee
Issa hal-a-li haa- toko Ik-sa illok isha shkee
Issa hal-a-li haa- toko Ik-sa illok isha shkee
Issa hal-a-li haa- toko Ik-sa illok isha shkee

Because you are holding onto me I am not dead yet

Love Can Build a Bridge

The Choctaws' Gift to the Irish in 1847

Phillip Carroll Morgan

> Love can build a bridge
> Between your heart and mine
> Love can build a bridge
> Don't you think it's time?
> Don't you think it's time?
>
> —Naomi Judd, Paul Overstreet, and John
> Barlow Jarvis, "Love Can Build a Bridge,"
> December 1990

I remember vividly, although it was eighteen years ago, my visceral reaction to televised images of mostly Muslim refugees streaming out of Kosovo under pressure of Yugoslav military forces who occupied their country. When I first saw newsreels of the refugees fleeing on foot with their remaining worldly possessions packed upon their backs, I uttered the words almost involuntarily under my breath, "Trail of Tears." In this age of fluid information, I have deeply felt sympathy for refugees from Syria, Iraq, Iran, Palestine, Afghanistan, Myanmar, Darfur, Libya, Rwanda, Somalia, Guatemala, and at least a dozen other places where people retreat from, or are driven out by war in their homelands where their families have lived for generations, centuries, perhaps millennia. These tragedies, played out before my eyes, help me visualize more realistically the perils my Choctaw ancestors faced when they were forced to give up their homelands in Mississippi as a result of the Indian Removal Act passed in 1830 by the United States Congress, and forced to relocate to Indian Territory.[1] The cooperative, forward-thinking Choctaws left their homes and all but a few possessions behind the following year, becoming the first tribe to emigrate en masse to Indian Territory after passage of the act. They carried few provisions because they were promised transportation, food, shelter, and supplies by the federal government, to be delivered along the way by contractors.

Indian Territory was an ever-dwindling federal reserve, never formally organized or chartered as a territory by the United States. Even though I value the five generations of family history here in Oklahoma and therefore my identity with what once was called Indian Territory and believed by my ancestors to be inviolable, this shrinking land base may be the classic example of smoke-and-mirrors negotiations by the United States in what American Indians have come to call the "trail of broken treaties."[2]

Choctaw chiefs and headmen of towns and districts signed the *Anumpa Bok Chukfi Ahilha*, the Treaty of Dancing Rabbit Creek, in late September 1830.[3] The Choctaws ceded the remainder of their land holdings in Mississippi to the United States in trade for the land west of Arkansas Territory, south of the Arkansas and Canadian Rivers and north of the Red River, roughly the southern half of present-day Oklahoma, and agreed to emigrate as soon as possible. The historic treaty promised perpetual title to the lands in fee simple, and perpetual rights of sovereignty and self-determination. In plain language, the Choctaws were promised that they could remain a self-governing people, with all the rights accruing to the citizens of their old and respected society.

Since most Choctaws were farmers or stock ranchers, they began their emigrations—the first Trail of Tears—during the fall and winter months after harvest time, and expected to be settled in their new homes early enough for planting in the spring. Their expectations proved naive. Government contractors clumsily and sometimes criminally failed to provide adequate food and shelter along the way, and more than a thousand Choctaw people died during that first bitter winter of removal.

In the latter part of that tragic winter, in February 1832, Choctaw chief George W. Harkins wrote a "Farewell Letter to the American People," which was published in newspapers across the country. In his letter, Harkins—educated at Centre College in Danville, Kentucky, before earning a law degree from Cumberland University in Lebanon, Tennessee—exposes the duplicity of U.S. officials who publicized as fact the half-truth that the Choctaws were giving up their ancestral homelands of their own free will.

> Yet it is said that our present movements are our own voluntary acts—such is not the case. We found ourselves like a benighted stranger, following false guides, until he was surrounded on every side, with fire and water. The fire was certain destruction, and a feeble hope was left him of escaping by water. A distant view of the opposite shore encourages the hope; to remain would be inevitable annihilation.
>
> Who would hesitate, or who would say that his plunging into the water was his own voluntary act? Painful in the extreme is the mandate of our expulsion. We regret that it should proceed from the mouth of our professed friend, for whom our blood was co-mingled with that of his bravest warriors, on the field of danger and death.[4]

His controlled but barely disguised rancor reveals that Chief Harkins clearly blames President Andrew Jackson for the cruelty of removing the Choctaws from their homelands. His disillusionment is apparently intensified by the fact that Native American warriors had fought shoulder to shoulder with southern state militias under Jackson's command in many important battles during the War of 1812; hence, Harkins's reference to "the field of danger and death." The tribal warriors and Jackson had regarded each other as comrades in arms, equals, and even personal friends during the tumultuous second decade of the nineteenth century.

Jackson's status as an American hero arose chiefly from victories in the Battle of Horseshoe Bend (1813) and the Battle of New Orleans (1815), either of which might have been impossible without his American Indian allies, the Choctaws, Cherokees, and Chickasaws. Regarding the Battle of New Orleans, for example, the Choctaws' and Chickasaws' knowledge of warfare on the lower Mississippi River, which they had defended for centuries, was invaluable in turning back an invading force of approximately ten thousand battle-hardened British marines, three times the size of Jackson's army. So when Jackson, who was a loyal friend of the Choctaws fifteen years earlier, became the prime advocate of Indian Removal after he was elected president of the United States in 1828, his change of colors was regarded as not just political, but a personal betrayal. Another thousand or more Choctaw refugees died emigrating during the winter following Harkins's statements, and the suffering of the initial removals extended into 1836.

The Gift

Little more than a decade after the tragic losses during emigration, when reports reached the Choctaws in Indian Territory during 1847 confirming the deepening famine catastrophe suffered by the people of Ireland, an advertisement was made asking concerned Choctaw citizens to bring or send donations to Skullyville, Choctaw Nation.[5] The tribulations of the Irish in 1847 struck a deep chord of sympathy with the Choctaws because they, too, had suffered greatly. Their dismal passages via largely unfamiliar routes that had periodically led them into poorly mapped wilderness, with few improved roads, were still raw memories.

Precise record-keeping during this most chaotic transition period, which spanned two harsh winters and a cholera epidemic, was impossible, but the total population of the Choctaw Nation in 1830 is accurately estimated at 25,000. The (conservative) estimate of 2,500 Choctaws who died during the exodus from Mississippi means that at least one Choctaw of every ten died during the fall of 1831 through the winter of 1832–33. This figure does not include the six hundred men, women, and children who died in the epidemic after the Arkansas River flooded in 1833, during the Choctaws' second summer in Indian Territory.

Americans remember vividly and painfully what it was like to lose three thousand U.S. citizens in a single day, September 11, 2001. To attempt to comprehend the Choctaws' scale of suffering during this short period in our history, we must imagine perhaps a similar scale. One in ten United States citizens, at present, equals 32,527,000 people. Therefore it is accurate to say that every Choctaw citizen was touched by tragedy. Smaller numbers of displaced Choctaws making the trek after 1834 and the years following resulted in fewer deaths. However, another relocation initiative to transport impoverished Choctaws from Mississippi to Indian Territory became necessary for several years during the mid-1840s.[6]

Skullyville, where donations to Irish Famine relief efforts were collected, derives its name from the Choctaw word for money, "iskulli," and was where citizens came from all over the Choctaw Nation to receive annuity disbursements, which were payments accruing from various treaties with the United States government.[7] On March 23, 1847, the Choctaw treasurer in Skullyville closed the collections for Irish

Famine relief and sent the money to the relief society, a gesture of compassion and friendship that both nations publicly value to the present day. In this essay I try to sketch, from a Choctaw vantage point, the landscapes and significant contexts of that day in 1847 when the Choctaw gift was officially made.[8]

The chief empathic commonalities shared between two seemingly disparate cultures separated by the Atlantic Ocean and half of North America can easily be traced to the collective outcomes of colonialism. The Irish had suffered since the eleventh century under the cultural extinction policies of the British, and the Choctaws suffered degradations since the seventeenth century forged by Britain's neocolonial descendants, the Anglo-Americans. The imperial model employed by the British to colonize the Irish—focused on gaining massive land cessions and legitimating aggressive assimilation policies to conquer indigenous tribes—was the same strategy the British brought to America. These aggressive policies did not cease after Anglo-Americans fought for and gained independence from Britain. The simple fact that United States citizens after 1783 could usurp indigenous lands and resources for their own immediate benefit, rather than for the benefit of the Crown, only accelerated the colonial enterprise north of Mexico.

The British frequently characterized the Irish as *savages*. Similarly, Anglo-Americans and other Euro-Americans often referred to Native Americans in public, or in private communications, as *savages, redskins, gut-eaters, blanket-butts*, and other pejoratives. To subvert the stereotype, I argue that the educational and political atmospheres in the Choctaw Nation during the 1840s, the formative years of the new Choctaw republic, combined to create goodwill toward the Irish during their Great Hunger. The simple facts that American Indian tribes are kinship societies, and that kinship considerations influence all aspects of their traditional politics and culture also contributed to their sense of commiseration with the Irish. Simply reading a partial list of nineteenth-century Choctaw chiefs' surnames such as McCurtain, McKinney, Kincaid, Garvin, Cole, Harkins, and McCoy suggests that kinship relations between Irish, Scots-Irish, and Choctaw people were well established.

To illustrate the strong analogies between the Choctaw and Irish nations, it's important to note that on the same day the gift was given, March 23, 1847, Peter Perkins Pitchlynn, one of the Choctaw Nation's most articulate diplomats,[9] and a company of men incorporated together for this single purpose were preparing several hundred destitute Six Towns Choctaws for the 600-mile emigration from Mississippi to the "Country in the West," the new Choctaw Nation in Indian Territory.[10] Approximately six thousand Choctaws, roughly a quarter of the tribe's population, had elected to remain in the Mississippi homelands under seemingly adequate provisions of the Treaty of Dancing Rabbit Creek. Instead of receiving peaceable possession of their allotted shares of tribal lands and fair treatment as citizens of Mississippi, as was promised by the treaty, these Choctaws suffered systematic assaults. They were physically abused by state-appointed bullies and methodically marginalized and impoverished by malicious state laws (reminiscent of the Penal Laws imposed by the Crown upon the Irish), all aimed at complete eradication of Indians from Mississippi, in defiance of federal treaty mandates.

My essay draws for source material upon letters between Pitchlynn and his business associates who had taken up the unenviable task of essentially rescuing impoverished and downtrodden Choctaw families from the backwaters of Mississippi and nearby areas of Louisiana, and of paying for their overland transportation and provisions. They also paid to lease, schedule, provision, supervise, and accompany the boarding and launch of steamboats hired to convey the refugees upriver on the Mississippi and then to Fort Coffee on the Arkansas River or Fort Towson on the Red River. The emigration contractors could not be paid until the long journey had been completed. The emigrating Choctaws carried with them government scrip or land vouchers, paid them for allotment farms they were entitled to, but cheated out of in Mississippi. The emigrants' uses of the scrip were heavily restricted by the federal government, and they could not trade it for cash until they reached Indian Territory.[11] Pitchlynn did his part of the work of the emigration from November 1846 until the end of March 1847, when he fell ill with cholera.

The centerpiece of the textual exhibits is Pitchlynn's eloquent letter written in November 1846 and mailed to his tutor and friend Dr. Gideon Lincecum, describing a beautiful tribal dance in Pitchlynn's honor on a moonlit night in a forest of tall pines on the north shore of Lake Pontchartrain in Louisiana, while he commenced his efforts to contact and aid his Choctaw friends in relocating to the "Country in the West." The letter is examined for its historical importance, its literary qualities, as evidence of the Choctaws' aspirations to, and achievements in, education, and for its bearing on the Choctaw–Irish exchange.

Background for This Study

My inquiry emanates organically from my ongoing seventeen-year study of Choctaw and Chickasaw intellectual traditions during the first half of the nineteenth century.

My training is in literary criticism, so my central focus has been on the writings of tribal intellectuals, an unexpectedly rich oeuvre of mostly letters, memorials, speeches, constitutions, and legal documents, but also yielding stories, poems, songs, and essays. Besides their value as literature, these written artifacts have languished in dusty, forgotten archives and represent a treasure trove of Choctaw history. My greatest find in the forgotten files was a small, four-by-six-inch, leather-bound journal upon whose 104 pages were inscribed the first written laws of the Choctaw Nation, all handwritten by Peter Perkins Pitchlynn in the Choctaw language during meetings of the National Council during the summers of 1826–28. The journal had been hiding in an unannotated folder since it was donated to the university library in 1962.[12] Apparently, I was the first person who had seen the journal in the forty-six years since its donation. I was also able to read it. To my further great astonishment, as I pored agape through the Choctaw masterpiece, I found as one of the signatories to the constitution, already using his English name as his legal name, my great-great-grandfather William Wade.[13]

Although less dramatic or overtly pathetic than losses of life from famine or dispossession, a perhaps more destructive and insidious effect of colonial hegemonies on indigenous people is the repression and obfuscation of their histories. Like many other Oklahoma Choctaws, I knew very little about my familial tribal ancestors in Mississippi until after I discovered Pitchlynn's journal. When the Choctaws were uprooted during the 1830s and removed to Indian Territory, though a significant number were already biliterate in English and Choctaw, tribal and family histories were transferred intergenerationally almost exclusively in stories, in the oral tradition. Without a paper trail to follow, historical records as basic as genealogies have been seemingly lost, and certainly obscure. I even had trouble tracking my ancestors in nineteenth-century Indian Territory (present-day Oklahoma, where I live and work). If Indian Territory is the metaphorical moon, from a research perspective, Mississippi is Mars, almost unattainable. Knowing that, it's not hard to imagine the epiphany I experienced when I found my own ancestor sitting right across the table from some more publicized Choctaw men of the period. Until that moment, the only detail of his life I had uncovered (in a dusty Mississippi courthouse archive) was that in 1825 he was living in Noxubee County. The Tribal Council drafting those first written laws during the summers of 1826–28 convened in Noxubee County.

My first focus in studying early Choctaw intellectuals was on those corresponding with each other during the pre-Removal period spanning the years 1824–31, and on Pitchlynn and Choctaw James L. McDonald (the first American Indian lawyer admitted in 1824 to the bar of U.S. courts). I had read the correspondence of the 1840s, but I had not found occasion to study it in any depth. I was intrigued by the agreement signed between Pitchlynn and five other men on December 17, 1846, for the purpose of "emigrating Choctaw Indians now in Mississippi to their Country in the West."[14] I did not know, for example, that this emigration company, and perhaps others like it, offered the last chance for Choctaws suffering in Mississippi to take advantage of federal government assistance in moving to Indian Territory. The partners in the company are an interesting lot, and I will present more about them later. Of the series of letters written between the summers of 1846 and 1847 regarding the emigration enterprise, including correspondence between business partners, I was most captivated by Pitchlynn's report to Dr. Lincecum of his interesting journey to find Indians who wanted to emigrate to Indian Territory.

Nothing to Be Seen but Ash, and Affectation

Pitchlynn's letter to his mentor and friend Gideon Lincecum outlines his travels around Mississippi after he last visited with Dr. and Mrs. Lincecum at their home in Columbus, Mississippi.[15] The letter, read with emotional sensitivity, is a narrative of the dispossessed. "I reached Louisville the same day I left your house, however stopped a few minutes at my old homestead and found it in a state of dilapidation, and the once beautiful scenery around it all despoiled," Pitchlynn writes.[16]

Fifteen years earlier, during 1832, Pitchlynn had left his old home in Mississippi to emigrate with his family to Indian Territory, where they immediately began to farm fertile bottom lands of the Arkansas River near Skullyville. After clearing trees and planting crops in the spring of 1833, one of the worst floods ever recorded on that river inundated the Pitchlynns' farm, destroying their crops, house, cattle, horses, and hogs. Six hundred people in the vicinity of the flood died from diseases it spread. A few devastated Choctaw families who had the means moved back to Mississippi, but Pitchlynn and his family decided to move later that fall to less flood-prone lands farther south in the new Choctaw Nation, near Eagletown on the Mountain Fork River, a tributary of the Red River.[17]

"Sadness came over my soul at the sight, but I will not trouble you with any whining sentimentalisms about the place or about myself, for every man of any sensibility who ever had a home and left it and saw it again years afterwards has had similar associations and feelings and there is no use in putting them on paper either in prose or poetry," Pitchlynn continues in fluent English. I will intrude here upon his narrative to report how I can feel the pathos of the moment my protagonist is recounting more intensely perhaps because I have stood on Pitchlynn's Prairie, ten miles west of Columbus, Mississippi, while listening to a dramatic story about Pitchlynn as a boy.

The story began during the Creek War of 1813–14, and he was seven years old, the story goes, hiding with his mother and sisters on Yokatubbe's farm several miles away from his father's home while an attack by Creek warriors appeared to be imminent.[18] John Pitchlynn, Peter's father, had been orphaned as a teenager when his father, a Scots trader named Isaac Pitchlynn, died on his first trip into Choctaw territory in 1774.

Choctaws welcomed John Pitchlynn into their society, and while still a young man, he married Sophia Folsom, a member of a prominent Choctaw family. He subsequently became the most influential intermarried white citizen of the Choctaw Nation, serving as the official interpreter for the Choctaws beginning with the Treaty of Hopewell in 1785. John continued to serve as a language interpreter trusted by both the Choctaws and U.S. agents for successive treaties up to and including the Treaty of Dancing Rabbit Creek of 1830, which initiated the great emigration of Choctaws to Indian Territory. John's home, about five miles north of Columbus, Mississippi, on the west bank of the Tombigbee River, had been fortified with a stockade and served as the rendezvous for several companies of Choctaw and Chickasaw warriors that had united to defend against an invasion by Creek warriors from east of the Tombigbee in 1813.[19]

Pitchlynn tells Lincecum that he spent the night at Louisville, Mississippi, and made his way south to Neshoba County (where the major part of the present-day Mississippi Choctaw Reservation is located). He said he stayed there "upwards of two weeks visiting the Indians in that region."[20] The presumed topics of conversation included discussion of their "last chance" to emigrate. Pitchlynn would certainly have had to communicate at length about life in Indian Territory in reports to Choctaws who had stayed in Mississippi. From Neshoba County, Pitchlynn set out on the longest leg of the journey. "From there I struck off Southward and after many long windings and twinings about in the country, I finally reached the shores of Lake Pontchartrain where I found Indians quite numerous." Pitchlynn's purpose along the way was to spread the word about the emigration opportunity, and I expect he was keeping careful records of families in the various Choctaw enclaves he visited who wanted to move to the new Choctaw Nation west of the Mississippi River, so that his company could lease transportation and more accurately calculate for necessary provisions.

"From here I traveled through swamps and canebrakes to Baton Rouge on the Mississippi River, at which place I took water up to Vicksburg and reached here [Jackson, Mississippi] last evening in the Cars."[21] Pitchlynn's matter-of-fact tone belies what by this time must have been a grueling and probably discouraging journey. "I saw Indians nearly every day on my route. They are indeed a scattered people, and I am certain there is no influence or inducement that will ever cause them all to emigrate. Many will remain in this country for years to come," he continues in a tenor of apprehension and resignation.

He communicates further in the letter to "Gid," as Pitchlynn always affection-ately addressed his mentor and friend Gideon Lincecum, that he will remain in Jackson for a week or so and then head back south again, presumably to begin the work of transporting refugee families overland to ports where they would begin the riverine portion of their journey to Indian Territory. He then nuances the letter in a way that might demonstrate skills to a teacher or mentor whom he wanted to impress with the quality of his education.

That nuance is a 185-word periodic sentence in which Pitchlynn describes the pristine beauty of a moonlit deep-woods stomp dance in his honor. He contrasts the rich cultural context of the stomp dance with the relatively dreary life he must endure in Washington, DC, where he has spent most of his time since 1845 as the Choctaw Nation's ambassador to the U.S. Congress. His rhetorical purpose in using the long, elegant sentence may also be to reflect the rich tradition of oratory that the Choctaws are famous for.[22] Pitchlynn's first wife, Rhoda, had been gravely weakened by disease, probably malaria, during the late 1830s in Indian Territory, and she died in 1842. After grieving for two years and having made arrangements for the care of his children, Pitchlynn took up his post and mission to Washington in 1845. His service as Choctaw ambassador to the federal government would continue for thirty-six years until his death in 1881, interrupted only by the American Civil War.

"The Indians at one place honored me with a big dance," Pitchlynn writes to open a paragraph roughly in the middle of the letter:

> The scene was a rich one . . . for it was at their incampment in a forest of long leaf
> pine, and not in a saloon such as I saw in Washington City, where all were pent

up in brick walls, and nothing to be seen but ash, and affectation, but here was a dance upon the green Earth, the pure air of the pine woods to be inhaled, and the full orbed moon and twinkling stars shedding their beams upon us and with those lights we had the lightwood fire flaring up red blazes—near which formed the moving circle of young men and women, who danced to their own songs, in which all united their voices, and ever and anon arose the shout of the warriors which rang loud and long upon the air, and on they moved with varied song and change of dance till at a late hour in the night when they closed with a grand flourish in the Man Dance, which I need not describe as you know all about it.[23]

Besides the rare and beautiful scene Pitchlynn describes, the probability that this may be one of the last stomp dances he ever experiences in Mississippi may be weighing heavily on his mind.

Here I ask the reader to pause for a moment and consider his or her preconceptions of Choctaws or other tribespeople in the American South more than a decade before the Civil War. I'm guessing that your preconceptions, like mine, did not envision a biliterate Choctaw intellectual penning 185-word periodic sentences in figurative but controlled English to his American frontiersman mentor Lincecum, who was an occasional correspondent with Charles Darwin.[24] You, like me, were probably also not envisioning a handsome, neatly but simply dressed Indian whose English diction alone identifies him within the educated elite living on the cusp of the Georgian and Victorian eras of fashion, and whom Charles Dickens described after their chance meeting on the Ohio River on board a paddle steamer traveling between Louisville and Cincinnati "as stately and complete a gentleman of Nature's making as ever I beheld, moving among the people in the boat as another kind of being."[25]

Pitchlynn notices that the warriors and old men are watching the festive dancing "like so many pictures of contentment." The *Nanena hitkla* (Man Dance) he alludes to starts with men and women locking arms and forming a ring. All sing, and the ring revolves rapidly until no one remains in it. "There was a wild inchantment about all this, yet the most natural and simple," he writes in the letter. "I wished when I was looking upon it that Gid was with me to see it."[26] The affection Pitchlynn has for his old friend and guide is obvious.

The Indians that Pitchlynn visited near Lake Pontchartrain, a 630-square-mile brackish estuary a few miles north of the Mississippi River and New Orleans in southeastern Louisiana, were most likely the Bayou Lacomb Choctaws, known also as the Acolapissas. Ethnographer David I. Bushnell found a few Choctaw families still living on the north shore of Lake Pontchartrain while he observed the Bayou Lacomb Choctaws for the Smithsonian Institution in 1909.[27] According to Bushnell, most who remained among the descendants of the "numerous" Indians whom Pitchlynn encountered there had taken the government's offer to move to Indian Territory after Congress passed legislation during the summer of 1902 that offered them financial aid to do so.

David Bushnell's narrative resonates with Pitchlynn's descriptions of the land some sixty-three years earlier. Bushnell continues:

> Until a few years ago, there were several hundred Choctaw living near Bayou Lacomb within a radius of a few miles. . . . Their dance ground was in the pine woods a short distance north of the place where the few remaining members of the tribe now dwell. There they would gather and with many fires blazing would dance throughout the night. No whites were ever permitted to witness the dance. It is said that if the Indians suspected that a white man was watching them, they would extinguish the fires at once and remain in darkness. During the dance one man acted as leader. He held two short sticks, hitting one with the other to keep time for the singing.[28]

The enchanting dances in Pitchlynn's honor at Bayou Lacomb in 1846 were already an old tradition with the Acolapissa Choctaws. Bushnell notes that the French officer Jean-Bernard Bossu observed similar dances in the same longleaf pine forest while touring the South during the third year of the French and Indian War, and that Bossu confirms that "nearly all the gatherings of the Chactas take place at night."[29] These accounts by Bossu in 1759, by Pitchlynn in 1846, and by Bushnell in 1909 show us a rich Choctaw ceremonial tradition that continued at Bayou Lacomb for at least 150 years. Historical documents attest to the continuous cultural practices of the Choctaws' ceremonies in the same place for at least two centuries before 1759, especially if one considers the Spanish documents concerning de Soto's expedition.

Pitchlynn closes his letter to Lincecum with his best sentiments for Mrs. Lincecum, and states that he hopes to visit their household in Columbus again "before I leave this country." He makes the cryptic statement "I have enemies in the field, but they are not open—however, know them and understand all their movements. I can hurt them more than they can me."[30] Apparently Dr. Lincecum would have understood whom his student was describing as enemies, but there are no clues in any of the other letters as to who they were.

Historical Mistreatment of the Choctaws

Much like the suffering of the Irish that reached a sinister peak in 1847, the misfortunes of the Mississippi Choctaws accumulated throughout the same period of time and took on ominous dimensions. With no access to white schools or facilities, the Choctaws who remained in Mississippi gradually gave up fighting the new system and withdrew into isolated areas in east-central Mississippi and formed subsistence enclaves on public lands along the Gulf Coast. They were forced to increasingly become strangers and exiles in their own country.

It had been fifteen years since Choctaws in large numbers began to emigrate west, and conditions for those who remained in Mississippi grew steadily worse. For those establishing new homes in Indian Territory, hunger was ever-present: one out of ten Choctaws had starved. They'd also died from exposure, disease, snakebite, or accident on the horrific removal treks during the winters of 1831–34. As previously mentioned, Pitchlynn's livelihood, as with many others, was washed away by the flooding Arkansas River during his family's first summer in the Territory. Disease and spoiled food, public hygiene challenges, whisky peddlers, the depredations of other, often criminal fugitives fleeing the United States, and bad weather were the routine perils of life Choctaws faced in their new home. The missionaries who had earlier established and maintained schools among the Choctaws in Mississippi removed with the tribe and built new schools and churches among the Choctaws in Indian Territory.[31]

One of the reasons Pitchlynn emigrated with some of the earliest groups was that he was perhaps the best-qualified and most strongly motivated citizen to guide the establishment of the new Choctaw school system in the west. My sense from reading his correspondence is that Pitchlynn, who was twenty-six years old during the season of emigration, along with his young-adult and well-educated Choctaw contemporaries were thrilled by the prospects of building a constitutional republic from their old and venerable society in a fairly new and exciting world.[32] Being overrun by multitudes of land-hungry Europeans did not make the Choctaws forgetful. The oral history of the tribe suggests that relocation is sometimes necessary. Some of the Choctaws' most cherished migration stories have them trekking from the south and west across mountain ranges and deserts and plains (in one version) and emanating from a coastal tropical lowland near a large ocean (in another), each suggesting that a large population of these people came up from Mexico, which some scholars have speculated was a retreat from the Spanish insurgency into Mexico early in the sixteenth century.[33] Pitchlynn is credited by one of John Swanton's informants with favoring the story that Choctaws came from tropical jungle lowlands, a Yucatan-type environment, to the Mississippi River Valley, where we separated from the Chickasaws to make two large and prominent tribes.[34]

One of the deleterious outcomes of colonialism for American Indians is that we, in the modern era, have been compelled to rely on history books written by the colonizers' scholars. In my own training at the University of Oklahoma I had to rely on these texts during the early stages of my research and was often offended by the scholars' interpretations of my ancestors. They invariably regarded any tribal leader who had both white and Choctaw ancestors as automatically corrupted.

I would never suggest that the authors of these works were personally racist, but I do believe they reflect, like a mirror, institutionalized racism in United States ideology. I regard the works as unreliable histories nonetheless, because they reflect one of the more sinister underbellies of colonialism: the presumption that white blood, white intelligence, white power always trumps red, or black, or yellow. We are woefully tired of the racist ideologies forged by the British Empire and its neocolonial offspring as much as by any other influence one might single out in history, and the caustic imprint of their radicalized caste systems never seems to completely go away anywhere throughout the modern world.

Pitchlynn continued in the work of emigration as long as he could. He wrote to Arnold Harris from New River on March 30, 1847:[35]

Dear Genl,[36]

I sent up on the Elk on last Sunday (day before yesterday) 144 emigrants—have with me now 6 others making in all of my party 150.

I stayed behind to gather up others but my health has failed, and I am compelled to leave the field with fair prospects of getting more behind.

I regret it very much.

I was attacked with the Cholera Morbus about a week ago—and have had some fevers, and dysentery, which together have reduced my strength very much.

Believing you have gone down to aid Major Hurst with his party, I send this to

New Orleans that you may know the extent of our operations. 'Tis small, 'tis true, but who has done better?

    I am yours respectfully,

    PP Pitchlynn[37]

Once again, we find Pitchlynn in a situation that would be hard even for those twentieth-century historians to interpret, despite his mixed-bloodedness, as anything other than admirable for its humanitarian dimensions. We may speculate that the last 150 Choctaws he was able to secure passage for before he fell ill with cholera were emigrating to Indian Territory in hopes of building a better life. It is a material fact that Pitchlynn made little or nothing in the emigration enterprise, and in fact was still owed $1,200 by Daniel Saffarans some years after the emigration efforts ended.[38]

Pitchlynn's Partners

In my studies of Pitchlynn correspondence, which is by no means comprehensive since he and his correspondents preserved hundreds of letters, I had run across no other letters to or from the partners listed in the "Articles of Agreement" signed in December 1846. I was skeptical that I could dig up any information on them because of the difficulties I had experienced in searches for my own ancestors and other persons among the Choctaws before the American Civil War.

    I was able nonetheless, while gladly confounding my skepticism, to locate some interesting stories about several of Pitchlynn's five copartners in the emigration company. I found a record about Daniel Saffarans, for example, the apparent scribe of the Articles of Agreement, which was a short contract describing the purpose of their company and pertinent terms. A descendant of Saffarans writes that he served at the age of sixteen in the War of 1812, was later an Indian agent with the Chickasaws and Choctaws, worked as a contractor of the Memphis Navy Yard, established a furniture factory, and oversaw the paving of early Memphis streets with gravel.[39] W. David Baird's biography of Pitchlynn identifies Saffarans as an influential Tennessee businessman who secured the removal contract with the federal government in the mid-1840s and who included Pitchlynn in the company as the one most likely to influence Choctaws remaining in Mississippi to emigrate to Indian Territory.[40] Saffarans apparently profited handsomely with a trading post that sold goods to Chickasaws on credit after their removal from Mississippi to Indian Territory in 1837. Pitchlynn had complained in Washington to the secretary of war in October 1841 about Saffarans and other traders' price-gouging of Chickasaws and Choctaws in Indian Territory, but trusted him enough to copartner with him in the emigration company during 1846–47.[41]

John J. (Jackson) Smith is probably the same John Smith Jr. as a white man who came to Mississippi from Boston, Massachusetts, as a Presbyterian missionary to the Choctaw Indians at Elliot Mission and School. Elliot School, founded in 1818, was the first mission school established in the old Choctaw Nation.[42] Arnold Harris, like Saffarans but to a lesser extent, had been embroiled in the controversies surrounding supplying goods and services to the Chickasaws in Indian Territory after their removal in 1837. The traders were often accused of taking advantage of the Indians, but none were ever charged with a crime, and most closed their businesses in the Territory before 1840. Harris moved on to become sutler at Fort Gibson in Indian Territory. I found nothing definitive on James W. Tate, even after a thorough search of Tate County, Mississippi. The most interesting stories besides Pitchlynn's turned up for Duncan Smith.

The name of Duncan Smith still raises controversy among his descendants and those of his southern contemporaries in Cameron Parish, Louisiana. The controversy spins around the question, was Duncan Smith, as his contemporaries called him, a Confederate traitor, or an American patriot? Duncan Smith may have been the most hunted man in Louisiana during the American Civil War. By 1863 he carried a Confederate bounty on his head of $10,000. The twenty-first-century equivalent, by the most modest conversion factors, is approximately $2,000,000.[43] He was labeled by critics loyal to the Confederate States of America as an arch-Unionist, and was opposed to human slavery, even though he was born and raised in the South. Besides, he had married a Methodist preacher's daughter from Charleston, South Carolina, and owned a lot of farmland in Rankin County, Mississippi, to which his wife's family and their entire Methodist church congregation had moved in 1825, a migration journey of about seven hundred miles. Smith had immigrated to Rankin County with his parents and brother Edmond earlier during the 1820s. He married Peggy Rhode Russell in 1834, two years after assisting some Choctaw citizens in their first removal treks to Indian Territory.[44] The *Beaumont Enterprise* reporter, who knew Smith in 1870, added this comment:

> Duncan Smith had opposed human slavery since long before John Brown's raid, and when the Civil War came on, his fiery opposition to it put him in bad odor with

the people who favored it and fought for it. He was a man of fixed and inflexible opinions, an Abolitionist bitterly opposed to slavery. He was ready at the drop of a hat to die for that principle![45]

Roughly between the time during which he assisted Choctaw families during 1832 in their emigration from Mississippi to Indian Territory and his Civil War experience of being shot at and hunted in the coastal marshes of Louisiana, Duncan Smith, who his descendants say was of Scots-Irish extraction, joined with Peter Pitchlynn and their four copartners in 1847 to help many of the embattled Choctaws who had remained in Mississippi emigrate to the friendlier environs of the new Choctaw Nation in Indian Territory, or the "Country in the West," as they often and poetically referred to it. Judging from the sparse details of their lives that began more than two centuries ago, it seems at least two common threads knit these men together. They were well-educated idealists, but also men possessing unusual entrepreneurial skills.

I take a lot of pride in my ability to perform research with a mind open to discovery, rather than a mind looking for support of foregone conclusions. I found an easy appreciation and felt a fuzzy, warm sentiment when I first learned of the friendship between the Irish and Choctaw peoples spanning 170 years, and still counting. I have read with great interest Peter Pitchlynn's letters, which give us a glimpse into the rich culture of the old Choctaw Nation, as well as into the suffering of his displaced countrymen. The fact that Pitchlynn and his company's complex rescue of destitute Choctaws from Mississippi was in progress simultaneously with the Choctaws' gift to the Irish relief society builds another layer of appreciation into the event. A few more corners of previously undernarrated Choctaw history have been brought into view, along with some interesting stories told of the people who volunteered to help refugees escape their oppression and make a new home in the Choctaw Nation of Indian Territory, in the Country in the West.[46] Some of the harmful and racist views of my Choctaw ancestors written as fact by misguided settler historians have been set aside. We have seen the literary qualities and surprisingly articulate writing in English by a classically educated, early nineteenth-century biliterate Choctaw intellectual.

In contrast to the warm sentiment, from a humanistic standpoint, in the Irish-Choctaw Exchange, however, difficulty arises in my attempts to draw meaningful conclusions about the long friendship from a political perspective. Every time I have tried to distill the seemingly profound circumstance of nearly two centuries of diplomatic relations between geographically distant nations into one or more useful conclusions, I have been stumped. Beyond the friendship, the exchange touches on so many of the gravest maladies of modern history—poverty, injustice, famine, blight, overpopulation, war, imperialism, religious persecution, racism, and classism—that searing accounts of virtually every form of human suffering are available within this story. Perhaps I am just avoiding the obvious conclusion that volunteers itself, but which I greatly resist. That conclusion is that the instances of compassion and friendship in this world are sadly few compared with the hatefulness and tragedy that characterizes too much of daily life everywhere. Stories of the Choctaws and the Irish raise painful questions, such as how is it possible that persecution of Irish Catholics by Protestants proceed from the same system of ethics, the philosophies of the forgiving, compassionate Jesus, that both adversaries embrace as the truth? Further, one may be able to comprehend how the British and their descendants, with their long history of colonial annexation and of forming hegemonic replacements of indigenous governments, could overrun American Indian tribes and take their homelands away from them. However, it is much harder to comprehend how Puritans, Russians, Jews, Germans, French, and even some of the Irish immigrants who fled horrific persecutions in their own homelands could willingly participate in the systematic rout of Native Americans from theirs.

Another reason the phrase "Irish-Choctaw Exchange" has an unexpected ring is that, historically speaking, Europeans of any stripe have not been high on the list of friends of American Indians. It is, after all, mostly Europeans, including millions of Irish, who came to America and usurped by various means, ethical or unethical, compassionate or cruel, the homes and livelihoods of American Indians. Perhaps as a Choctaw citizen, I should resist celebrating the heartwarming goodwill that the Choctaw–Irish Gift Exchange represents because it is a relatively trivial anomaly compared to the vast sums of land, natural resources, treasure, sacred sites—and the less tangible but immeasurable wealth reposing in our indigenous languages—that have been destroyed or taken over by Europeans and their descendants. Perhaps any acknowledgment of compatibility among Irish and Choctaws should be resisted until Euro-Americans have significantly redressed the crimes of colonialism. Euro-Americans in the United States, by now, officially and constitutionally have acknowledged and rejected the evils of human slavery, but American Indians are still waiting for the first official policy or constitutional amendment that acknowledges and redresses the evils of colonization heaped on our Native nations.

One must consider and consume the paradox of giving and taking in America with a healthy salting of irony. One person's redemption is sometimes another person's damnation. Consider the words of an immigrant Irish American in a letter to the editor of the *Times* of London in 1850:

> I am exceedingly well pleased at coming to this land of plenty. On arrival I purchased 120 acres of land at $5 an acre. You must bear in mind that I have purchased the land out, and it is to me and mine an "estate forever" without a landlord, an agent or tax-gatherer to trouble me. I would advise all my friends to quit Ireland—the country most dear to me; as long as they remain in it they will be in bondage and misery.
>
> What you labour for is sweetened by contentment and happiness; there is no failure in the potato crop, and you can grow every crop you wish, without manuring the land during life. You need not mind feeding pigs, but let them into the woods and they will feed themselves, until you want to make bacon of them.
>
> I shudder when I think that starvation prevails to such an extent in poor Ireland. After supplying the entire population of America, there would still be as much corn and provisions left us would supply the world, for there is no limit to cultivation or end to land. Here the meanest labourer has beef and mutton, with bread, bacon, tea, coffee, sugar and even pies, the whole year round—every day here is as good as Christmas day in Ireland.[47]

As students growing up in public schools in the United States, my contemporaries and I were presented daily with material to read or hear that proved what a blessing it was to be American. It is easy for me to feel joy when I read the formerly starving Irishman's letter. I truly exult in what must have seemed like a divine miracle to him, a god-sent transformation from starving tenancy to landed prosperity. Unfortunately, the Native tribespeople of America experienced essentially the opposite transformation—from centuries of relative freedom and abundance to dispossession, disenfranchisement, death, and almost extinction. From the time that sustainable European colonial enterprises began in North America during the early seventeenth century to the polling of the U.S. Census in 1900, Native American population plummeted from 10 million, by conservative estimates, to four hundred thousand, with the majority of the survivors speaking only English. Natives went from living in a land of linguistic diversity that held at least one hundred different languages to a land desolate of Native languages in less than a century. This is a 96 percent loss in population, genocide if you will, for which I need not offer comparisons for scale. The disappearance of diverse languages, along with the knowledge and culture that inheres in those languages, has been compared in equal terms to the survival-as-a-species risks associated with losses in biodiversity—but I will digress no further.

The creator religion that I received through oral tradition, family culture, and from the Earth herself during my lifetime has been enriched by the interesting cosmologies and worldviews of the tribes of Africa, Asia, India, the desert tribes, the Pacific Islands people, the Arctic tribes, the southern continents, and Europeans. I have had the privilege of knowing some of their views because of the educational opportunities I have been blessed with—books, schools, broadcast radio and television, movies, and the Internet. The Dalai Lama in a recent interview was asked if he thought modern people were becoming more cold-hearted, and the Earth a more cynical place. He replied that the truth was quite contrary to that assertion. With advanced information technology deployed around the globe, no earthquake, hurricane, tsunami, or airline disaster strikes without the whole world knowing about it, he said. The outpourings of sympathy and aid are unmatched in history, and it caused him to be filled with great hope.

More than one Muskogean-language tribe in the southeastern United States, the homelands of the Choctaws, traditionally extinguishes all their home fires once a year, usually at harvest time. Also extinguished are unpaid debts, grudges, and other hard feelings between individuals in the community. During the harvest celebration, when the home fires are ignited anew with coals from the one central sacred fire, this represents spiritual unity. The entire community vows to move together forward into the next new cycle together, as one. In the spirit of my religion and my best ethics, and according to my best analyses and estimations of greatest benefit, I will report that I have extinguished any grudges I ever held against any people and choose to embrace and celebrate the *virtues* of history, such as a longstanding friendship between nations, the people of Ireland and the Choctaw people, who bear the ancient mantles of their histories and sovereignty, and who remain loyal, sacrificial, and contributing citizens of their respective modern republics.[48] Inspired by the Dalai Lama's optimism, I will hope that the ever-shrinking human village will learn to make peace and not war, make music and not noise, and to reach out to each other in times of need. It is incumbent upon each of us, however, especially we who are elders, to demand that the aggressive, war-hungry, and hateful members of our societies sit down and be quiet. The horrific and deracinating tragedies of the Great Famine and of the Trail of Tears have not gone away, have not vanished from the Earth. The United Nations Refugee Agency (UNHCR) declares that there are currently more refugees, more people displaced by war, famine, and senseless violence than at any other time in history, exceeding a staggering 65 million and counting.[49] So, let us celebrate our Choctaw-Irish friendship and shared hopes, but at the same time let us become more active in diminishing fear and greed, as well as more active in establishing compassion and friendship as shared central values.

The imperative to cultivate traditions of compassion and friendship between the tribes, bands, and nations of Earth, of *Yaknimoma*, has never been more important, nor the need more apparent, than it is now in our densely populated world. The growing tendency to return to the imagined security of isolationism and protectionism should be resisted. The trends toward increasingly polemical "othering" of people of different ethnicity, religion, or tradition must be dismantled, examined, and replaced with attitudes of sharing and mutual respect.

People widely acknowledge the convincing evidence revealed by modern geneticists that all members of the only surviving species of the genus *Homo*, *Homo sapiens* (Latin: "wise men"), human beings, are descended from one common ancestor. Perhaps rather than beating our chests with complaints of our seemingly irreconcilable differences, what wise men and women need to do is to recognize and affirm our undeniable commonalities.

Tribes are kinship societies, and nothing is more important in indigenous societies than identifying with, and caring for, one's relatives. If the geneticists are correct, the people of Earth are one very large kinship society. If we truly value civilization in our world, we must never betray or abandon our relatives. The Choctaws in 1847 shared some of their modest sustenance with the suffering people of Ireland, because they were, and are, our relatives. The Choctaw–Irish Gift Exchange we celebrate here is a model worthy of preservation and emulation throughout *Yaknimoma*, the world.[50]

NOTES

1. Indian Removal Act, May 28, 1830, Library of Congress, *Statutes at Large*, Twenty-First Congress, Session 1, ch. 148, 411–12.

2. The Trail of Broken Treaties (also known as the Trail of Broken Treaties Caravan and the Pan American Native Quest for Justice) was a cross-country protest staged in the autumn of 1972 in the United States by American Indian and First Nations organizations. Designed to bring national attention to American Indian issues such as treaty rights, living standards, and inadequate housing, it brought to the national capital the largest

gathering ever of American Indians presenting their hopes. For a fuller account, see Vine Deloria Jr., *Behind the Trail of Broken Treaties: An Indian Declaration of Independence* (New York: Delacorte Press, 1974). Well-known American humorist Will Rogers, a Cherokee from Oklahoma, said, "The United States never broke a treaty with a foreign government and never kept one with the Indians."

3. Treaty with the Choctaw, Sept. 27, 1830, 7 Stat., 333, Proclamation, Feb. 24, 1831. Read the treaty in Charles J. Kappler, *Indian Affairs: Laws and Treaties*, vol. 2 (Washington, DC: Government Printing Office, 1904), or online at https://www.tngenweb.org/cessions/18300927.html.

4. George W. Harkins, "Farewell Letter to the American People," *American Indian* magazine, December 1926. Reprinted in *Great Documents in American Indian History*, ed. Wayne Moquin and Charles Van Doren (New York: DaCapo Press, 1995), 151.

5. Citizens may have been asked to contribute a fraction of their annuities distributed at Skullyville. I have not yet found a physical record, if any exists, that might reveal the method of collection for the offering.

6. Arthur H. DeRosier, *The Removal of the Choctaw Indians* (Knoxville: University of Tennessee Press, 1970); Mary Lou Stahl, *The Ones That Got Away: A Choctaw Trail of Tears* (Angleton, TX: Biotech Publishing, 1996). John R. Swanton tabulated 3,284 Mississippi Choctaws who emigrated during the period 1846–49; Swanton, *Choctaw Social and Ceremonial Life* (Washington, DC: Smithsonian Institution, Bureau of American Ethnology, 1931), 5.

7. Skullyville was near Fort Coffee on the Arkansas River, the port where Choctaws, Creeks, Chickasaws and some of the Seminoles fleeing the war in Florida arrived on river boats to enter Indian Territory. New Hope Academy for girls and Fort Coffee Academy for boys, to which young Choctaws eagerly applied for admission, were built near Skullyville. The Choctaws, during their first fifteen years in Indian Territory, established numerous neighborhood schools and ten male and female academies, boarding schools, which were originally staffed by missionary teachers, who were gradually replaced by Choctaw teachers. Oklahoma Historical Society, "Choctaw Schools," http://www.okhistory.org/publications/enc/entry.php?entry=CH049.

8. March 23rd is also my birthday, so I drink a toast to the gift and to the friendship of Choctaws and Irish every year during my birthday celebration. ("And I've drunk so many times to your health, I've ruined my own.")

9. Charles Dickens, who in 1842 met Pitchlynn on a steamboat on the Ohio River while traveling between Cincinnati and Louisville, described him at length:

He was a remarkably handsome man; some years past forty, I should judge; with long black hair, an aquiline nose, broad cheek-bones, a sunburnt complexion, and a very bright, keen, dark, and piercing eye. There were but twenty thousand of the Choctaws left, he said, and their number was decreasing every day. A few of his brother chiefs had been obliged to become civilised, and to make themselves acquainted with what the whites knew, for it was their only chance of existence. But they were not many; and the rest were as they always had been. He dwelt on this: and said several times that unless they tried to assimilate themselves to their conquerors, they must be swept away before the strides of civilised society.

When we shook hands at parting, I told him he must come to England, as he longed to see the land so much: that I should hope to see him there, one day: and that I could promise him he would be well received and kindly treated. He was evidently pleased by this assurance, though he rejoined with a good-humoured smile and an arch shake of his head, that the English used to be very fond of the Red Men when they wanted their help, but had not cared much for them, since.

He took his leave; as stately and complete a gentleman of Nature's making, as ever I beheld; and moved among the people in the boat, another kind of being. He sent me a lithographed portrait of himself soon afterwards; very like, though scarcely handsome enough; which I have carefully preserved in memory of our brief acquaintance.

—Charles Dickens, *American Notes for General Circulation*
(London: Chapman and Hall, 1842).

10. Arnold Harris wrote to Pitchlynn from Vicksburg, MS, on March 23, 1847 (the day the Choctaw gift was sent from Skullyville, Indian Territory, to the Irish relief society): "I send you the Steamboat Elk for your Indians. Col Stone will be down in a day or two but in the meantime you can be getting them on board and preparing for a start. By the time you get here McRae will be in with 100 more Six towns." The *Elk* was apparently the steamboat intended for the Bayou Lacomb Choctaws who Pitchlynn succeeded in boarding at New River near Lake Pontchartrain before he fell ill himself with cholera and withdrew from the enterprise on March 30, 1847. Peter Pitchlynn Collection, University of Oklahoma.

11. A. H. H. Stuart, *Annual Report of the Secretary of the Interior* (Washington, DC: US Department of the Interior, 1851), 300–301.

12. The journal was originally donated to Bizzell Memorial Library, University of Oklahoma,

as part of the Lester Hargrett Collection.

13. After discovering the journal, I immediately requested from the archivist a photocopy of all its pages. I delivered the pages to Marcia Haag, Choctaw linguist, and she collaborated on the translation to English with Henry Willis, a Native speaker who had become Dr. Haag's primary language consultant with the tribe. The product of their significant labor was: Peter Perkins Pitchlynn, *A Gathering of Statesmen: Records of the Choctaw Council Meetings, 1826–1828* (Norman: University of Oklahoma Press, 2013).

14. "Articles of Agreement between A. Harris, D. Saffarans, P. P. Pitchlynn, John J. Smith, Duncan Smith and James W. Tate," December 17, 1846, Peter Perkins Pitchlynn Collection, Bizzell Memorial Library, University of Oklahoma, https://digital.libraries.ou.edu/cdm/singleitem/collection/pitchlynn/id/884/rec/5.

15. Letter from P. P. Pitchlynn to Gideon Lincecum, November 12, 1846, Peter Perkins Pitchlynn Collection, Bizzell Memorial Library, University of Oklahoma.

16. Louisville, Mississippi, 60 miles southwest of Columbus, where Lincecum lived.

17. W. David Baird, *Peter Pitchlynn, Chief of the Choctaws* (Norman: University of Oklahoma Press, 1972), 49–51.

18. The Creek War, which began as a civil war between the "Red Stick" Creeks, located mostly in northern and central Alabama and allied with British and Spanish interests in North America against the south and westwardly expanding United States, and the Lower Creeks (lower because they controlled Creek territory in southern Alabama including around Mobile Bay). The Lower Creeks counted among their numbers the slave-owning minority of the tribe and were loyal to the United States. The war has generally been viewed by historians as a subset of the War of 1812 between the United States and Great Britain. This was a time of world war, and the complex theaters of war in America were parallel and similar to the complex coalitions and battle lines that formed all over Europe during the Napoleonic Wars (1803–15).

19. The story was told to me during 2010 by Rufus Ward, a retired district attorney of Clay County, Mississippi, and a respected local historian whose ancestors in 1856 had purchased Yokatubbe's allotment farm and whose family had owned it ever since.

20. With a little sensitivity, a reader can feel the burden of Pitchlynn's colonized self riding in between old Choctaw towns recently renamed after Italian explorers and French emperors offering empty-handed Choctaws a means to escape their colonial oppressors.

21. The "Cars" were stagecoaches and other wagons designed to carry passengers. Construction of the first railroads, consisting usually of only a few miles of track, did not get underway until the 1850s. Interestingly, one of the first railroads in northern Mississippi was chartered in 1871 by William Clark Falkner, the great-grandfather of

twentieth-century Nobel- and Pulitzer-prize-winning author William Cuthbert Faulkner.

22. The great war chief of the Choctaws, Pushmataha, was considered the greatest orator of the tribe until his untimely death in Washington, DC, in 1825. Choctaw scholar Don Birchfield argues that Pushmataha's famous speech of 1811, imploring the Choctaws and other southeastern tribes to reject Tecumseh's impassioned plea to join forces with his military alliance aimed at driving the Americans back to the Atlantic coast, may have saved the young republic of the United States from conquest by the British. D. L. Birchfield, *How the Choctaws Invented Civilization and Why Choctaws Will Conquer the World* (Albuquerque: University of New Mexico Press, 2007).

23. Letter from P. P. Pitchlynn to Gideon Lincecum, November 12, 1846.

24. Interesting works by or about Gideon Lincecum include his edited autobiography, *Adventures of a Frontier Naturalist: The Life and Times of Dr. Gideon Lincecum*, ed. Jerry Bryan Lincecum and Edward Hake Phillips (College Station: Texas A&M University Press, 1994); Lois Wood Burkhalter, *Gideon Lincecum, 1793–1874: A Biography* (Austin: University of Texas Press, 1965); Gideon Lincecum, "The Agricultural Ant of Texas (Myrmica Molefaciens)," *The Friend; a Religious and Literary Journal* [1827–1906] 40 (June 1, 1867): 315.

25. Dickens, *American Notes for General Circulation*, 191–93.

26. Letter from P. P. Pitchlynn to Gideon Lincecum, November 12, 1846.

27. Spelled "Lacombe" in the present day.

28. David I. Bushnell, *The Choctaw of Bayou Lacomb, St. Tammany Parish, Louisiana*, Bureau of American Ethnology Bulletin 48 (Washington, DC: Smithsonian Institution, 1909), 20–23.

29. Bossu was a French officer on duty in Louisiana during the early years of the French Indian War (1756–63). Bushnell's footnote for Bossu's text on page 23 in *The Choctaw of Bayou Lacomb, St. Tammany Parish, Louisiana* is: "*a Nouveaux voyages aux Indes occidentales*, n. 104, Paris, 1768 [written in 1759]."

30. Letter from P. P. Pitchlynn to Gideon Lincecum, November 12, 1846.

31. For a more complete discussion of Choctaw educational history, see Clara Sue Kidwell, *Choctaws and Missionaries in Mississippi, 1818–1918* (Norman: University of Oklahoma, 1995).

32. James L. McDonald, the first Choctaw lawyer admitted to the bar in 1824, was a frequent correspondent of Pitchlynn's. In his opening salutation to Pitchlynn in a letter of December 17, 1830, as they were making initial plans to move with their whole nation to Indian Territory, McDonald writes: "Esteemed friend: I resume the task which I left unfinished (or rather untouched) a few days since, in an attempt to prove that

our vernacular tongue is more expressive than the English. Should you coincide with me in opinion who shall gainsay our decision? It may indeed be said that the parties interested will generally decide in their own favour. But let the question for the present rest." For more examples of the fascinating written work of Peter Pitchlynn and James L. McDonald, I invite you to read my doctoral dissertation: Phillip Carroll Morgan, "Who Shall Gainsay Our Decision? Choctaw Literary Nationalism in the Nineteenth Century," University of Oklahoma, 2009, available online at https://shareok.org.

33. Chickasaw author and scholar Stanley Nelson pointed out to me that the mature characters of southeastern cultures, languages, and tribal customs noted in and about the time de Soto (1540–42) made contact with tribes of the Southeastern Ceremonial Complex render the idea of a migration from Mexico in response to the Spanish insurgency rather unlikely. The oral tradition story of migration from a tropical coastal jungle geography could, nonetheless, be rooted in a much earlier migration from the south.

34. Swanton, *Choctaw Social and Ceremonial Life*, 30–31.

35. New River was a tributary of the Mississippi River in Louisiana with a port capable of boarding emigrants on a steamboat, and in this case, mostly Bayou Lacomb Choctaws bound for Indian Territory. New River has changed course since 1847 and is no longer a viable connection to the Mississippi. Swanton, *Choctaw Social and Ceremonial Life*, 5.

36. The history of Arnold Harris is obscure enough not to yield any findings regarding Pitchlynn's salutation of Harris as Genl, the common abbreviation in that day for the rank of general. One record I found on an Arnold Harris that might be a clue recounts a story of a man by that name traveling to Texas on horseback from Indian Territory with Sam Houston during the spring of 1832, which was Houston's first entry into Texas. Edwin Legrand Sabin, *With Sam Houston in Texas* (Philadelphia: J.B. Lippincott Co., 1916), 51–52.

37. Letter from P. P. Pitchlynn to Arnold Harris, March 30, 1847, Peter Perkins Pitchlynn Collection, Bizzell Memorial Library, University of Oklahoma. Pitchlynn's report of his emigration-project-ending affliction with cholera was written one week after the Choctaws' gift to the Irish.

38. Baird, *Peter Pitchlynn, Chief of the Choctaws*, 79.

39. Pat Goitein, http://www.findagrave.com/cgi-bin/fg.cgi?page=gr&GRid=93721190.

40. Baird, *Peter Pitchlynn, Chief of the Choctaws*, 76–79.

41. Amanda L. Paige et al., *Chickasaw Removal* (Ada, OK: Chickasaw Press, 2010), 248–49.

42. Choctawnation.com.

43. Measuringworth.com.

44. W. T. Block, "Duncan Smith: Calcasieu Parish's Confederate Traitor or American Patriot?,"

http://files.usgwarchives.net/la/cameron/history/popular.txt.

45. The quoted passage first appeared in the *Beaumont (Texas) Enterprise* on January 30, 1907, and was cited in W. T. Block, "Great-Grandpa Wasn't Popular in the South," which appeared in the *Beaumont Enterprise*, September 28, 1998, 6A.

46. Often when I reread the phrase the "Country in the West," which Pitchlynn and his correspondents often used, it resonates with the title of Louis Alberto Urrea's stirring novel *Into the Beautiful North*, whose main characters are Mexican emigrants. The book was published by Little, Brown & Co. in 2009.

47. "Irish and German Immigration," http://www.ushistory.org/us/25f.asp.

48. Native Americans, many doing so even before they were granted U.S. citizenship in 1924, volunteered in significant numbers to serve in the Armed Forces of the United States during every American war of the twentieth century. According to war historian Thomas D. Morgan, during World War II, roughly 84,000 Native American men and women participated in the war effort, roughly one quarter of the entire population. Some 99 percent of Native American men registered for the draft, and many enlisted before they could be drafted. My father and uncle, for example, each beyond draft age in 1942, volunteered for service and served in the Pacific Theater throughout the remainder of the war. My father, Raymond Wade Morgan, survived. My uncle, Robert Allen Morgan, was killed in action in April 1945, two months before the war ended. "Native Americans in World War II," *Professional Bulletin of Army History*, no. 35 (Fall 1995): 22–27.

49. "One in every 122 humans is now either a refugee, internally displaced, or seeking asylum." UNHCR, The UN Refugee Agency, "Worldwide Displacement Hits All-Time High as War and Persecution Increase," http://www.unhcr.org/en-us/figures-at-a-glance.html.

50. *Yaknimoma* is a Choctaw word meaning "the whole world." It is a compound word constructed with *yakni*, meaning land, and *moma*, meaning all, and most colloquially translated as "all lands."

Famine pot courtesy of Eleanor Hooker, Tipperary, Ireland (2017). According to Ms. Hooker's research, famine pots were made in a Quaker foundry in the Severn Valley in Great Britain and were supplied/donated to Irish communities.

An Ocean of Benevolence

Christine Kinealy

This chapter was part of a larger project to explore the incredible, and largely untold, story of private charity during the Great Famine. While donations came from all over the world, from India to Venezuela, from New Zealand to the Caribbean, the largest number came from America, many given by people who had no direct association with Ireland. Of the thousands of contributions sent to help the Irish poor, a number stand out as remarkable, as they came from people who were themselves impoverished, marginalized, and dispossessed. The gift made by the Choctaw Nation is an example of this spirit of altruistic kindness and compassion. Their generosity was noted at the time, sadly through a racialized prism. The local newspaper the *Arkansas Intelligencer* commented that

> What an agreeable reflection it must give to the Christian and the philanthropist to witness this evidence of civilization and Christian spirit existing among our red neighbours. They are repaying the Christian world a consideration for bringing them out from benighted ignorance and heathen barbarism. Not only by contributing a few dollars, but by affording evidence that the labours of the Christian missionary have not been in vain.[1]

Alex Pentek's sculpture *Kindred Spirits*, courtesy of Gavin Sheridan (© Gavin Sheridan, @ gavinsblog).This memorial, which celebrates the relationship between the Choctaw and the Irish, is installed in Bailic Park, Midleton, Ireland.

More recently, the Choctaw donation has been remembered for the extraordinary gesture that it was. A plaque at the Lord Mayor's Mansion House in Dublin, which commemorates the Choctaw gift, was unveiled in 1992. Irish presidents from Mary Robinson to Michael D. Higgins have expressed the gratitude of the Irish people to representatives of the Nation, while in March 2017, during a visit to the Choctaw Nation, *an Taoiseach*, Leo Varadkar, announced a scholarship for Choctaw students to study in Ireland.[2] The $174 donation from the Choctaws has also been commemorated in art. In 2005, Quinnipiac University in Connecticut purchased Kieran Tuohy's beautiful carving in Irish bog oak entitled *Thank you to the Choctaw*.[3] In June 2017, the sculpture *Kindred Spirits*, a 6-meter circle of tall feathers, was unveiled in the small town of Midleton, in east Cork.[4] The kindness of these strangers to Ireland has not been forgotten.

The General Relief Committee of New York

Throughout 1846, newspapers in the United States were carrying reports from Ireland that chronicled the deteriorating state of the people. In the wake of the first appearance of blight, there had been some suggestions that American people should send aid to Ireland, but the second failure of the potato crop provoked a widespread and spontaneous response. For some Irish Americans, the reaction was not quick enough: the *Boston Pilot* asserted, "We confess we have been astonished at the apathy and indifference with which the people of this country have regarded the horrible conditions of their fellow beings in Ireland."[5] The formation of the Central Committee of the Society of Friends in Dublin in November, and their circular to Friends throughout the world confirmed the gravity of the situation and resulted in a number of donations being made from all parts of the United States. In New York, the Quakers' circular prompted a number of "benevolent gentlemen" to ascertain "the exact losses with a view to institute measures of providing relief."[6] The outcome of this investigation was the founding of a committee that put New York at the forefront of international fund-raising efforts for Ireland. Interestingly, the man responsible for this initiative had no direct connection to Ireland.

Myndert Van Schaick, a member of one of New York's oldest Dutch families, was a successful businessman who was associated with bringing drinking water to New York. Reports of the worsening conditions in Ireland prompted him to take a more professional approach to providing aid. He commenced by opening a subscription list on February 7, 1846.[7] He invited fellow members of the New York elite to assist. His request was followed by a meeting on February 12 in Prime's Building in Wall Street, which was provided free of charge. This, in turn, led to the formation of a "special committee" consisting of Jacob Harvey, George Griffin, Theodore Sedgwick, and John Jay, all of whom were successful businessmen. Van Schaick acted as both chairman and, briefly, treasurer of the Standing Committee. On February 12, the ad hoc committee issued an appeal on behalf of the Irish poor, which they entitled an "Address to the Public."[8] It pointed out that four million people were on "the verge of starvation," and that "Neither the energy of the father, nor the tenderness of the mother, avail anything—young and old, the strong and the feeble, are involved in this common ruin."[9] The justification of American involvement was explained thus:

> It is to God alone that we can ascribe the fertile soil, the boundless prairies, the infinite mineral wealth, which makes our country the garden of the world.

... Our fellow citizens, generally of the agricultural and commercial classes, are making large gains by the advance in foreign prices. What is death to Ireland is but augmented fortune to America; and we are actually fattening on the starvation of another people.[10]

The appeal concluded by stating, "Every dollar that you give, may save a human being from starvation!"[11]

The committee, together with John A. King, a former assemblyman, decided to call a public meeting at the Tabernacle (the United Church of Christ) on Broadway on February 15.[12] The Tabernacle had been founded in 1832 by Lewis Tappan, a leading abolitionist.[13] The meeting on behalf of Ireland was attended by the cream of New York society, and cut across divides of religion and nationality. It was chaired by Robert Minturn, a wealthy merchant. According to one newspaper, "he expressed in a beautiful manner the duty the people here owe in connection with the great claim Ireland presents to us."[14] Among those who addressed the gathering at the Tabernacle was Rev. (later Bishop) Jonathan Wainwright of St. John's Episcopal Chapel.[15] The next day, local newspapers carried a message explaining that "the standing committee for the relief of sufferers in Ireland, have permission to occupy an office on the second floor of Prime's Buildings, no. 54 Wall Street, opposite the Merchant's Exchange, where attendance will be given from 10:00 am to 2:00 pm each day, to receive contributions for that object."[16]

A further large meeting was held in the Tabernacle on February 23. Van Schaick was confirmed as president, with a committee of twenty-two vice presidents and five secretaries. Van Schaick called on the public, without reference to "customs or creed," to contribute to the new committee established to help the starving in Ireland. He pointed out, "The Irish cabin of 1847—without food for the living, or coffins for the dead—exhibits a picture more heart-touching than perhaps misery ever before presented to the eye of philanthropy."[17] During his speech, Van Schaick, alluding to the political situation in Ireland, criticized absentee landowners:

On the liberal aid of the Irish absentees, who have habitually deserted their home to spend abroad that overflowing wealth which should have enriched, or at least saved from want, their native land—who have broken asunder those ties of patronage and reciprocated affection that should consecrate the relation of landlord and tenant—we have no reason to suppose that the Irish peasantry can confidently rely in this extremity of their need. England has nobly headed the list of charity for the relief of her suffering sister, thus redeeming in part the debt, ancient and vast, which she owes to Ireland.[18]

Questioning how a famine on such a scale could exist in the center of civilization, he added:

How would the world exclaim, with England at its head, should our Southern negro slaves be fed solely on the potato, and be left, upon a failure of that crop, to starve and die in masses by the road side, or in crowded and nauseous hovels, without even a poor candle for the last rites of their religion, and there to be gnawed by rats or buried with no covering save their rags![19]

According to Van Schaick, in the preceding year Irish house servants and laborers in the United States had contributed over one million dollars, which he attributed to a "deep-seated love of country."[20]

The new organization was to be known as the General Relief Committee of New York. A number of resolutions were passed, including:

That Ireland, the hospitality of whose people has been long proverbial, now stricken by the hand of Providence, and filled with the starving, the dying, and the dead, has a peculiar right to sympathy and aid; and that to this Republic, whose wealth is increased by their want, it especially belongs to contribute of the abundance where-with God has blessed us, to the necessities of the Irish people.[21]

The committee included John Jay, James King, and Stewart Brown. George Barclay, James Reyburn, and Robert Minturn also assisted as donations started to pour in from the rest of the country. Minturn, of the shipping agents "Grinell, Minturn and Co.," took charge of commissioning the ships to carry the foodstuffs to Ireland. The fact that everything arrived intact was later attributed to his careful choice of sailing vessels.[22] The ecumenical nature of the committee was manifest in its composition. One of the secretaries was an Irish-born merchant, Jacob Harvey, whose family were members of the Society of Friends in Limerick.[23] He worked in this capacity until his premature death in 1848, which was mourned by people on both sides of the Atlantic.[24] Another founding member of the committee was August Belmont. He had been born in Europe, but, following emigration, had changed his surname from Schoenberg to avoid anti-Jewish prejudice. In the United States, he acted as agent for the Rothschild Banking House. In addition to offering administrative support, Belmont made a personal donation of $500.[25] Some years later, he became embroiled in controversy with the Irish American community as a result of looking after the "Fenian Fund."[26]

The ecumenical nature of the New York Committee was enshrined in the resolution that "customs" or "creed" does not "absolve us from the duties of common brotherhood."[27] Letters were to be sent to the clergy of all denominations in the city, asking them to make collections in their respective churches.[28] It was further decided that all food and money raised would be sent to the Central Relief Committee of the Society of Friends in Dublin. From the outset, it was apparent that American relief efforts would cut across economic and political boundaries and would involve people who had no direct connection with Ireland. Van Schaick, the president of the General Relief Committee, was a former Democratic assemblyman and senator. He was a member of one of the city's oldest and wealthiest Dutch families who belonged to the Dutch Reformed Church.[29] He was also a noted philanthropist who had no direct association with Ireland. Responding to a donation from Pensacola in Florida, Van Schaick outlined some of the reasons for his involvement: "We hope that our operations will save some lives, will heal some broken hearts, and in the performance of a Christian duty will exhibit the character of American freemen in no disadvantageous light abroad."[30]

When about to resign his position, he offered further insights into his personal motivations for working on behalf of the Irish poor:

> Supposing that I might be able to accomplish some good to a greatly abused and suffering people, my employment has been to me a source of unmixed gratification and happiness, and now that I am about to resign my trust into the hands of another, I cannot leave my post without conveying to the true and disinterested friends of Ireland my ardent hope that the education of the people with Bible in hand, and irrespective of religious dogmas and sectarian interests, may be made to constitute one of the measures, as it is an indispensable preparation by which the population are to be enabled to provide for their own subsistence, without depending too much on human aid, advice or direction, which is quite as likely to be selfish, as disinterested.[31]

The work of the New York Committee began immediately. On February 24, Van Schaick wrote to Jonathan Pim and Joseph Bewley, secretaries of the Quaker

Committee in Dublin, addressing them as "Christian Friends"; they responded by addressing him as "Respected Friend." Van Schaick's letter included a contribution of £3,000 ($14,066.67), explaining "our fellow-citizens of every name and creed, deeply sympathizing with the distresses of the Irish people, have with the greatest alacrity come forward to contribute their mite towards the alleviation of a misery, which we fear, no human aid can reach in all its depths and recesses."[32] Although the New York Committee preferred to send aid in food, they felt that sending cash would provide more immediate relief and help the most remote districts. The majority of the food aid was to be given to families who were totally destitute, but the committee had agreed that a smaller portion would be sold to "poor families who are still able to buy at such reasonably reduced rates as may be consistent with the humane intention of the contributors."[33]

The initial response to the appeal was so great that the committee was forced to meet daily. By the end of February, they had raised over $45,000. By March, that amount had more than doubled, rising to over $105,000.[34] At the end of the month, Van Schaick informed the Dublin Committee that:

> The cry of Ireland for assistance will be answered with great liberality from every quarter of this country—even I hope from the defaulting States, who in their infancy are unable to pay the debts which they were induced to contract by their evil counselors.[35]

By mid-April though, donations were beginning to taper off, which Van Schaick attributed to two reasons, "because all tides ebb and flow" and "the unusually great numbers of poor people that have been landed on our shores from British traders since 1 April."[36] On May 11, Van Schaick confirmed that the charitable impulse in New York was slowing down, and informed the committee in Dublin, "This City is filling fast with foreign poor, and I am sitting frequently the whole morning in this room, without receiving any money excepting occasionally a remittance coming in from the country or from a distant state."[37]

Regardless of the reduction in donations, by May 18 the total had reached $144,450.30.[38] By June 25, the committee had raised $156,581.65 in cash on behalf of "the famishing poor of Ireland without distinction of sect, creed or opinion."[39] At this point, James Reyburn took over as treasurer, although Van Schaick remained as chairman. On February 2, 1848, Reyburn reported that $19,037.37 had been received.[40] In total, $171,374.24 in cash had been collected; $156,581.65 had been received by Van Schaick in the early months up to June 25, 1847, and $14,792.59 added in the following twelve months, when Reyburn was treasurer. During this period, donations in the form of provisions amounted to $242,042.79 in value.[41] However, the freezing weather in the west of the country meant that the canals and rivers were not navigable, and so, much of the foodstuffs could not be transported until spring.[42]

The New York Committee worked closely with the Quakers in Dublin. As Van Schaick explained to one of the American donors, "In the impartiality, judgment and discretion of the Central Committee of the Society of Friends, all our committee have unlimited confidence."[43] Bewley and Pim, in turn, responded:

> We sensibly feel the large responsibility which devolves upon us, in endeavoring, as we are bound to do, to carry out faithfully and with due promptitude the designs of those who are thus pleased to make us the almoners of their bounty. We can gratefully appreciate the confidence of a community to whom we are comparatively unknown.[44]

The impact of the American donations in Ireland was considerable, as Jonathan Pim, writing from County Mayo at the end of March, explained:

> Your assistance comes at a most opportune time, as I quite think that the coming month will be really the period of trial; and I trust that your contributions, stimulating our Committee and the other bodies to whom they may be sent, to increased exertions to meet the crisis, will be the means of greatly lessening the suffering, and of saving many lives.
>
> I enclose copy of a circular which we have sent out a few days since, and will give thee some idea of our course of action. I also send a copy of the Government instructions under the new act, which will enable thee to form some opinion of its object and probable effects. If we can get tolerably well over the coming month, I shall have great hopes that our difficulties will be greatly lessened by the general working of the new act.
>
> Your contributions are truly noble, and are felt and acknowledged by all here to be such. They put many of our rich people here to shame—or at least they ought to do so. The warm and generous sympathy which extends throughout the Union, springing from those brotherly feelings which a common language, a common origin, and kindred institutions naturally inspire, will, I trust, have effects long,

out lasting the misfortunes which have drawn it forth and may hereafter tend to neutralize the jealousies, which conflicting interests must occasionally produce.[45]

Only a few days later, the Quakers in Dublin acknowledged:

> We can truly say that the munificence of your City and its vicinity, and of the citizens at large in many other parts of the United States as exhibited by the immense supplies of food they are sending for our starving people, surpass all the expectations that we had ventured to form on the subject.[46]

In 1847, the General Relief Committee decided to publish their proceedings.[47] A purpose was to show the donors that their contributions had been received and let them know how these subventions were being utilized in Ireland. A further reason for making the information available was to disabuse some people in Britain of the idea that there had been a selfish motive behind the donations.[48] The report also explained that initially the committee had intended to act only on behalf of New York City, but,

> from being the representatives of a single City, they became the almoners as will appear from the contributions they now acknowledge, of large numbers of their fellow-countrymen in the states of Connecticut, Massachusetts, Vermont, New Hampshire, New York, New Jersey, Pennsylvania, Maryland, Virginia, North Carolina, South Carolina, Georgia, Florida, Alabama, Mississippi, Kentucky, Tennessee, Arkansas, Indiana, Illinois, Wisconsin, Iowa, Michigan, and Ohio, as well as residents of Canada and the District of Columbia—and of officers and sailors attached to our navy on foreign stations—and of the Choctaw tribe of Indians in the far West.[49]

Occasionally, special requests were made on behalf of particular districts in Ireland. In early March, the Irish Relief Committee of Salina and Syracuse donated $1,200. In the accompanying letter, James Lynch, on behalf of the committee, stated:

> The committee have the utmost confidence in the prudence and humane feeling of that society, and feel assured that they will make a fair and impartial distribution of everything sent them; but some of the members of our committee are particularly acquainted with the province of Munster, and believe that the greatest destitution and distress prevails in the counties of Cork, Kerry and Tipperary, and would (if not

inconsistent with the action of the Committee of Friends in Dublin) wish one-half of our contributions sent to the starving poor of Cork, Kerry and Tipperary.[50]

The inhabitants of Morganton, North Carolina, donated $210 and requested that one-half be sent to the parish of Inniscoffey, County Westmeath, and the other half to the parish of Milltown, in the same county. Van Schaick apologized to the Dublin Committee for special requests, but explained, "It is difficult for us to avoid giving you some trouble in this way. But we make no promises, and keep these local feelings as much as possible at a distance from our system of operations."[51]

Nonetheless, on April 29, Van Schaick wrote to the Dublin Friends:

> I have promised two old Irish gentlemen who came to this room abounding in sympathy and thankfulness, that I would say to you that a letter had been received from Thos. Swanton of Cranlieth, county Cork, representing the extreme destitution and misery of the large parish of Skufl [*sic*], East Skull [*sic*], a half parish, containing 8000 inhabitants, is particularly recommended to your attention, Though I clearly see the danger and the impropriety of interfering with your system by giving special instructions, yet less than this I could not do at the request of "two gray haired old men."[52]

The towns of Schull and Skibbereen were to achieve notoriety in 1847 for the suffering and mortality of their populations.[53] The Dublin Committee agreed that this was one of the poorest districts in Ireland and responded by sending members of their Cork Society to the areas to distribute relief as requested.[54]

As was frequently noted in 1846 and 1847, many Americans were becoming wealthy because the food shortages in Ireland and other parts of Europe had doubled the value of food exports from the United States. Philip Hone, a former mayor of New York and noted diarist, confessed to feeling guilty for eating sumptuous dinners while the Irish were starving. He attributed the recent increase in America's prosperity to a sharp increase in food and freight prices.[55] Hone was one of the founding members of the General Relief Committee of New York. In February, he made a personal donation of $25 to the committee.[56] Hone was given a chance to do something practical to help Ireland when he was asked, in spring 1847, by the Lisburn-born merchant prince Alexander Turney Stewart, to preside over a raffle for a rosewood piano. It was to be held in Stewart's showcase store, the Marble Palace in New York City.[57] Like Hone, Stewart was involved in fundraising for Ireland, being a member of the General Standing Committee of the New York Relief Committee.[58] The piano had been donated by Horatio Worcester, a pianoforte maker also based on Broadway.[59] The raffle raised $1,275.[60] Stewart personally contributed "generously" to the day's proceedings.[61] The raffle was not the end of Stewart's involvement in famine relief. An early biography stated that in 1847 he chartered a ship, which he filled with provisions and sent as a gift to Ireland. Nor was this the last time that Stewart demonstrated that he had not forgotten his roots.[62] During the industrial downswing in Ireland in 1863, he arranged for a ship loaded with foodstuffs to be sent to unemployed mill workers and weavers in the Lisburn and the Maze districts. In addition, he offered free passage to New York to those who wanted to emigrate.[63]

At the beginning of 1847, as news reached the United States of the cost of foodstuffs in Ireland, appeals were made that assistance should be given as far as possible in provisions rather than money, so that food prices in Ireland did not rise further. In Ireland, Indian corn was selling at 74 shillings a bushel, double the price of that in the States.[64] Money donations in New York were collected at 54 Wall Street, while provisions or clothing to be sent to Ireland were to be left at the store of Joseph Naylor at 18 Broadway and marked "relief for Ireland."[65] Inspired by the activities in New York City, Brooklynite R. J. Todd offered to receive or collect provisions in that town until a vessel could be obtained to carry them to Ireland.[66] The donations received by the New York Committee up to May 27, 1847, were used to fund the sailing of fourteen ships, either fully or partly loaded with provisions. The cargoes consisted primarily of Indian corn, flour, cornmeal, barley, and beans, with smaller quantities of cheese, pork, and beef. Cartons of clothes were also included. The New York Committee left it to the committee in Dublin to "determine the best course to pursue in applying our consignments so as to save life, and shed some small rays of comfort into the abodes of your desolate people."[67] Once the foodstuffs arrived in Ireland, they were transported to the interior by inland navigation.[68] The Irish Committee had asked if the first cargoes could go to Dublin, which had good links via inland navigation to some of the remotest parts of Ireland.[69] Subsequent ships were sent to Liverpool in England, the port being the center of the transatlantic trade and having close trading links with Dublin.[70] The initial cargoes arrived in April.[71] Part of the money raised was used to offset freight charges, but this became unnecessary when the government announced that, on production of a consular certificate, they would pay freight charges on aid sent to Ireland and Scotland.[72] The request for the government to pay these charges had been made by the London Committee of the Society of Friends.[73] As soon as a cargo arrived, it was taken charge of by the agents of Government, at their respective ports of destination, so as to relieve us from all expenses attending the landing, storage, costs of agency, and transporting it to the distressed districts [the name given to the twenty-two poorest Unions] an arrangement which will contribute essentially to facilitate the proper distribution whilst it will divest these operations of almost all cost.[74]

Importantly, the agreement of the Treasury meant that the cargoes from America could be distributed without "delay, risk or expense." Moreover:

The food put on board at New York, may be considered as laid down almost at the doors of the sufferers for whom it is intended, without any material diminution from the expenses attending its transport across the Atlantic, or the cost and delay inseparable from its conveyance into the remote and mountainous districts of this country, where the distress is of the most severe character, and the channels of internal communication very imperfect.[75]

The Quakers were permitted to make use of the many commissariat depots established in the previous year for the holding and distributing of food. The British Treasury, however, refused to accept the charges for insurance.[76] The Quakers were appreciative of these arrangements and praised "the liberal spirit on the part of our Government, to which we are indebted for such important facilities, and as the fact of so many of the vessels delivering their cargoes to the agents of Government, would, in itself, if unexplained, furnish occasion of uneasiness."[77]

By the beginning of 1848, the freight charges paid by the British government for goods coming from North America totaled £42,673 17s. 6d.[78] This amount represented 119 ships, which had sailed from a variety of ports, including 36 from New York, 27 from New Orleans, 18 from Philadelphia, 6 from Charlestown, 5 from Baltimore, Savannah and Mobile, 4 from Boston, 4 from Wilmington, 3 from Toronto, 2 from Montreal and Alexandria (Virginia), and one each from Newark and Richmond. An overwhelming number of these cargoes—sixty-three in total—were consigned to the Society of Friends in Ireland, while smaller amounts were sent to the mayor of Cork (four shiploads), the mayor of Belfast (two shiploads), the General Central Relief Committee in Dublin (four), the Irish Relief Association (four), and the Dublin Parochial Association (two). Single cargoes were also sent to the archbishop of Tuam and the archbishops of Armagh and Dublin. Four shiploads destined for Belfast were delivered to the care of "Mr Allen," while two shiploads sent to Cork had been consigned to local individuals—to a "Mr Barry" and "Misses Cox" respectively. The Cox sisters of Dunmanway in West Cork had achieved some notoriety in the United States by making an appeal to the American vice president for assistance, which had been widely reported.[79] The Reverend P. Murphy in Wexford received two consignments.[80] Four shiploads were designated for Scottish relief, with three being sent to the Highland Destitution Committee and one to the Glasgow Relief Committee.[81]

The approach of the 1847 harvest was watched with trepidation, not only in Ireland, but among those who were involved in fundraising elsewhere. In August, Reyburn informed the Dublin Committee that "we are all alive to the prospect of your harvest—the result of which will make it necessary to continue or wind up our committee, most of whom are now absent from the city, in order to escape our very hot season."[82] The harvest, although it contained relatively little blight, was small. The closing of the soup kitchens and the transfer to Poor Law relief again placed pressure on private charities, although, as was evident from the experience of the New York Committee, the charitable impulse was slowing down.

Donations to the New York Committee were not only made in money or provisions. Some of the more unusual contributions included a concert by the Musical Society, a piano, expensive jewelry, a barge (which proved to be useful for conveyed foodstuffs), an offer by the French Consulate to convene a meeting of French citizens, and the assistance of the Mercantile Library Association.[83] As was generally the case, aid to the committee cut across social and political groups. The "Descendants of the Pilgrims" donated $10, and "officers, cadets and laborers at West Point" contributed $312.43.[84] A "Relief Ball" held in Castle Garden, the Emigrant Receiving Station in New York City, raised $1,420.25. The jury and clerk in the case of "Griffin versus Mutual Life Insurance" gave $2. The Temperance inhabitants of Norfolk, Litchfield County in Connecticut, contributed $475 on February 26, 1847. They requested that breadstuffs to that value should be given to the Reverend Theobald Mathew, the Irish Temperance leader, to be used by him in such manner as he deemed fit.[85] A number of journals and papers, including the *Journal of Commerce* and the *Tribune*, organized collections, while staff in the office of the *New York Observer* gave $17.[86]

Women were significant contributors to the committee, although many gave anonymously. One of the largest individual donations came from a "Lady" who gave $1,000. Other donations from women included $133 received from "the Ladies of Burlington, Vermont." "The ladies of Monticello, Sullivan County" held a donations party that raised $5. Teachers and Scholars of Madame Chegary's French School, a seminary for young women, raised $47.25. Mrs. Van Cortlandt, a resident of Sing Sing, New York, organized a collection of $45.50. Children and young people also joined in the fundraising. This included "two little self-denying girls" of Rhinebeck, Duchess County in New York, who gave $10. The boys of Ward School No. 3 in the 10th Ward raised $1.54 in one-cent coins. Amenia Seminary, a private Methodist coeducational secondary school and college located in Duchess County, raised $20.[87] The principal of the school was Erastus Otis Haven, who had an illustrious career as an educationalist.[88] Pupils of a George P. Quackenbos donated $7. Two of the smallest donations came from "a little boy" and "a little Irish emigrant," both of whom contributed 50 cents. Pupils of St. Matthew's Lutheran Academy in Walker Street, New York City, raised $14. A school for young ladies run by Charlotte M. Havens, and located at 263 Ninth Street, New York City, held a fair that raised $287. The donors stipulated that $50 of this was for "the Scotch."[89] Charlotte's younger sister, Catherine, later noted in her diary:

> Four years ago there was a dreadful famine in Ireland, and we gave up our parlor and library and dining room for two evenings for a fair for them, and all my schoolmates and our friends made things, and we sent the poor Irish people over three hundred dollars. My brothers made pictures in pen and ink, and called them charades, and they sold for fifty cents apiece; like this: a pen, and a man, and a ship, and called it, "a desirable art"—Penmanship. The brother, who used to be so mischievous, is studying hard now to be an engineer and build rail-roads. He draws beautiful bridges and aqueducts.[90]

Donations came from rich and influential citizens. Van Schaick contributed $500, as did a number of other businessmen. The latter included $2,000 from the Board of the New York Stock and Exchange. Theodore Frelinghuysen, then chancellor of the University of the City of New York and a successful politician known for his evangelical Christian views, donated $5. Horace Greeley, founder of the *New York Tribune*, gave $6.50.[91] Greeley, known for his radical politics, was an avid champion of the Young Ireland group and their demands for an independent Ireland.[92]

In June, the Washington City company of Corcoran and Riggs donated $5,000.[93] William Wilson Corcoran, one of the owners, had been born in Georgetown, Washington, in 1798.[94] His father, Thomas, had emigrated from Limerick to Baltimore in 1783.[95] William Wilson Corcoran was a renowned philanthropist and art collector.

Although not a Catholic, in 1851 he gave $500 to Father Mathew's temperance movement. This marked the beginning of a friendship between the men, with a planned meeting in Ireland in 1853, although Father Mathew cautioned, "I now hope that you will not visit Ireland until next July, at which season the beloved country of your ancestors will appear in all its beauty."[96]

Many well-known people gave their support to the fundraising. Irish-born Richard Pakenham, who had been appointed envoy extraordinary and minister plenipotentiary to the United States of America in December 1843, gave £100, which was the equivalent of $469. William Colville Emmet, son of the Irish-born veteran of the 1798 Rebellion, Thomas Addis Emmet, contributed $400, which was followed a few weeks later by an additional $25.[97] A number of musical concerts were held in New York and the surrounding areas. A performance of Handel's oratorio *Messiah* (which had its premiere in Dublin in 1742 to raise money for an earlier famine in Ireland) was given at the New York Tabernacle on February 27, 1847, and "In a rare show of unanimity, both the Sacred Music Society and the American Musical Institute generally volunteered to pool their resources, as did the conductors."[98] Dr. Edward Hodges, a noted organist, was one of the organizers. Unfortunately, terrible weather kept potential audience members at home and the hall was virtually empty.[99] The concert raised a disappointing $24.[100] Kip & Brown, Proprietors of the Greenwich & Broadway Stages, donated the proceeds of one day's performance, which amounted to $295.46.[101]

The poor of the city also contributed, as did various groups of workers, with donations for the "hands of Philip Hone" ($360), "clerks, Maiden Street" ($6), "hands in Bowne and Co.'s bindery" ($30), "Workmen and hands of Mrs G. B. Miller and Co.'s Manufactory ($27.50), "the workmen in the employ of Peckham and Runville" ($76.26), "workmen in the employ of Moses G. Baldwin, manufacturers and jewelers, 145 Reade Street" ($32), "the hands of Pearse and Brooks, paper mills" ($57), "the hands of the manufactory of H.P. Leake, 164 Broadway" ($100), "the men employed in Allaire Iron Works, New York" ($157), "lithographers of New York" ($5), "the employees of the Eerie [*sic*] railroad at Pierpoint" ($100), "workmen in the employ of NY dyeing and printing establishment on Staten Island" ($106.50).[102] Donations were made also by police of the First Ward ($71), the officers and crew of the U.S. steamer *Michigan* ($10), "workers in the employ of the New York Screw Company" ($60), "the agents and drivers of the Harlem Railroad Company" ($76).[103] French residents and workmen gave $637.55. The money was donated on their behalf by Victor De Launay, who, with his brother, owned a company in New York and Le

Havre. B. P. Haatmgs & Co., of Detroit, sent a donation made by "A Committee of Miners on south side of Lake Superior," who raised funds to pay expenses on 60 bbls (barrels) of flour to be transported to Ireland.[104] The officers and workmen of the Dry Dock Navy Yard in Brooklyn gave $530.61, which was used to purchase 120 barrels of cornmeal to be transported on the *Victor*. On its arrival in Dublin, the Society of Friends wrote to the workers in the Navy Yard thanking them for their generosity.[105] A donation of $57.42 was raised from Moira in Franklin County, New York, the cover note explaining that it was "mainly contributed by those who depend upon their daily labor for their daily bread." Van Schaick responded, "May their bread never fail and their cup be always full."[106]

Inevitably, Irish groups and societies were prominent in the relief efforts. The Irish Relief Committee of Galena in Illinois sent $1,000. A ball organized by the Independent Sons of Erin raised $420. The Hibernian Providence Society in New Haven, which had been founded in 1842, donated $200. An interesting donation of $385 was made by the Benevolent Order of Bereans.[107] This newly formed Protestant secret society was similar in outlook to the Orange Order and was known for its anti-Catholic views.[108] They had links with the larger American Protestant Association.[109]

Public figures were important in assisting in promoting the work of the New York Committee. Local mayors, in particular, acted as a conduit for many donations.[110] Andrew Hutchins Mickle, a tobacco merchant and mayor of New York from 1846 to 1847, gave $40 on behalf of "Tammany Hall."[111] While later remembered as an example of institutionalized corruption, Tammany Hall (also known as the Society of St. Tammany) was renowned at the time for helping immigrants, especially Irish immigrants. It had close links with the Democratic Party, and both were known for holding proslavery views.[112] In addition, the Society donated the proceeds of a ball held on St. Patrick's Day, which raised $200. In contrast, the Friendly Sons of St. Patrick in New York forsook their annual ball in 1847 and instead donated the $215 worth of food "to their suffering brethren in Ireland."[113] The money was channeled through James Reyburn, who had been president of the Friendly Sons since 1843 and was treasurer of the Irish Emigrant Society.[114] Reyburn had also replaced Van Schaick as treasurer of the General Relief Committee.

Public lectures were another way of raising money for Ireland. At the end of March, Rev. Giles, a Unitarian minister who had been born in County Wexford, lectured before the Society of the Young Friends of Ireland in the Broadway Tabernacle. It brought in $378.50. Giles, a noted orator, had earlier raised money for the Philadelphia Relief Fund by giving a public lecture.[115] However, Giles was not the only Irish-born man of the cloth to lecture. John Hughes, the flamboyant Irish-born bishop of New York, lectured at the Tabernacle on March 20.[116] Hughes's father had emigrated to the United States in 1816, and John had joined him a year later. Hughes had entered the priesthood in 1820 and he had been ordained a bishop in 1838. In the intervening period, he had gained a reputation as an outspoken and effective defender of the Catholic Church, his robust approach earning him the nickname "Dagger John."[117] When anti-Catholic rioting had erupted in Philadelphia in 1844, Hughes had taken an uncompromising stand, warning the perpetrators that if the violence spread to New York, the city would become "a second Moscow."[118] Hughes's topic was "On the antecedent causes of the *Irish Famine* in 1847." He commenced by saying, "The year 1847 will be rendered memorable in the future annals of civilization by two events; the one immediately preceding and giving occasion to the other; namely, Irish famine and American sympathy and succor."[119]

Despite his deeply held religious views, Hughes did not take a providentialist view of the food shortages, instead warning:

> Let us be careful, then, not to blaspheme Providence by calling this God's famine. Society, the great civil corporation which we call the State, is bound, so long as it has the power to do so, to guard the lives of its members against being sacrificed by famine from within, as much as their being slaughtered by the enemy from without.[120]

Although he defended the rights of property, he qualified this with:

> Still the rights of life are dearer and higher than those of property; and in a general famine like the present, there is no law of Heaven, nor of nature, that forbids a starving man to seize on bread wherever he can find it, even though it should be the loaves of proposition on the altar of God's temple.[121]

One Washington newspaper observed:

> The tickets were a dollar each, and the proceeds, quite handsome, were appropriated to the great object. The bishop is a very agreeable speaker; his voice is clear and musical. He is about fifty years of age, of dark complexion, Milesian features,

stoops slightly, and has very much of that air which somehow always characterizes the Romish ecclesiastic.[122]

However, Hughes's strong defense of his countrymen and their human rights was a powerful call to the people of New York to act.[123] The lecture raised $529.11, of which $4.50 was deducted for advertising.[124]

In addition, Catholic congregations, some of which were newly formed, contributed. One of the largest individual donations came from St. Patrick's Cathedral in New York City, which gave $1,350.87 in March 1847, followed by an additional $20. On St. Patrick's Day 1847, a collection was made in St. James's Catholic Church in New York that raised $100. On the same day, the Temperance Society attached to the church collected $94.[125] The pastor of the church was Reverend John Smith, who, like Hughes, had been born in County Tyrone.[126] Many other Catholic congregations, predictably perhaps, raised money for Ireland. St. Joseph's Catholic Church on Sixth Avenue ($800); St. Mary's Catholic Church, Grand Street ($2,250.72); St. Peter's Catholic Church ($1,083); the Nativity Catholic Church, a Jesuit church on Second Avenue ($2,060.62); Wallabout's Catholic Church, Brooklyn ($125.60); St. Nicholas (German) Catholic Church on Second Street ($42.23); and St. Peter's Catholic Church, Staten Island ($143) all contributed to the General Relief Committee. The recently opened St. Francis of Assisi Church in Midtown Manhattan raised $22. This church had been established in 1844 by Father Zachary Kunz, a Hungarian Franciscan priest. The majority of the congregation consisted of poor German immigrants.[127] These fund-raising efforts benefited from the fact that in the preceding decade a number of new Catholic churches had been built in the United States, reflecting the large-scale Catholic immigration to the country even before the Famine and European revolutions of 1848.

The ecumenical nature of the response was evident in the donations received from diverse religious congregations, including Baptists, Episcopalians, Dutch Reformed, Presbyterians, Methodists, Congregational Christians, and Unitarians.[128] A number of local synagogues also contributed.[129] Reverend William Stevens Balch of the Universalist Church in Bleeker sent $38.55 to the Relief Committee.[130] Balch, who had been at Bleeker Street since 1841, was a renowned journalist, politician, teacher, historian, and educationalist who helped to found St. Lawrence University. Even before the influx of immigrants caused by the Famine, he worried about the undemocratic influence that Catholic immigrants were having on American politics, leading him to write in 1842, "Native American Citizens: Read and Take Warning!"[131]

Nonetheless, he felt moved to donate to relieve Irish suffering. A number of churches made more than one donation. St. Paul's Episcopal Church in Ossining, New York, built with local marble quarried by inmates of nearby Sing Sing Prison, donated one week's offering of $59. They made a subsequent donation from their Sunday collection of $5.[132]

An unusual donation came from the *John Wesley*, a Bethel ship moored in New York. Bethels were discarded ships that were reused as floating chapels for resident and visiting seafarers. The *John Wesley* had been made into a floating Methodist chapel in 1845, especially for the use of sailors.[133] At this time, the ship was moored at the foot of Carlisle Street, on the North River.[134] The *John Wesley* was the first Bethel ship to be fitted out and dedicated for this purpose. It flew American, Norwegian, Danish, and Swedish flags.[135] The pastor was the Swedish-born O. G. Hedstrom, and his congregation was described as being comprised of "wayward sailors." On March 7, 1847, they donated $11.25 to the General Relief Committee.[136] The following day, the sailors made an additional donation of $6.[137] Further donations were made, bringing the seamen's contribution to over $22. The congregation on the *John Wesley* had been informed of the suffering in Ireland and Scotland during a sermon by Rev. George Lane, a Methodist minister, on March 7.[138] Hedstrom wrote on their behalf to a local evangelical newspaper, pointing out:

> Let our neighbours and brethren know on the other side of the Atlantic that the poorest of us think of them and pray for them; trusting that the merciful father of us all will, for the sake of our Lord Jesus Christ, cause his face to shine upon them, and give them fruitful seasons again, that their hearts may rejoice in him.[139]

It was not only Christian communities who contributed. A number of synagogues made collections. At this time, there were less than 50,000 Jews throughout the United States, about 13,000 of whom resided in New York City.[140] The Crosby Street Synagogue, which was the third to have been built in the city, donated $175.[141] The donation was the outcome of a specially convened meeting for the purpose of "taking measures for the relief of the famishing thousands of their fellow mortals in that unfortunate and destitute country, Ireland."[142] The prayer and address were delivered by Jacques Judah Lyons, the *hazan*, or prayer leader. Lyons, who had been born in Surinam, Dutch Guiana, had joined the Congregation Shearith Israel of New York City in 1839. In his address, he made an impassioned plea for the Irish poor:

A nation is in distress, a nation is starving. Numbers of our fellow-creatures have perished, *dreadfully, miserably* perished from hunger and starvation. Millions are threatened with the same horrid fate, the same dire calamity. The aged and the young, the strong and the feeble alike are prostrated. The heart of civilization is touched by the distress and woe of the sufferers. Relief, and if not relief at least alleviation, is the first sentiment to which utterance is given, and in obedience to that sentiment are we, my brethren, assembled this evening.[143]

Lyons was followed by Jonas B. Phillips, the assistant district attorney, who delivered a speech of "great beauty and eloquence."[144] Other synagogues contributed, including members of the Franklin Street Synagogue, who collected $80.[145]

Many small towns assembled their own committees to raise money on behalf of the General Relief Committee. This included the New Haven Irish Relief Committee, which gave several donations, and committees based in Morristown, New Jersey ($114.75), Waterbury, Connecticut ($460), Morgantown, Virginia ($220), Toledo, Ohio ($331.71), and Plattsburg in New York ($50). Further donations came from the Ninth Ward of New York City ($397.70), the Haverstraw Irish Relief Society ($220), committees formed in Honesdale, Pennsylvania ($1,000), in Onondaga, New York ($1,200), the Citizens of Chicago ($1,687.44), South Bend, Indiana ($111.75), Montgomery, Alabama ($575.62), Jonesboro, Alabama ($350), Wooster, Ohio ($117.84), Danville, Kentucky ($363.30), Louisburg, North Carolina ($36.25), Tallahassee, Florida ($800), Petersburg, Virginia ($722.88), and Mackinac Island, Michigan ($200).[146] The mayor of Cleveland, Ohio, sent $121.16. On May 4, the large sum of $1,302.64 was received from Vicksburg in Mississippi. The citizens of Quincy, Florida, raised $125.81, the proceeds of one meeting.[147] The meeting had been chaired by Charles H. Dupont, a local lawyer, businessman, and Democratic politician. Dupont was also a plantation owner who kept 108 slaves.[148]

The population of Richmond, Virginia, provided relief in the form of foodstuffs, giving 2,600 barrels and 150 bags of kiln-dried cornmeal, in addition to 324 barrels of Indian corn, two barrels of peas, two hogsheads and one box of bacon, 40 barrels of flour, as well as 16 boxes of clothing.[149] George Barclay, a member of the New York Committee who was in charge of provisions, responded:

The people of this country deserve great credit for the prompt and liberal contributions made by them for the relief of our suffering fellow beings in good old Ireland, a country to which I am warmly attached, having spent many happy days there between the years 1815 and 1819, and received very kind attentions.[150]

Similarly, a committee in Milwaukee, Wisconsin, donated flour, to be distributed thus: 50 bbls to Dublin, 50 bbls to Belfast, 50 to Cork, 75 to Waterford, 100 to Galway, 60 to Valencia in Kerry, and 50 bbls to Westport, County Mayo. The Milwaukee Committee requested "these donations to be given in their names to the Roman Catholic and Protestant ministers of the above-named places, or to some other prominent gentlemen."[151]

One of the largest single contributions was made by the City of Albany, the state capital of New York. On April 19, their donation of $16,000 was recorded by the General Relief Committee. This was followed by $4,000 on May 14, $2000 on July 2, and $400 on September 13. Their final donation of $282.78 was received on February 2, 1848.[152] The Albany Committee for the Relief of Ireland had been founded in February 1847 in response to the appeal from New York. The chairman of the Albany Committee was Robert M. Jenkins, a successful local lawyer. Other members of the executive committee included Edward Delavan, a wine merchant and temperance advocate, bank presidents Thomas Olcott and John Norton, and James Dexter, an attorney. John Ford, also an attorney, served as the committee's secretary, and Theodore Olcott, director of the Canal Bank, served as treasurer. The committee appointed an official collector to each ward within the city, and a circular was issued asking for donations, which could be in cash, food, clothing, or provisions (usually grain or flour). The names of individuals who donated over $5 were listed in the local newspapers. Thomas James, a prosperous flour merchant, was a member of a subcommittee that oversaw the collection and transfer of goods from Albany. As was the case elsewhere, fund-raising efforts included special concerts, lectures, and church sermons. More unusually, the three Roman Catholic churches in Albany took part in a "benevolent race" to raise funds. Together, they donated $5,329 to the committee.[153]

Due to the size of the first donation from Albany, a complete vessel was able to be filled with provisions and sent to Ireland, it being known as the "Albany ship." The Albany ship, which was the British brig *Minerva*, sailed to Cork and, as requested by the Albany Committee, its cargo of 2,000 barrels of meal was to be distributed among the poor in Dublin, Cork, Tuam, and Cashel.[154] The British government paid the freight.[155] A second Albany ship, the *Malabar*, sailed at the end of May.[156] It was carrying provisions to Dublin valued at $24,013.08.[157] The final Albany ship, the *Ashburton*, left for Ireland in the latter part of December 1847. It was carrying 715 barrels of cornmeal and $212.78 in cash. Following this shipment, the Albany Committee dissolved.[158] In total, the city had raised approximately $25,000 on behalf of the Irish poor. Van Schaick, who was a native of Albany, commented, "I feel proud of the good conduct of the ancient Dutch city."[159] Undoubtedly, the generosity of the people of Albany helped to save many lives throughout Ireland.

On May 10, $103.30 was received from Richard H. Coolidge, the assistant surgeon of Fort Gibson in the Cherokee Nation. The individual donors were not named.[160] The fort, situated at what was referred to as the "Indian frontier," was coping with unrest from the local Cherokee Nation while many of their men had been deployed to fight in the Mexican-American War.[161] Coolidge, who had been born in New York City in 1816, had been appointed assistant surgeon in the United States Army in 1841. He was highly regarded in the army and, later, promoted for his bravery during the Civil War, but he died prematurely in 1866.[162] Captain Silas Casey of the 2nd Infantry sent $112 on behalf of the officers, soldiers, and Sunday school scholars at Fort Mackinac, Michigan, on May 10.[163] A committee for Ireland had also been founded in the frontier town of Fort Wayne in Indiana. The town had grown as a result of the Erie Canal, which had brought German and Irish immigrants to the area. The committee consisted of Allan Hamilton, Hugh McCullough, and Henry Colmick, who raised $150.[164]

A donation of $653 was made by members of the U.S. naval forces serving on the west coast of Africa on board USS *United States*, sent there to suppress the illegal slave trade. Three-quarters of the money donated was for Ireland and one-quarter was for Scotland.[165] The captain, Joseph Smoot, was a hero of the War of 1812.[166] The author Herman Melville had enlisted as a seaman on this frigate in 1843.[167] The commanding officer of the USS *United States* explained their motivation:

The distressing accounts brought from the United States, of the sufferings of the poor in Ireland and Scotland, have caused a deep feeling of concern for their unfortunate condition, which has been manifested in a substantial manner by the officers and crew of this ship.

Without having been prompted, they came forward and offered to raise a contribution in money. The amount collected might have been larger, but for the necessity of limiting and regulating subscriptions made by seamen, in consequence of the unequal donations which they would other-wise make. It was therefore found proper to fix the amount which each should give.

A bill drawn upon the Hon. Secretary for the sum of $653 is herewith enclosed. We are aware that it is but the "widow's mite" when compared with the amount subscribed by our kind hearted people at home; yet, we trust that it will effect some good, and that it may reach its destination in time to relieve the sufferings of many individuals.[168]

The Ireland Relief Committee of Nashville, Tennessee, proved to be both active and generous, raising a number of large contributions for the Irish poor. On April 15, the New York Committee noted the receipt of $1,200, forwarded by a subcommittee comprised of William Gowdy, Benjamin Litton, and William Eakin.[169] This was not their first donation for Ireland. On March 27, they had sent $2,500 to the Central Relief Committee of the Society of Friends, "to be distributed among the suffering Irish in such a way as in your opinion may be productive of the greatest relief." The accompanying letter explained, "The donors sympathize most heartily with the sufferings of the people of Ireland; and hope that they, in connection with their fellow countrymen of other states, may be able to alleviate them in some considerable degree, until more permanent means of relief may be found."[170] An Irish relief committee had also been founded in Memphis, and throughout April, it sent several separate donations. By April 21, the Memphis Committee had donated $1,376, which, by the middle of May, had reached $2,374.61. The Memphis Committee suggested that because so much aid was going to the south of Ireland, a portion of their funds should go to Belfast and to Londonderry.[171] Van Schaick assured them that:

Concerning the mode, time, amount and plan of distribution to each locality, the best judges in Ireland are that Committee. As they are entirely disinterested and conscientious in their proceedings, they will do perfect human justice to all parts of the Island. I shall take care to give them extracts from your letter concerning your views, which they will treat with candor and respect, and will conform to, if it be possible and consistent with duty.[172]

He added:

I glory in your liberality to the abused and suffering people of Ireland, and in the consideration that it is an offering of that divine sensibility of soul which is not confined to country, but would extend its beneficence to every oppressed and famishing people, and not merely to a sect or a party.[173]

An example of disproportionate generosity by people who had few resources themselves was provided by the Navy Yard in New York, where the officers and workmen raised $530.61. They had already contributed $604. The accompanying letter explained:

Upon any occasion, to be the medium of presenting a donation for the relief of the distressed and the unfortunate, would afford me pleasure; but in the performance of the duty now devolving upon me I experience the more satisfaction in saying that I believe none have contributed more willingly, or in a spirit of truer philanthropy than those at this Yard; for it is not of their abundance, but of their penury, that many have responded to the appeal which has been made in behalf of the famishing people whom your Committee seek to relieve.[174]

Van Schaick thanked them, saying, "Your noble contribution from your generous and valiant associates and men will largely aid in the blessed work of our meek and humble friends in Dublin."[175]

One of the most remarkable donations to Ireland was made by people who were themselves disenfranchised, impoverished, and marginalized. As was the case generally, it was groups who were themselves poor that proved to be most generous in relative terms. Captain William Armstrong, the Indian agent near Fort Smith in Arkansas, sent $10, "a large portion of which was contributed by our red brethren of the Choctaw nation."[176] This donation was also reported in sections of the American press.[177] Van Schaick, when writing to the committee in Dublin at the end of May, referred to the donation from "the children of the forest, our red brethren of the Choctaw nation."[178] On May 21, the New York Committee recorded receipt of $170 from Captain Armstrong, noting, "A large portion of this sum was contributed by our red brethren of the Choctaw nation."[179]

The Choctaws were not alone in their generosity. The Cherokee Nation held a meeting in Tahlequah on May 5 to raise money for the hungry in Scotland, explaining, "the very considerable number of the descendants of Scotsmen among the Cherokee is calculated particularly to awaken our sympathy towards that people."[180]

Tellingly, the chief was himself named John Ross (his Cherokee name being Coowescoowe or Tsan-Usdi). English-educated Ross had led the Cherokee Trail of Tears from their ancestral homes in 1838, a move that he had strongly resisted. During the journey, thousands died, including Ross's wife.[181] The money raised by the Cherokees was forwarded to the Scottish Relief Committee in Philadelphia.[182] When urging people to contribute, reference was made to the Choctaws' support for Ireland, and an appeal was made to other parts of the Nation to become involved.[183] Within a month, the Cherokees had raised $245.25.[184]

The generosity of the Choctaws and Cherokees was described in the press in terms of their civilizing encounters with the white man. The U.S. *Gazette* acknowledged their intervention, patronizingly averring:

> Among the noble deeds of disinterested benevolence which the present famine has called forth, none can be more gratifying to enlightened men than the liberality of our red brethren in the Far West. . . . The unexpected contribution is the more acceptable that it comes from those upon whom the white man has but little claim. . . . Christianity has taught them that "God hath made of one blood all nations of men to dwell upon the face of the earth."[185]

N. Chapman, of the Philadelphia Committee, was more unequivocal, but similarly insensitive, informing Chief Ross:

> How sensibly they are affected by this act of truly Christian benevolence on the part of the Cherokee nation. Especially are we gratified by the evidence it affords of your people having already attained to higher and purer species of civilization derived only from the influence of our holy religion, by which we are taught to view the sufferings of our fellow beings wherever they exist as our own.[186]

The work of the General Relief Committee was not without controversy. In March 1847, Congress agreed to the former ships of war, the *Jamestown* and the *Macedonian* being used to take supplies to Ireland, although they declined to pay any charges associated with the voyages. In May, articles appeared in various New York newspapers written by Commodore DeKay, criticizing the New York Committee for refusing to use his services on the *Macedonian*, without offering any explanation. The committee refuted his version of events.[187] They claimed they had rejected his offer on the grounds that it would be quicker to employ a number of smaller vessels. Moreover, they believed that if the *Macedonian* was used by the committee, it would be impossible for the British Treasury to pay the freight charges.[188] DeKay remained unsatisfied, publishing more critical articles and blaming the New York Committee for the delay in the *Macedonian* sailing to Ireland. The committee again refuted DeKay's accusations, but in more detail. One of their criticisms was that DeKay had expected that the committee would pay salaries to him and his officers, which they considered an inappropriate use of the monies that had been raised.[189] In retrospect, the committee believed that their judgment had been correct and that they had sent relief "in the most rapid, direct and economical manner, and with as little ostentation as possible, than to devote any portion of a fund so sacred, under circumstances so imperative to the transmission of any part of these provisions in a costly manner, for the gratification of personal, municipal or national feeling."[190] Nonetheless, DeKay's complaints added a bitter note to what had been a glorious and charitable venture on behalf of the starving poor in Ireland.

The final donation to the General Relief Committee in New York was received on February 2, 1848. It was for $282.78 and came from the chairman of the Albany Committee.[191] As was the case with other fund-raising organizations, the bulk of the committee's work had been carried out in the early months of 1847; while $156,581 was raised up to the end of June 1847, the total raised after this date was $19,037.[192] News from Ireland throughout August appeared to be positive, with a large, healthy harvest expected.[193]

The hope that the 1847 harvest would mark an end to the famine proved to be illusory. The smallness of the potato crop, coinciding with a more general economic downturn meant that the poor in Ireland were facing the third consecutive year of famine. Moreover, Ireland was facing this crisis largely unassisted; the amended Poor Law was intended to throw the financial burden for relief onto Irish taxpayers, while the international fund-raising drive had mostly dried up. In its relatively brief existence, the General Relief Committee had provided an efficient and effective conduit for getting much-needed food to Ireland. The thousands of people in the United States who came together on behalf of the starving Irish resumed their lives. In the longer term, the contributions of many of them were forgotten. When Van Schaick, the inspiration behind the New York Committee, died in 1865, his long obituary made no reference to his work on behalf of Ireland in 1847.[194] However he, together with thousands of other Americans, many of whom had no connection with Ireland, and others whose names have not been recorded or have been forgotten, helped to save the lives of the suffering Irish. Charity, it appears, was more important to them than publicity. Impressively also, differences of religion, class, and ethnicity were cast aside in favor of helping a starving people three thousand miles across the ocean. As the committee declared in its report, "Let Ireland's extremity be America's opportunity to teach the nations a magnificent lesson in human brotherhood by her mighty deeds of brotherly love."[195]

NOTES

A version of this chapter first appeared in Christine Kinealy, *Charity and the Great Hunger in Ireland: The Kindness of Strangers* (London: Bloomsbury, 2013).

1. *Arkansas Intelligencer*, May 8, 1847.
2. Michael D. Wilson, "President of Ireland Mary Robinson Addresses the Choctaw People," June 1995, http://people.uwm.edu/michael/choctaw-homepage/president-of-ireland-mary-robinson-addresses-the-choctaw-people; James Wilson, "President of Ireland Thanks Oklahoma Tribe for Their Generosity during the Great Famine," June 27, 2017, www.irishcentral.com/roots/history/president-of-ireland-thanks-oklahoma-tribe-for-their-generosity-during-the-great-famine; "Varadkar Announces Scholarship for Choctaw Students," *Irish Times*, March 12, 2018.
3. "The 1847 Choctaw Gift to the Irish," http://indianyouth.org/news/detail/the-1847-choctaw-gift-to-the-irish.
4. The unveiling was featured in BBC news, "Sculpture Marks Choctaw Generosity to Irish Famine Victims," June 18, 2017, www.bbc.com/news/world-europe-40304645.
5. *Boston Pilot* [hereafter *Pilot*], November 28, 1846.
6. General Relief Committee of the City of New York, *Aid to Ireland: Report of the General Relief Committee of the City of New York, with Schedules of Receipts in Money, Provisions and Clothing* (New York: The Committee, 1848), [hereafter *Report of GRC*], 7.
7. Gerard T. Koeppel, *Water for Gotham: A History* (Princeton, NJ: Princeton University Press, 2012), 145.
8. *Report of GRC*, appendix.
9. "To the Public," February 12, 1847, *Report of GRC*, 147.
10. *Report of GRC*, 148.
11. Ibid., 149.
12. Ibid., 8.
13. The Broadway United Church of Christ, Broadwayucc.org.

14. *Brooklyn Eagle* [hereafter *Eagle*], February 16, 1847.

15. *Report of GRC*, 8.

16. *Eagle*, February 16, 1847.

17. *Report of GRC*, 152; speech by Van Schaick, 154.

18. Ibid., 155.

19. Ibid., 156.

20. Ibid., 157.

21. Ibid., 156.

22. Ibid., 14–16, 91.

23. Some of Jacob's papers are held by the American Philosophical Society, www.amphilsoc. org/mole/view?docId=ead/Mss.Film.1111-ead.xml.

24. James C. Bell, New York, to Society of Friends, Dublin, May 16, 1848, *Transactions of the Central Relief Committee of the Society of Friends during the Famine in Ireland, in 1846 and 1847* (Dublin: Hodges and Smith, 1852), 327.

25. *Report of GRC*, 17, 149.

26. Perry Belmont, *Public Record of Perry Belmont, a Member of the House of Representatives in the 47th, 48th, 49th, 50th Congress etc.* (Albany, NY: Lyon Block, 1898), 80–83.

27. *Freeman's* (NY), February 16, 1847.

28. *Report of GRC*, 8.

29. Obituary of Van Schaick, *New York Times*, December 3, 1865.

30. *Report of GRC*, Letter to Van Schaick, New York, April 9, 1847, from Messrs. C. F. Peake, P. Donan, J. M. Portine, Committee of Pensacola, Florida, 84.

31. Ibid., Van Schaick to Bewley and Pim, Dublin, April 7, 1847, 80.

32. Ibid., Van Schaick, Primes Building, NY, to Pim and Bewley, February 24, 1847, 67.

33. *Report of GRC*, 69.

34. Ibid., 27, 43.

35. Ibid., Van Schaick to Bewley and Pim, March 29, 1847, 79.

36. Ibid., Van Schaick to Bewley and Pim, April 15, 1847, 86.

37. Ibid., Van Schaick to Bewley and Pim, May 11, 1847, 88.

38. Ibid., Van Schaick to Bewley and Pim, May 22, 1847, 91.

39. *Report of GRC*, 54.

40. Ibid., appendix 2, 59.

41. Ibid., appendix 3, 65.

42. *Report of GRC*, 83.

43. Ibid., Van Schaick to Mayor of Hartford, February 24, 1847, 72.

44. Ibid., Bewley and Pim to Van Schaick, April 4, 1847, 118.

45. Ibid., extract from a letter from Jonathan Pim to Jacob Harvey, Westport, County Mayo (Ireland), March 31, 1847, 120.

46. Ibid., Central Relief Committee of the Society of Friends, 57 William Street, Dublin, April 1, 1847; M. Van Schaick, Chairman of Irish Relief Committee, New York, April 19, 1847, 121.

47. *Report of GRC*, 3.

48. Ibid., 6–7.

49. Ibid., 5–6.

50. Ibid., Van Schaick to Pim and Bewley, March 16, 1847, 82.

51. Ibid., 87–88.

52. Ibid., Van Schaick to Bewley and Pim, April 29, 1847, Dublin, 87.

53. See Patrick Hickey, *Famine in West Cork: The Mizen Peninsula and People, 1800–1852* (Dublin: Mercier Press, 2002).

54. *Report of GRC*, Bewley and Pim to Van Schaick, May 5, 1847, 130.

55. Diary of Philip Hone, quoted in Merle Curti, *American Philanthropy Abroad* (St. Louis: Transaction, 1963), 55.

56. *Report of GRC*, 149, 22.

57. Stephen N. Elias, *The Forgotten Merchant Prince* (Westport, CT: Praeger, 1992), 165.

58. *Report of GRC*, 162.

59. Vera Brodsky Lawrence, *Strong on Music: The New York Music Scene in the Days of George Templeton Strong*, vol. 1, *Resonances, 1836–1849* (Chicago: University of Chicago Press, 1995), 400.

60. *Report of GRC*, 35.

61. Elias, *The Forgotten Merchant Prince*, 165.

62. Francis Samuel Drake, *Dictionary of American Biography, Including Men of the Time: Etc.* (Boston: James R. Osgood, 1872), 868.

63. Elias, *The Forgotten Merchant Prince*, 164–65.

64. *Eagle*, February 16, 1847.

65. Ibid., February 17, 1847.

66. Todd's premises were at 83 Fulton Street, Brooklyn; *Eagle*, February 18, 1847.

67. *Report of GRC*, Van Schaick to Bewley and Pim, February 24, 1847, 69.

68. Ibid., Pim and Bewley to Van Schaick, April 1, 1847, 119.

69. Ibid., Bewley and Pim to Van Schaick, April 4, 1847, 119.

70. Ibid., Reyburn to Bewley and Pim, August 13, 1847, 113.

71. Ibid., appendix 3, 60–61. The ships were the *Victor*, the *Fame*, the *Duncan*, the *Boston*, the *New Haven*, the *Lisbon*, *Bavaria*, *Europe*, *Express*, *Liverpool*, *Siddons*, *Minerva* (Albany ship 1), *Anna Marie* (Albany ship 2), *Malabar* (Albany ship 2).

72. *Report of GRC*, 73.

73. Ibid., 119.

74. Ibid., Bewley and Pim to Van Schaick, April 19, 1847, 122.

75. Ibid., Bewley and Pim to Van Schaick, May 3, 1847, 124.

76. Ibid.

77. Ibid., Bewley and Pim to Van Schaick, May 3, 1847, 125.

78. Ibid., Bewley and Pim to Reyburn, February 24, 1848, 179.

79. See Kinealy, "'How Good People Are': The Involvement of Women," in *Charity and the Great Hunger*, chap. 7, 143–66.

80. This was possibly Father Patrick Murphy, the priest of Barntown, Wexford, http://taghmon.com/vol4/chapter07/chapter07.htm.

81. *Report of GRC*, "Food from America. Return to the House of Commons," November 7, 1847, appendix, 180–87.

82. Ibid., Reyburn to Bewley and Pim, August 13, 1847, 113.

83. Ibid., 9.

84. Ibid., 27, 30.

85. Ibid., Van Schaick to Pim and Bewley, New York, March 13, 1847, 78.

86. Louis Dow Scisco, *Political Nativism in New York State*, vol. 13, *Studies in History, Economics, and Public Law* (New York: Columbia University Press, 1901), 68.

87. *Report of GRC*, 29–50.

88. Rev. C. C. Stratton, ed., *Autobiography of Erastus O. Haven: With an Introduction by the Rev. J.M. Buckley* (New York: Phillips & Hunt, 1883).

89. *Report of GRC*, 24, 33, 34, 50.

90. Catherine Elizabeth Havens, *Diary of a Little Girl in Old New York*, 2nd ed. (New York: Henry Collins Brown, 1920), 84–85.

91. *Report of GRC*, appendix 1, 17, 21, 36, 43.

92. See Christine Kinealy, *Repeal and Revolution: 1848 in Ireland* (Manchester: Manchester University Press, 2009).

93. *Report of GRC*, 52.

94. Corcoran School of the Arts and Design, https://corcoran.gwu.edu/history.

95. William Wilson Corcoran, *A Grandfather's Legacy: Containing a Sketch of His Life and Obituary Notices* (Washington, DC: H. Polkinhorn, 1879), 3.

96. Ibid., 99, 100, 110.

97. *Report of GRC*, 29–31, 36.

98. Lawrence, *Strong on Music*, 480.

99. Ibid.

100. *Report of GRC*, 31.

101. *Minutes of the Common Council of the City of New York, 1784–1831*, vol. 17 (New York: City of New York, 1917), 620; *Report of GRC*, 41.

102. $10 was received from "a few poor Christians in Brooklyn," *Report of GRC*, 18; "a poor man gave $3," ibid., 23.

103. *Report of GRC*, passim.

104. Ibid., appendix 2, 58.

105. *Eagle*, May 12, 1847.

106. *Report of GRC*, Van Schaick to Henry Burch, Esq., Moira, Franklin Co., NY, June 14, 1847, 96.

107. Ibid., 29, 34, 45, 36.

108. Albert Clark Stevens, *The Cyclopædia of Fraternities* (New York: E.B. Treat and Co., 1907), 300.

109. Scisco, *Political Nativism*, 68.

110. *Report of GRC*, 40.

111. Ibid., 34. For more on Mickle, see The Political Graveyard: A Database of American History, http://politicalgraveyard.com/bio/micheau-middleswarth.html.

112. See Christine Kinealy, *Daniel O'Connell and Anti-Slavery: 'The Saddest People the Sun Sees'* (London: Pickering and Chatto, 2011).

113. *Report of GRC*, 43, 51.

114. John D. Crimmins, *St. Patrick's Day* (New York: Self-published, 1902), 97.

115. *Report of GRC*, 43, 10.

116. Ibid., 44.

117. New Advent Catholic Encyclopedia, www.newadvent.org/cathen/07516a.htm.

118. Quoted in J. J. Lee and Marion R. Casey, eds., *Making the Irish American: History and Heritage of the Irish in the United States* (New York: New York University Press, 2006), 278.

119. John Hughes, "'On the Antecedents of Famine,' delivered under the auspices of the General Relief Committee for the relief of the suffering poor of Ireland," in *The Complete Works of the Most Rev. John Hughes, D.D., Archbishop of New York, Comprising His Sermons, Letters, Lectures, Speeches, etc.* (New York: American News, 1864), 544.

120. Ibid., 556–57.

121. Ibid, 556.

122. *National Era*, March 25, 1847.

123. For more on Irish involvement in abolition, see Kinealy, *Daniel O'Connell and Anti-Slavery*.

124. *Report of GRC*, 44.

125. Ibid., 35, 41–42.

126. Catholic Editing Company, ed., *The Catholic Church in the United States of America: Undertaken to Celebrate the Golden Jubilee of His Holiness, Pope Pius X* (New York: Catholic Editing Company, 1908), 3:432.

127. History of St. Francis of Assisi, www.stfrancisnyc.org/history.

128. For example: included the Bridgeport Congregational Church ($83), St. Luke's Episcopalian Church in Catskill, Church of the Holy Communion in New York ($403.45), the Norfolk Street Methodist Church ($12), the Church of the Ascension, Fifth Avenue ($645.53 and four barrels of bread stuffs), Trinity Church, New York ($334.82), Protestant Episcopal Free Church of the Holy Evangelists ($95.38), St. Paul's Episcopal Chapel ($265.55), Unitarian Church of the Messiah ($481), St. John's Church ($556 and $13.60), St. Matthew's Episcopal Church on Christopher Street ($83.37), Presbyterian Church of Morris County in New Jersey ($18), Duane Street, Presbyterian Church ($273.31), Second Wesleyan Chapel, Duane Street, New York ($700.75), the Methodist churches in Middletown, Connecticut ($62), St. Annis [*sic*] Church, Fishkill ($40.86), Congregational Society, Meriden, Connecticut ($76.35), the Episcopalian Grace Church in New York City ($1,912.38), St. Mary's Catholic Church, Brooklyn ($230), the Catholic churches of St. Columba's, the Church of the Transfiguration, St. Andrew's in New York City ($435.88, $531, and $276.07 respectively), the Methodist Episcopal Church on Forsyth Street ($102.50), the Commercial Congregation of South Amherst in Ohio ($37), the Episcopal Churches of Southport, Connecticut ($30) and Calvary in New York City ($1 and 375 barrels of cornmeal), Christ Church at Syosset, Long Island ($64), the Reformed Dutch Church on Houston Street, New York City ($37.57 and later, $3), Unitarian Church ($91), Methodist Episcopal Church ($30), Unitarian Universalist Church ($33), North Congregational Church, Connecticut ($171.33), St. John's Church ($148), Christ Church ($363), Centre Church ($244.66 for Ireland and $100 for Scotland), Mercer Presbyterian Church ($381.38), St. Stephen's Episcopal Church, near Sixth Avenue ($186), St. Mark's Church, New York ($250), Christ Episcopal Church in Norwich, Connecticut ($100), St. Paul's Church, St. Lawrence ($24), St. Thomas Episcopal Church on Broadway ($319.38), St. Peter's Episcopal Church ($150.62), the Methodist church on Seventh Street ($35), St. John's Episcopal Church in Bridgeport, Connecticut ($120), St. John's Episcopal Church, Staten Island ($65.75), St. John's Episcopal Church, Stamford, Connecticut ($110), First Presbyterian Church, Mercer Street, New York ($153), St. John's Episcopal Church, Delhi, Delaware ($15.36), St. Vincent ($150), St. John the Evangelist ($61.25), the Methodist Episcopal Church in Cayuga in New York ($15), St. Matthew's Episcopal Church, Westchester, Bedford ($10.25), St. George's Episcopal Church on Long Island

($23.50), St. Paul's Catholic Church, Harlem ($358.86), Reformed Dutch Church on Staten Island ($25.50), St. Bartholomew's Episcopal Church, Bowery, New York ($354.25), Christ Episcopal Church in Tarrytown, New York ($115.50), Union Episcopal Church in Humphreysville, Connecticut ($14), Mercer Street Presbyterian Church, New York ($25), Protestant Episcopal Church of the Holy Cross in Troy ($108), Reformed Dutch Church in Kinderhook ($36.80), the Congregational Society and the Methodist Society of Essex in Connecticut ($90.75 and $20.50 respectively), the Baptist Church in Amity Street ($275). See *Report of GRC* for more churches and congregations that gave.

129. *Report of GRC*, 9.

130. Ibid., 47.

131. William Balch, Dictionary of Unitarian and Universalist Biography, http://uudb.org/articles/williamstevensbalch.html.

132. *Report of GRC*, 44, 53.

133. Henry C. Whyman, *The Hedstroms and the Bethel Ship Saga: Methodist Influence on Swedish Religious Life* (Carbondale: Southern Illinois University Press, 1992), 77.

134. *Report of GRC*, 37.

135. Whyman, *The Hedstroms and the Bethel Ship Saga*, 77.

136. "Sailor's Union Bethel Methodist Church," www.federalhillonline.com/tourstop04.htm.

137. *Report of GRC*, 37.

138. George Lane (1784–1859) was influential in Joseph Smith's founding of the Mormon Church. Larry C. Porter, "Rev. George Lane: Good Gifts, Good Grace, and Marked Usefulness," *Brigham Young University Studies* 9, no. 3 (Spring 1969): 321–40.

139. *NY Christian Advocate*, March 24, 1847.

140. American Jewish Historical Society, *Publications of the American Jewish Historical Society* 6 (1897): 143.

141. American Jewish Historical Society, *American Jewish Historical Quarterly* 27 (reprint by Nabu Press, 2011): 251.

142. "Meeting of the Jewish Population of New York in Aid of Ireland," *Occident and American Jewish Advocate*, vol. 5 no. 1 (April 1847).

143. Ibid.

144. Ibid.

145. *Occident and American Jewish Advocate*, vol. 5, no. 5 (August 1847); *Report of GRC*, 40.

146. *Report of GRC*, 24, 30, 35.

147. Ibid., 24, 30, 35, 39, 48, 47.

148. Florida's Ante Bellum Plantations, www.dejaelaine.com/abplantations.html.

149. *Report of GRC*, Van Schaick to Bewley and Pim, May 14, 1847, 103.

150. Ibid., George Barclay to Bewley and Pim, May 14, 1847, 104.

151. The Milwaukee Committee consisted of Richard Murphy, John White, and Rufus King. *Report of GRC*, Reyburn to Pim and Bewley, July 14, 1847, 106.

152. Ibid., 47, 59.

153. Albany Committee for the Relief of Ireland: A Guide to the Albany Committee for the Relief of Ireland Records, www.albanyinstitute.org/tl_files/pdfs/library/Library%20Collection%20Finding%20Aids%20Albany . . . Irish%20Relief%20CD%20528.pdf.

154. *Report of GRC*, Van Schaick, NY, to Bewley and Pim, Dublin, May 15, 1847, 89.

155. Ibid., Van Schaick to Charles M. Jenkins, chairman of executive committee for relief of Ireland, Albany, April 10, 1847, 85 (the real name of the vessel was the British brig *Minerva*).

156. Ibid., Van Schaick to Pim and Bewley, May 22, 1847, 91.

157. Ibid., Van Schaick to Pim and Bewley, May 26, 1847, 94.

158. Committee for the Relief of Ireland, Albany.

159. *Report of GRC*, Van Schaick to Pim and Bewley, April 15, 1847, 86.

160. *Report of GRC*, 49.

161. Richard L. Trotter, "For the Defense of the Western Border: Arkansas Volunteers on the Indian Frontier, 1846–1847," *Arkansas Historical Quarterly* 60, no. 4 (Winter 2001): 394–410.

162. Coolidge was promoted to brevet lieutenant-colonel for faithful and meritorious services during the Civil War: http://www.civilwarmedicalbooks.com/Principles_of_Surgery.html; Coolidge, Fort Gibson, Cherokee Nation, to Adjunct General of the Army, *United States Congressional Serial Set*, vol. 483 (Washington, DC: U.S. Government Printing Office, 1892), 5–51.

163. *Report of GRC*, appendix 2, 56.

164. Ibid., 53.

165. Ibid.

166. Harry Wright Newman, *The Smoots of Maryland and Virginia: A Genealogical History of William Smute, Boatright, of Hampton, Virginia, and Pickawaxon, Maryland, with a History of His Descendants to the Present Generation* (Washington, DC: J. P. Bell, 1936), 31.

167. Herman Melville used his experiences to inform his novels *White-Jacket* and *Moby Dick*.

168. *Report of GRC*, George C. Read, U.S. Naval Forces, West Coast of Africa, United States frigate *United States*, Porto Praya, Cape Verde Islands, to Jacob Harvey, Esq., 14 May 1847, 117.

169. Ibid., 46. Litton had been born in Ireland in 1799; www.findagrave.com/memorial/34690836/benjamin-litton.

170. Irish Relief Committee, Nashville, Tennessee, March 27, 1847, appendix 5, *Transactions*, 238.

171. *Report of GRC*, 51, 92.

172. Ibid., Van Schaick to D. Dark, Chairman, and Charles Goffland, Treasurer, Memphis Irish Relief Committee, Tennessee, May 21, 1847, 90.

173. Ibid.

174. *Report of GRC*, Isaac McKeever, Captain, U.S. Navy, to Myndert Van Schaick, Esq., March 12, 1847, 76.

175. Ibid., Van Schaick to McKeever, March 12, 1847, 77.

176. *Report of GRC*, 51.

177. For example, *Arkansas Intelligencer*, April 3, 1847; *Niles National Register,* May 1, 1847.

178. *Report of GRC*, Van Schaick to Bewley and Pim, May 22, 1847, 92.

179. *Report of GRC*, 51; some newspapers gave the figure as $710, for example, *Connecticut Courant*, April 24, 1847.

180. *Cherokee Nation*, May 6, 1847.

181. John Ross, chief of Cherokee Nation, in *Encyclopædia Britannica* online, https://www.britannica.com/biography/John-Ross-chief-of-Cherokee-Nation.

182. *Cherokee Nation*, May 6, 1847.

183. Ibid., May 13, 1847.

184. Ibid., June 10, 1847.

185. Ibid., July 15, 1847.

186. N. Chapman, Philadelphia, to Chief John Ross, June 11, 1847, in *Cherokee Nation*, July 15, 1847.

187. These accusations were made by Commander DeKay and published in the *New York Sun. Report of GRC*, 165–66.

188. *Report of GRC*, Resolution of Standing Committee, March 10, 1847, 166–69.

189. Ibid., Letter of GRC, May 31, 1847, 169–74.

190. Ibid., 175.

191. *Report of GRC*, 59.

192. Ibid., 54, 59.

193. *National Era*, August 5, 1847.

194. Obituary of Van Schaick, *New York Times*, December 3, 1865.

195. This is a quote from Elihu Burritt on behalf of Ireland. *Report of GRC*, 15.

Ishki, Mother, Upon Leaving the Choctaw Homelands, 1831

LeAnne Howe

Right here is where I once suckled babies into Red people
Right here we grew three sisters into Corn, Beans, and Squash
Right here we gave foods to all who hungered
Right here we nurtured abundance.

Right here my body was a cycle of giving until
Torn from our homelands by the Naholla, and
Andrew Jackson, the duteous seamster
Intent on opening all veins.

Right here there's a hole of sorrow in the center of my chest
A puncture
A chasm of muscle
Sinew
Bones

Right here I will stitch my wounds and live on
And sing,
And sing,
I am singing, still.

I Should Have Known

Tim Tingle

In 2013, I was among the featured performers invited to Ireland to the Cape Clear Storytelling Festival. I took the long but loaded-with-anticipation plane trip from San Antonio, Texas, to Cork Airport, Ireland. This was followed by a pleasant, though map-crazy, drive in a rented car from Cork to Baltimore. We had done our research, my traveling partner and I. We knew how often the ferry paddled from Baltimore to Cape Clear Island, the southernmost floating fist of Irish soil.

I should have known that so much more awaited us. I had asked for, and received, five additional days on the mainland, following the festival. I was, and still am, researching book four of the *How I Became a Ghost* series, partially set in Ireland, shifting back and forth from the Choctaw Trail of Tears to the Irish Potato Famine. Yes, I know they were sixteen years apart, and that's why I write fiction, where time-traveling is not only allowed, but greatly appreciated by my middle-grade school target audience. And ghosts aplenty line the roads of both Ireland and Choctaw country.

And this leads me to tell of another commonality, one of many we Choctaws share with traditional Irish folks. Our journeys together beginning in 1847 is not, nor has it ever been, about the money, whether it be $710 or $170 as some scholars have questioned. It is about the Choctaw Gift of Famine Relief. Now that I have gotten that out of the way, I want to say why I write this story: to uncover stones, to teach the untaught, to educate with feelings and living winds, the rain and the pain of cold and hunger, and for ghosts still thriving in our woods and mountains—and, as I would soon find out, ghosts thrive among the hills and valleys of Irish burial sites. Still they rest on tiny mounds of rising ground; still they surround those willing to listen.

Maybe that begins to explain why the 1847 Choctaw gift stands out as borne of angels. Choctaws and Irishmen are kinfolks in suffering, yes, but so much more. We are kinfolks in the joy of human contact, of expressive smiles and lively conversations, of reaching down to help the young, the old, be they family or foreign.

I should have known—when the ferry ticketmaster explained, having seen us arrive in an auto, "No cars allowed on board, ya know. No cars allowed on Cape Clear, only those belonging to residents."

And where did my mind go? Yep, "how much money have I wasted on this rental car that will now sit here for what, a week?"

Praise the divine that I was allowed no car—no car to speed by the Gaelic hillsides. I soon discovered I was floating to an island of the past, to graveyards filled with hard-boned memories. Choctaw graveyards of Oklahoma have been my inspiration for decades. Not glorious monument-filled graves, with stone entryways and mausoleums. No, I was called by former residents of the small, and often unseen gravesites, covered by fallen trees and leaves and soil erosion.

One night, a decade ago, I will always remember as a turning point in my life. 'Twas Sunday evening, Labor Day weekend near Tushkahoma, the old Choctaw capital, following a day of talking and dancing and playing Choctaw Rabbit Trickster jokes on my best friends, all while celebrating our Choctaw Nation's independence. My friends, storytellers Greg Rodgers, Stella Long, and a few other older kinfolks, were following the path of the moon, after midnight and away from the busy lights of Ferris wheels and outdoor cooking pits and overhead lights of campers, a temporary home to two hundred thousand celebrants, mostly Choctaws.

Lured by the silence, we circled the old stone capitol building and trudged up the winding road. We knew where we were going, though no one spoke of it. We were nearing the graveyard, a seldom-seen blanket of trees and stone fences and thick iron gates. Tucked away on the edge of the blanket was a small tombstone with a young girl's name notched in the stone.

We walked together, but when we entered the graveyard we separated, wandering in silence and led by the whisperings. Most people are attracted to the light—*the goodness*, they say—but my friends and I were attracted to the darkness, where in our minds goodness lies deeper, as yet unseen.

I neared the wall on the east side of the graveyard and stood by the grave of a young girl. She had died when she was seven or eight, and the words on the tombstone were simple and tender. I felt grief, living grief. But something made me smile and I felt the little girl rising from the ground and laughing.

I should have known. I turned away and walked to the center of the graveyard, waiting on my friends. I know I laughed out loud, realizing *how silly am I!* We're in a graveyard! I might wait till dawn.

Hoke, I strolled to the far west wall of the site, circled a few tombstones, then stopped and whisper-sang "Shilombish Holitopama"—"Amazing Grace" in Choctaw. Our nation's national anthem. As I walked slowly to the gate I noticed Stella, the eldest among us, kneeling at the grave of the young girl. *She's getting to know her, too,* I thought. Most of our circle was now waiting at the gate, casting their eyes toward Stella.

Someone said softly, "Is she hoke?" No one replied, but we all strolled in her direction, not with a sense of urgency, more with a feeling of night-family.

Stella approached us, telling of the girl, the dates of her birth and death, and whispering her name.

"You read that from a gravestone?" asked Jay.

"Yes," she said, turning and pointing to the tree shadows near the eastern wall.

"I don't see any tombstone," he replied. "Show us."

We followed Stella to the Choctaw girl's burial site, the site I had stood over and felt the little girl's sense of joy—joy at finally being noticed.

Stella looked at me. I looked at Stella. The small stone marker was gone, stolen years ago or perhaps it was never there. We looked upon the grassy spot by the stone wall and saw no indication of a grave.

Stella laughed and turned to the gate. Our conversation as we walked the mile or so to our campsite was full of Choctaw memories, burial tales, and rising spirits—but not one word did we say about the girl. We let the blessing hover in the goodness of the dark.

How Many Bodies Are Buried?

After an hour at sea we spotted Cape Clear in the distance. As we sat on the deck and watched the waters rise and fall and felt the ferry sway with the rhythm, I returned to that night near the old Choctaw capitol. *How many bodies are buried,* I thought, *and no one knows where?*

We neared Cape Clear and my eyes were drawn to the beauty of the high cliffs, rugged and with no sign of human invaders. Waves crashed on the shore and clouds of steamy water rose high. The ferry circled the island, and the captain steered us into a small inlet, approaching a long wooden pier.

"Careful as you step," he warned, and rightly so, for the waves still ruled and the ferry rocked.

"You must be Tingle," a smiling gray-haired gentleman said, stretching out his hand to both shake mine and steady my leap to the shore.

How many times in life do we take a step that will forever change us? I took that step that afternoon, from the ferry to Cape Clear, aided by my host Jack Lynch.

"I'm taking you to the bed and breakfast where you'll be for the next four days," Jack said. We loaded the luggage and pulled away, on a barely paved road that circled the cliffs. In thirty minutes I flopped down on the bed, grabbing a quick nap before my first performance that evening.

Jack Lynch, himself an Irish storyteller, clearly understood that being entertained by eager-to-please hosts is the biggest nightmare most tellers face. He left me alone, making sure I knew when to be ready and where to stand outside for my ride.

"If you're not there, she might assume you've walked or found another ride," he said, "so if you don't want to be left, be there and easy to spot."

A British teller, Ursula Holden-Gill, and her husband were staying in the same two-storied stone bed and breakfast as myself, with an Italian teller, Paola Balbi. The two Irish performers, Batt Burns and singer/storyteller Ger Wolfe, were nestled somewhere else, as best I can recall.

The rooms were tiny, wonderfully tight and wooden, and the bath was a makeshift shower or a clutch-your-knees tub. The food was made by the hostess and *oh so delicious*—creamy and thick and served with wine—and any thoughts that "potatoes never returned" were soon boiled away. I gobbled down supper and hurried upstairs for my drum and flute.

I did catch my ride, and the opening concert, at a small venue, was a sometimes noisy and sometimes tearfully moving affair. Long before I stepped onto the stage

I felt the hum of rising joy from the Irish crowd, eager to hear a Choctaw's vision of the world.

I chose to open with a "Trail of Tears" story, based on family memories passed down from almost two centuries ago. John Carnes, my great-great-grandfather and ten years old at the time, carried the bones of his mother on the journey; she had died of smallpox on the trail. It is believed by many that the epidemic of smallpox was deliberately spread by infected blankets passed out to Choctaws by soldiers selected for their immunity to the disease.

President Andrew Jackson had worked closely with Choctaw soldiers, many of whom fought on the side of the United States Army during the War of 1812, and he knew of their lack of resistance to smallpox. Thousands of Choctaws died on the Trail from starvation and injuries suffered on the freezing winter's walk, and disease. We lost one-quarter of our population on the Trail of Tears; Choctaws had to walk from our Mississippi homelands to Indian Territory. And cruelty claimed many lives, as soldiers grew impatient with the old. The slow. The under-nourished.

As storytellers we hope to resurrect the dead with our narratives, and often we are inspired by those well-trod and well-mentioned graveyards—and even, in my son's case, the songs we hear and sing at Irish bars.

Tim Finnegan lived in Wattling Street
A gentle Irishman mighty odd
He'd a beautiful brogue so rich and sweet
To rise in the world he carried a hod

My son, Jacob Tingle, spent five years courting his bride and attending grad school at the University of Maryland, not far from Washington, DC. He also spent, by his own admission, two nights a month at Dubliners Restaurant and Pub, a famous Irish bar.

"They even passed out song sheets, so you'd get the lyrics right," he said, and that's how he became familiar with "Finnegan's Wake," the drinking song.

Now Tim had a sort of a tripling way
With a love for the liquor poor Tim was born
To help him on with his work each day
He'd a drop of the whiskey every morn

"Jen is Irish on her mother's side," said Jacob, referring to his wife, "as am I. So we decided, since her last name would be Tingle, to honor the Irish side by giving our first child an Irish name, Teagan. Baby Teagan," he said in a whispery voice.

Four months following Teagan's birth, we spent a wonderful Christmas Day together, in the hills of Canyon Lake, Texas, passing giggling Teagan back and forth and chasing her crawling over the carpet. Three days later I received a phone call from Jacob, at two o'clock in the morning. He was howling and crying and I could barely make out his words.

"Dad, please come over. Please, we need you."

Teagan, Baby Teagan, died on December 28, three days after Christmas. Asleep in her mother's arms she left this world. The tragedy gripped the family and I prayed that my son and his wife would survive.

> One morning Tim felt rather full
> His head felt heavy which make him shake
> He fell from the ladder and broke his skull
> And they carried him home his corpse to wake

On Christmas morning, a year following the loss of Teagan, Jacob rang my doorbell and woke me up at 5 a.m. I lived an hour's drive from my son, so this was rather unexpected. We had coffee, spoke quietly, and never mentioned Teagan, though her spirit hovered over every word, every glance. As he said goodbye and stepped to the door, he turned to face me.

"I'm breaking a promise with Jen," he said, "but I have to tell you. Teagan would not let us have even a single unhappy Christmas."

"What do you mean, Jacob?"

"We loved our time with her last Christmas, and a few weeks ago we learned Jen is pregnant again, so this is a very special Christmas. Jen wanted me to keep it a secret, but I can't. I want you to be happy, too, Dad."

I hugged my son, we both shed a few tears, and I wished him well. "When we found out Jen was having a boy," Jacob later revealed, "our search for just the right name for our next baby became all-important. We searched for an Irish name, made secret lists, and decided to share them one evening. Finnegan was the first name on both of our lists, so it was settled."

I knew right away the reason for the choice—the resurrection of the baby who left us far too soon.

They wrapped him up in a nice clean sheet
And laid him there upon the bed
A bottle of whiskey at his feet
And a gallon of porter at his head.

His friends all gathered at the wake
And Missus Finnegan called for lunch
First they brought in tay and cake

Jacob and Jen spoke to themselves, only to themselves, of the resurrective power and beauty of the name Finnegan, as they longed to let Teagan know they would never forget her.

Mickey Maloney raised his head
When a bottle of whiskey flew at him
It missed him falling on the bed
The liquor scattered over Tim

Tim revives, see how he rises
Timothy rising from the dead
Whirl your whiskey around like blazes
Tonamondeal, do you think I'm dead?

The strength and power of belief, of never allowing tragedy to rule your vision, is both Irish and Choctaw, and feeds families and individuals with a taste of hope. We also share an eerie understanding of life's arc—the expectation of tragedy.

My grandmother warned us "to see the world through Choctaw eyes only sometimes, when you are surrounded by family and friends." Though the Trail of Tears and the Irish Famine are often ignored in our teachings, to avoid the pain they carry, we know that we are meant to endure sorrow, and we use whatever tools we can to light those tiny, flickering flames of joy.

On that first evening of the Cape Clear International Storytelling Festival, I shared in a bonfire of joy, as each performer tossed new logs upon the fire. Ger Wolfe sang songs in Gaelic with the audience joining, sometimes clapping and rocking with the strums of his guitar, and sometimes with tearful whisperings.

During breaks in the performance, several audience members gave me warm shoulder hugs; others mentioned The Gift, the Choctaw collection of money sent to aid the Irish in the midst of the Famine in 1847.

"I've heard there's to be a sculpture made, honoring the Choctaws for The Gift," said one.

"I've heard the same," I said, "and I'm staying after the festival to learn some details of the Famine."

"Oh, there's quite a story there."

There Is Quite a Story There

Indeed. Monies were collected in Skullyville, Choctaw Nation, and on March 23, 1847, the gift of $170 was sent to an Irish relief society in Boston. The gesture of caring, the message that *somebody cares*, was carried across the Atlantic, and has been remembered as an indestructible bridge between the Irish and the Choctaw people for 170 years and counting.

"On Sunday, June 18, [2017] the Choctaw Nation was honored at a dedication of the sculpture 'Kindred Sprits' in Midleton, County Cork, Ireland." Thus begins an article by Charles Clark, published in the August edition of the tribal newspaper, *Biskinik*. The sculpture, of nine 20-foot-tall stainless-steel feathers, was created by Irishman artist Alex Pentek, who said, "I think . . . today as much as ever, standing together against adversity from those who are persecuting, is perhaps a message we can still move forward."

Seamus McGrath, mayor of County Cork, stated beautifully the tragedy of the Famine and the link between our two peoples. "We have a shared past as people who have experienced unwelcome intrusion and a shared sense of injustice. During the great Famine, up to one million people perished. . . . and approximately 600,000 emigrated."

Choctaw Chief Gary Batton added, "We endured and overcame; we came across the Trail of Tears where we lost one-fourth of our people. When our ancestors heard of the Famine and the hardship of the Irish people, we knew it was time to help. . . . The Choctaw people and the Irish people are still here today."

We celebrate to remember, and hopefully to halt the flow of blood on the river of greed. I have known of the Choctaw Gift to the Irish for at least a decade, but I only recently realized that the monies were collected in the town of Skullyville, a town I know well.

I will never forget the decade I spent researching and exploring the present-day remains of Skullyville, working on my novel fifteen years in the making, *House of Purple Cedar* (2014):

> The hour has come to speak of troubled times. Though the bodies have long ago returned to dust, too many ghosts still linger in the graveyards. You are old enough. You need to know. It is time we spoke of Skullyville.

By the 1890s, Skullyville was booming and prosperous, the third-largest town in all of eastern Oklahoma. It was home to New Hope Academy for Girls, a popular Indian boarding school with hundreds of Choctaw girls in attendance, and Fort Coffee School for Boys was less than ten miles away. "Iskulli" is the Choctaw word for money, and Skullyville was "money town," where allotment payments were passed out to Choctaws on a monthly basis. Each week of allotment payments the town was flooded with Choctaws with money to spend.

Though many historical revisionists claim the United States federal government was giving unearned benefits to "Indian People," these payments were compensation for Choctaw land following our removal from Mississippi, as well as from various other treaties we signed.

Skullyville had a bustling Main Street, with clothing and hardware stores, feed stores, restaurants—even the stagecoach connecting major cities from St. Louis to California stopped first in Skullyville before heading west. Imagine the scene: hundreds of Choctaws scurrying about and making monthly purchases at the stores downtown.

But that was half a century later, after the Gift to the Irish. Such was the prosperity of Skullyville, when the Union Pacific Railroad announced a plan to build a cross-continental railroad, Skullyville was chosen as the first Oklahoma stop. If Skullyville was "money town" now, a railroad would bring with it unbelievable wealth to the community.

Lingering in the shadows was the small town of Spiro, populated by white settlers—*illegal immigrants* to Choctaw Nation. When residents heard of the railroad's plans to build a station in Skullyville, greed began to grow. Choctaw homes were burned, people were threatened, and just before midnight on New Year's Eve, January 1, 1897, New Hope Academy for Girls was burned to the ground. Twenty little Choctaw girls lost their lives in the fire.

Knowing there was no justice in United States federal courts across the river,

Choctaws moved away by the thousands, and today Skullyville is home to the Choctaw National Cemetery, the New Hope Academy Cemetery, and little else. What was once the third largest town in Eastern Oklahoma is today obliterated from even the state map.

We must never forget to honor those who lived good and decent lives, our Choctaw ancestors, our Irish kinfolks. We will continue to survive. As stated in *House of Purple Cedar*, "once we were alive, all of us, and when good people, Choctaws and nahullo (white) both, step over our Skullyville graves, we sing as best we can. . . . We Amen! At the top of our lungs beneath the brush arbors, we sweat and toil in our gardens and fields and brood over our livestock and our babies both"

On the second day of my Cape Clear journey, I walked a few miles uphill from my lodging and came upon the largest graveyard on the island. Not knowing if I should be wandering among the graves, I sat on the stone wall and felt the wind, smelling of the sea.

Somehow I did miss my ride for the evening concert, located on the far side of the island. I checked my watch and gave myself thirty minutes, hoping I could remember the directions of my bed-and-breakfast hostess.

I speed-walked and made it!

I recall thinking, as I entered the bar, *No featured storyteller from across the ocean would ever be treated this way in America!*

And in case you're suspecting that a bit of Yankee egotism had crept into my thinking, you'd be wrong to go there. No, my next thought was *I love it here!*

No one's a star, not here on Cape Clear Island. Or *maybe*—everyone's a star. We populate the heavens, not solo but as part of constellations, adding to the purpose of the whole.

I performed a Choctaw folktale that evening of a young man striving for the respect of his father, who scornfully calls him "No Name," as the boy has never earned a name. After giving his life to save another, as I am certain so many did during both the Trail of Tears and the Irish Famine, he finally earns his father's respect. I also shared an old Choctaw belief with my Irish audience of nodding heads and tearful faces—the belief that the ghosts of deceased kinfolks are never far away.

Oh, That I Could Be There Once Again!

The next morning I joined a group on a walking tour of coastal sites, among them a small graveyard overlooking the harbor. The tour guide had grown up on the island, as his family had for generations. He ushered us through a narrow stone gate and gestured to a grave, which we encircled.

"This is my family's grave," he said, "where I hope to be buried someday. My uncle lies here, and his father before him, and maybe a dozen others, maybe more. Especially during the Famine, and certainly after, the land was scarce, as you see. Gardens and farms and livestock and homes, no room for graves. Here's how we do it. Every family has their own gravesite, not a wide expanse of many graves, but a slab as big as a coffin. Only one.

"But it wouldn't work if we used coffins. Not on Cape Clear. No, the bodies must—and pardon my language—the body must rot and work its way into the soil. That makes room for the next family member, who dies and is buried atop the other, and down we travel through the family tree.

"Gives a whole new meaning to researching your roots, *eh*?" We all laughed softly, but he was only just beginning.

"I was maybe ten years old," he continued, "and my uncle Derek died long before his time. He was not yet sixty, as I recall. And Granddad was buried here only a year before, so there was no time for his body to—shall we say decompose?

"No, no time. And after laying Uncle Derek on top of Granddad and tossing dirt on them both, the gravediggers looked at each other. Frustrated they were. The mound refused to settle. So they struck the stony soil with picks and shovels.

"We stood watching, for the preacher had yet to say his words and no songs had we sung, though most heads were bowed. But not all!

"From beneath the mound of dirt Uncle Derek's head came rolling! I picked it up and held it high. 'Hey, look! It's Uncle Derek!' I will cherish that moment for the rest of my life, though I'm sure my mom and dad would just as soon forget it."

He looked at the mound of dirt at his feet and smiled. Uncle Derek, he knew, was smiling back at him.

We walked for what must have been several miles that day, from cliff overlooks to narrow roads surrounded by stone walls. From a cliffside path, our guide pointed across a small bay inlet—to a stone church building that looked like nothing else on the island, a majestic structure boasting of its beauty with a thrust of its towers above a stone stairway winding to the ground.

To enter me, you must stare at your feet, bowing your head in thankful prayer that you are entering the temple of glory, not A temple of glory, not on this impoverished island, but The Temple of Glory, or so it seemed to say.

Our guide cast his eyes around our circle—as I later realized—looking for another among us who knew the story of this church. "It is the only Protestant church on Cape Clear," he said. "Even you Choctaws know we are standing on Catholic soil," he said to me, good-naturedly.

I nodded and returned the smile.

He took a deep breath and continued. "As you see, we will not tour the church. The doors are nailed shut and no services have been held there for at least a century. A British nobleman, during the worst days of the Famine, when mothers and fathers watched their children starve, had the church built.

"In those days you didn't have to *spread the word*, like today. When news circulated that a church was being built, a glimmer of hope spread across Cape Clear.

"And when it was announced that the church was bringing food from Britain to help the poor and starving, you can imagine the joy. As the church neared completion and a shipload of English Protestants disembarked for the first Sunday service, the church was surrounded by townsfolk hoping for food.

"Before the service began, a well-dressed man stepped from the church, unrolled a sheet, and began reading. In summary, he announced that food aplenty, fresh-cooked meats and breads and soups, would be passed out twice a week, *enough to feed your family.*"

"Wow," I said, glancing about and expecting nods of approval. But my fellow walkers on the tour were Irish. They waited, tight-lipped and thinking *at what price?*

Indeed, there was a price.

"In order to receive the food and keep their children from starving, a mother and father had to renounce their Catholic faith and join the Protestant church. That was the choice. Turn your back on the God you knew and become essentially a Britisher, a Protestant. A traitor, not only to your faith, but to your countrymen."

He paused, tightened his lips and nodded to me, then looked to the glassy waters far below. I thought of Teagan, little grandbaby Teagan, and shivered back the tears.

"How many?" someone asked.

"No records were kept, or none that can be trusted. The goal was not to relieve people of their suffering, but to humiliate them, to challenge their most cherished beliefs, their belief in a God looking over all people equally."

And where did my mind go? Of course the Trail of Tears was foremost in my thinking, but time traveling often involves pit stops.

Hollywood, my first stop as I soared backwards to the Trail. There stands Gene Hackman, in 1995 and deprived of his well-earned Oscar by *Forrest Gump*!

The film, *Mississippi Burning*, was made only a few miles from the Mississippi Band of Choctaw Indians, where the civil rights workers were shot and their bodies tossed in a lake bordered by Choctaw lands.

A key scene of the film occurs inside a church, as Christian members of the Ku Klux Klan gather to discuss the murders they had committed. I revisited the movie and watched the scene, as church pews rippled on the waters below—hearing of the Protestant churchgoers agreeing to feed the starving and save the children only if they renounced their version of Christianity and joined the British Protestants.

I was reminded of a term paper I wrote in a history class at the University of Houston in 1969, entitled "Jesus and the Viet Nam War." I cried softly as we turned away from the church overlooking Cape Clear Bay and made our way to town.

My dream world grew, and I said a prayer for my brother Danny, a player on the first major college integrated basketball team in Texas, the 1969 Houston Cougars. He saw prejudice firsthand. When he spent Christmas week with an African American teammate in north Louisiana, my mother began receiving phone calls, at 3 a.m. every morning.

"You will never see your son alive again," a voice said. "I am with the Ku Klux Klan and you will never see him alive."

After several more calls, at the same early morning hour, my mother found the courage to answer. "I am going to call the local police and have your number traced. You will not get away with this."

She later said she heard loud laughter before the man replied, "Lady, I am calling from the local police department. I am an officer; how do you think we traced your son's license plate? And I am also an officer in the local KKK. You will never see your son alive again." Then, like always, he hung up.

He was lying, of course, but also dangling the body of guilt—guilt for raising a son who made no judgments based on race—in front of my mother. A year later my brother Danny, with two weeks between Basic Training and his first tour of duty in Viet Nam, drove to Mississippi and attended the trial of the KKKers accused of murdering the civil rights workers.

He was there when the verdict was announced.

"Not guilty!"

He turned away and two weeks later caught a plane to Viet Nam, *to fight for freedom.*

Faith and Greed and Politics, and Now Religion

The final concert of the Cape Clear International Storytelling Festival was jam-packed. Story-lovers arrived long before we were scheduled to begin, and the wooden walls of the restaurant/bar were three deep with a standing-room-only audience. A gratifying aspect of a tight and crowded facility is the closeness the performer feels with the audience. No longer strangers, we are friends for the night, sharing our deepest feelings, enjoying a brief moment of respite from the everyday to the eternal—that is the essence of storytelling.

After a rousing set of Gaelic music by Ger Wolfe, I told a favorite of mine, "Crossing Bok Chitto," of a young Choctaw girl who reaches across racial and national boundaries to rescue a family of slaves. I closed the story with a Christian hymn sung in the Choctaw language, and as I whispered the words into the microphone I recalled my day's walk, crossing the graveyards where unknown numbers of Irishmen, turned away from churches built to humiliate, now blend with the soil.

At the close of the evening, as we returned to our lodge on a bumpy road in a crowded car, I envisioned my few days on the island as a heavy stone door slowly creaking open—a stone door lying flat across a grassy green field, slowly opening to reveal the bones beneath it.

If we are to be truly informed about the Irish Famine, we must know details of the pain and suffering. As Choctaws, we are continuously frustrated by the almost total ignorance, even among the educated, of the causes and events on the Trail of Tears. And truthfully, we fertilize the ignorance; we smother truth with downward glances, choosing not to show the scars.

Pondering the unwillingness to talk of the Irish Famine, Mark McGowan of the University of Toronto compared survivors to "soldiers who have gone to war and when asked about their experiences prefer, for the most part, to change the topic because the experience was so deeply hurtful."[1]

In the words of Gerald O'Brien, a local Skibbereen historian, "The retrieval of the past is a great challenge—and we are in Ireland something of a secretive people; and because of this almost universal reluctance to talk about the crisis, it suffered an early death in the collective memory."[2]

I should have known, I was on the verge of encountering brave souls willing to speak.

The next morning, as we caught the ferry to the mainland, Jack Lynch became my guide to coastal sites related to the Famine. Also a storyteller, Jack has appeared several times as a featured teller at Cape Clear. He is well known throughout Ireland, and has also appeared at the Smithsonian Folklife Festival in Washington, DC.

During a hectic week—just as I had hoped for—following the festival, Jack Lynch drove me from museum to lunch, from afternoon interviews with writers and folklorists to evening events and dinner. We stayed busy and Irish pubs were common stops.

I'm certain I was the *strange American Indian* when I ordered tea at every meal, and I must admit the beer was alluring. I should probably share a little life detail of my heart attack in a sweat lodge in Montana, in 2001, on the shores of a Rocky Mountain lake. The night before, I had consumed two six-packs of stout German beer, and was still staggeringly drunk as I tossed off my clothes and entered the Shoshone sweat lodge.

As the steam grew thick and the oxygen thinned, my heart burned and throbbed, so strong I could see the pounding back and forth on my naked chest. Rather than alarm my hosts, I wrapped a towel around myself and crawled uphill to die. I didn't. As I lay on my back on the mountainside, I saw kinfolks who had passed on—my Choctaw grandmother, my brother, my father. They were reaching out to welcome me. I shook my head and said, "Please, I don't want to die."

They soon disappeared, and to my left, as clear as if he were standing at his desk in the classroom, was Dr. Fergusen, my recently deceased creative writing professor at the University of Oklahoma. I took a deep breath and spoke to him. "You always promised you would help with my writing. Can you give me any advice?"

He smiled and nodded, and as I passed out I heard him say words I will never forget. "Stop your drinking."

I survived the heart attack and two hours later stumbled wide-eyed down the mountainside. From that day to the present, I have enjoyed the taste of beer through the joy on others' lips. Only.

Another communality between Choctaws and Irish folks, I discovered, is good-natured teasing. Silence and look-away eyes are a method of insult, but teasing is a warm social embrace.

"Must be a souper," said a friend of Jack's when he saw me sipping tea instead of Irish brew.

Everyone at the table laughed.

"Souper?" I asked. "Hoke, what's souper? I'm not sipping soup!"

There followed another round of laughter. And thus began my education on a still unresolved controversy regarding the Famine. How widespread and how deadly were the acts of the Protestant Church?

And why the term "souper?"

In the early decades of the nineteenth century, Protestant colonies were established, most notably on western Irish land. Funded by British churches, the intent, by many observers, past and present, was to gradually eliminate the Catholic Church from Ireland.

With the onset of the Irish Potato Famine, and the deaths by starvation, these new church communities set up soup kitchens, asking only that, as discussed above, the recipients of the charity join the Protestant Church.

In one case new clothing was even offered, and many Irish Catholics, mostly men, accepted the faith of the Protestants, leaving with crisp new clothing. The next Sunday, when they attended their local Catholic church, the clothing donors reported them to legal authorities as "thieves." Since religious conversion is often a nonpermanent state, no charges were ever filed.

Many conditions of life we share, we Choctaws and Irish, and insofar as our prosperity is concerned, we share a common plight. We both struggle to maintain our culture and our life values in the shadow of a dominant power—a power that ignores our needs and even sometimes our right to life. We are both determined people and will never give up our right to sovereignty and self-determination.

As the British have been to the Irish way of life, so have the Americans been to Choctaws. We are so often ignored in public education, we are never taken seriously as a voting block, and when we are acknowledged, it is with a small flair of condescension. We are *Redskins*; we are *Braves*; we are mascots in the eyes of most, rather than people. But in response to these untruths, we, the Choctaws and our friends the Irish, share a common and no-need-to-speak-it vow: We will never give up.

Back to Jack

Jack Lynch was well aware of my reasons for staying the extra week on the mainland for my research. I arrived in Ireland hoping to find the ideal location to set my latest novel, a location wrought with the tragedies of the Irish Potato Famine.

I had just completed the manuscript for *How I Became a Ghost* (2013), based on the death of Isaac, a ten-year old Choctaw boy on the Trail of Tears circa 1831–32.

I was researching book four of the series, and the new book would introduce a young Irish girl, near Isaac's age. He's a ghost and watches as the young Irish girl struggles to feed her family. She is sent to a food kitchen, and passes by the bodies, some dead and some so close to death they barely move. Their crying, moaning voices are painful to the young girl's ears. She stumbles and falls, dizzy from lack of food and water, and Isaac assumes she has died and her spirit, her *Shilombish* (Choctaw), has reached out to him.

Isaac asks Pushmataha, a Choctaw chief who died in 1824, now also a ghost, for permission to travel to Ireland. Pushmataha consents, and as Isaac knows, the chief will oversee his every move.

Imagine my bewilderment and gratitude, my feelings of "this is a sign," upon learning that the southernmost tip of Ireland, where I now stood, bore witness to the cruelest life-ending practices on the part of the British. I arrived in Ireland hoping to find the ideal location to set the novel, and I was standing on it.

Jack took me to a powerful one-man play, with a strong young Irish actor portraying scenes on the "coffin ships." And, of course, the pub visit following the show included a lively conversation about the deception and greed of those who watched so many Irish people die from yet another source, the disease-ridden coffin ships.

Liverpool, the first destination of many of the vessels, became in many respects an international gathering sight of Irish victims. American author Herman Melville, after a visit to Liverpool, described the city in his novel *Redburn: His First Voyage.*

> It seemed hard to believe that such an array of misery could be furnished by any town in the world. Old women, rather mummies, drying up with slow starving and age; young girls, incurably sick, who ought to have been in the hospital; sturdy men with the gallows in their eyes, and a whining lie in their mouths; young boys, hollow-eyed and decrepit; and puny mothers, holding up puny babies in the glare of the sun, formed the main features of the scene.[3]

His good friend and neighbor, Nathaniel Hawthorne, had quite a different perspective, more like the British attitude. Describing Irish people lying about on the docks, he wrote: "The people are as numerous as maggots in cheese; you behold them, disgusting, and all moving about."[4]

Though I find the above so infuriatingly offensive, if we are to be truly informed about the Irish deaths, the causes, the pain and suffering, we must know what the

Irish had to endure at the hands of colonizers. As Choctaws, we are continuously frustrated by the almost total ignorance of Americans, even educated Americans, concerning the effects on our people from the forced march on the Trail of Tears.

In the minds of many, we also share victimhood from a common source—King Cotton. In the Deep South, Indian lands were stolen and thousands marched to their deaths for the sake of King Cotton and plantation owners. And the primary buyer of King Cotton? The British. They bought the cotton, made the cloth, sold the garments for their own use and for export.

The plantation owners of the South elected Andrew Jackson to the U.S. Congress for one principal reason: to increase their landholdings and increase the shipment of King Cotton to Great Britain. The most desirable land in the South was owned and settled, for centuries, by Indian nations, with governments, often elected, and civilized communities. The Choctaws, Cherokees, Chickasaws, Creeks, and Seminole nations were targeted by President Andrew Jackson (1829–37), who threatened death to all Indian nations in the form of federal Indian policies. He made good on his threats through our removal from our ancient homelands.

And Now a Confession

It was after midnight, and Jack, before returning us to our small bed and breakfast, left the table for a bathroom stop. He left his half-filled mug of dark Irish brew, still slightly foaming at the top. "Don't do it," I whispered to myself, as my fingers crept like a silent, deadly spider across the boards of the table.

I felt the cool welcome of the mug as I wrapped my thirsty fingers around it, *fingers denied this feeling for more than a decade.* I tightened the grip and prepared to lift the mug, licking my lips in anticipation. I first glanced to the door, making certain Jack was still filling another mug with Irish brew.

"Maybe buy your own and leave Jack's alone!" shouted a voice from across the pub. I didn't even turn my head; I was caught and Jack would learn of it, *of this I was certain.* I waved over my shoulder and laughter filled the pub. Jack Lynch, apparently, was well known in the pubs as well as on the storytelling stage.

As the evening drew to a close, Jack reminded me of the next day's adventures. "You're on your own for most of the day tomorrow," he said. "I'll pick you up early and we have a meeting with the director of the Skibbereen Heritage Center. She'll probably give us a museum tour, then I'm off. A walking tour starts at the museum and you'll be on that one, both to learn and to teach. The walkers will enjoy hearing of the Choctaw Gift to the Irish, and you might add a bit about the Trail of Tears. I'll meet you at the pub for dinner. It's not far from the museum."

So I fell asleep that night wondering how to summarize fifty years of rolling away the stones in seeking the truth of my family's and my nation's history—my Choctaw Nation.

Early morning.

I rose early and was off to the Skibbereen Heritage Center. There we met museum manager Terri Kearney, who joined Jack and me for coffee. She had heard of my intent to write a middle-grade novel based on the Irish Famine, and I soon knew, by her body language and the lack of small talk, that she felt strong opposition to my project.

She allowed me two sips before saying, "I have read several middle-grade and young-adult books on the Famine, and they all grossly misrepresent. Especially those written by outsiders."

Being Choctaw, being Native American, and living in the United States, I am quite accustomed to doubt. *Indians are primitive peoples; Indians can't write* seems to be the national attitude. I smiled inside and waited. When she paused, I sighed and replied.

"Nothing makes me feel better about the day, about your museum, than what you just said. I write for exactly that reason. Non-Indians know so little about us, and where do they go for research? To other books or documents written by *nahullos*. Non-Indians.

"My purpose in writing is to uncover unknown and hidden truths, and if you or someone you recommend would agree to help edit my book before it goes to publication, my trip here is worthwhile. My trip to Ireland, I mean."

"You write fiction?" she asked.

"Yes, because the kids read fiction, and hopefully seek the truth *because* of the fiction."

Ms. Kearney rose and returned with *Under the Hawthorn Tree*, by Marita Conlon-McKenna. "This is a juvenile novel from our bookstore," she said, "and I do recommend the series."

As Jack departed and we circled throughout the museum, stopping for short films and exhibitions, I felt the emotions behind her words, as strong as my own feelings when I drive across state lines to Mississippi, retracing the Trail of Tears. Before I left the museum, Ms. Kearney offered to help me find someone qualified to read my manuscript before it went to the publisher, to fight the ever-present stereotypes and confirm an accurate depiction of events.

A group was gathering outside the museum for a walking tour of downtown Skibbereen, and I introduced myself and joined the twenty or so walkers. My strongest memory of the tour is the site of the former workhouse, which housed hundreds of people and was "a breeding house for disease."

According to Joe Lee, history professor at University College Cork and NYU,

> From January of 1847 and throughout 1848, society as we know it really broke down. Conditions were so bad in the workhouse there were accounts that men were causing disturbances there so they'd be arrested and sent to jails where conditions would be better; they'd be fed. There was a death cart left the workhouse every day with the bodies of the dead, and in January 1847, in one week in the Skibbereen workhouse there were 46 deaths recorded. And on one day, January 30, there were 16 deaths. . . . conditions were getting worse and worse. For every death in the workhouse, there was a multiple of that outside the workhouse.[5]
>
> People were just dying on the streets, the death carts would go through the town every day and collect the dead bodies. Society had broken down. Most of the deaths weren't recorded at all and there were stories of people burying loved ones at night, because there was a stigma attached to people dying of hunger or dying of fever.
>
> People came to graveyards. . . . to bury their family at night. Other people just died in ditches and were forgotten about. It was. . . . horrific. You are watching death creeping up on you all the time.

Later that same afternoon, Jack Lynch met me at The Paragon, a local pub and restaurant, and we drove to Abbeystrewry Abbey, a Famine burial plot where between eight and ten thousand are buried, though many believe the number of unknown corpses is much higher.

Jack parked his car by the roadside, high above the gently sloping graveyard, and we strolled down the hill, past what appeared to be a grassy rise of real estate. Never have I witnessed a more palpable vision of silence and denial than the flowing green blades of grass, giving a natural beauty to the tens of thousands of unnamed, unmarked, unacknowledged men and women and children, of every age, whose last remains were tossed into a giant canyon of bodies.

I sat upon a bench and stared and sighed and recalled the pencil sketches I had seen at the museum: bodies carried by wagons to the graves, with arms and legs hanging over the sides; of workers tossing bodies from the roadside as if they tossed unwanted stones or tree stumps.

Jack tapped me on the shoulder and pointed to a small building down the walkway. "The museum is open," he said. "Come on."

I shook my head and waved an "it's fine, you go ahead," which he did. I had seen enough of museums and heard enough lectures. I wanted to spend time with the Irish people at rest before me, to let them know they will never be forgotten.

My mind went back and forth—from the living bones beneath the surface to Skibbereen and Ms. Kearney, with whom I knew I shared a common vision. She spoke of one Dr. Donovan, who was a hero of the Famine and "saved thousands of lives. He wrote extensively in medical journals, and of discovering that people, especially children, were being buried alive."

According to historian Philip O'Regan, local Skibbereen historian, "In 1848. . . . in the Dublin Medical Press, [Dr. Donovan] gives an account of being in the square in Skibbereen when a young girl was being loaded in the death cart. He examined the body and felt there were signs of life. He revived the little girl and she lived in the workhouse for seven or eight days. In the article in the *Dublin Medical Journal*, Dr. Donovan points out that people should be acutely aware of this phenomenon, of people being buried alive."[6]

> Tom Guerdin was another young boy, thought to be dead, . . . taken to the death cart and he tumbled out at Abbeystrewry, to be buried with the other bodies. And as the gravediggers were tapping down the bodies, they hit his knees and he let out a little cry, and he was taken from the grave, taken to the hospital and . . . Tom Guerdin lived on in this area until 1910.[7]

I pictured Dr. Donovan in my mind, and I wondered what were his thoughts as he saw the faces and absorbed the smells of bodies, the living and the dead. And then I realized we Choctaws, who lost one-quarter of our people on the Trail of Tears, and our Irish friends, who lost even more people over a decade, share another startling truth—an unspoken truth. *No one had to die. We were systematically killed.*

Wagons and horses and soldiers were available to attend to the walking thousands, and food enough to feed the entire population of Choctaws. Why then death? Why the cruelty from *nahullos* to Choctaws? From the leaders in the capital, the answer is abiding, insatiable greed. Reduce the population, save money—and if the victims are *savages* and not truly *human*, the colonizer feels no guilt.

Yes, the potato blight killed the crop, and yes the Irish depended on the potato for the principal source of food, of nutrition. But other crops were readily available. Why were poverty-stricken Irishmen not allowed to eat the crops they had themselves grown, in fields they worked? Abiding greed. And if Irish people were on equal footing with the Brits, as human beings rather than as "savages," the stench of bodies would certainly have made its way across the sea.

I stood and wandered up the hill to wait for Jack Lynch. On the return drive to Baltimore I was struck with a most powerful memory, my personal recollection of the unmarked grave of my great uncle, Clarence Carnes. *Another Gift of the Irish if ever there was one*, I thought.

My great-uncle Clarence Carnes, a criminal whose life was not discussed in our Choctaw family gatherings when I was growing up, was buried in an unmarked grave in Kansas, in a cemetery for the deeply impoverished. When an old friend of his, an Irishman from Boston, heard the news, he rented a hearse and drove halfway across America. He paid for the disinterment of my great-uncle, whereupon he drove the hearse from Kansas to the tiny hometown of Daisy, Oklahoma, where my uncle was raised. I am indebted to Tony Byars, a Choctaw elder, for telling me of the mistreatment Clarence received as a young boy in Jones Academy, a Choctaw school near Hartshorne, established in 1891. Not an excuse, but it helped me understand.

Back to the Irishman

Whitey Bulger, also a criminal, paid for a new coffin for Clarence Carnes, and a burial plot in a small hillside cemetery. He arranged for an unforgettable all-day burial service, with a Choctaw preacher and a Choctaw choir singing hymns in Choctaw. And another detail making this venture even more of a *Gift* from an Irishman to his Choctaw friend—Bulger risked both his life and freedom in making the journey.

As I sit at my desk in Canyon Lake, Texas, I am only three weeks away from my annual visit to Daisy, to the gravesite of Clarence Carnes. On my way home following our Choctaw Labor Day celebration, I always wander slightly off route to spend a quiet time sitting at the gravesite of Clarence—at peace with my great-uncle, a man whom I forgive and respect. He lies buried only two hours from the old Choctaw capitol grounds at Tushkahoma.

COURTESY OF CHOCTAW AUTHOR IAN THOMPSON.

"Choctaw Corn Soup."

I Should Have Known

Whatever high crimes and mass deaths and lasting pain can be attributed to the perpetrators of genocide on innocent people, the truth is, we must forgive.

And what of the Choctaw-Irish connection? We cannot blame the people standing before us for mistakes their ancestors made. The wrong we are attempting to right in this volume is ignorance. Ignorance of the truth about the Irish Potato Famine, and the cruelty and deaths that resulted from the Choctaws who were forced on the Trail of Tears.

In the words of historian Terry Eagleton, "If the famine stirred some to angry rhetoric, it would seem to have traumatized others into muteness. The event strains at the limit of the articulable, and is truly in this sense an Irish Auschwitz."[8] One of the great difficulties in discussing and writing about or researching a tragedy as horrendous and widespread as the Irish Famine, or the Trail of Tears, is the fog of blindness that surrounds us. If we narrow our vision, we cannot see the millions lying dead beside the road; yet if we broaden our vision to include statistics and numbers, we cease to feel the moment-by-moment wrenching pain of hunger, of freezing cold, the silent stalking of inevitable death. Our own death.

We forgive, for that is how we lighten the burden and allow our own lives to proceed; but we will never forget. And why? So it will never happen again. That is our hope, our wish, our prayer.

May the tragedies of our peoples never happen again. Our gift, the Choctaw Gift to the Irish, is a gift of love. Love and respect for you, your children, your husbands, wives, your ancestors, those buried and those hovering about. We send you blessings and hope that the spirit of joy will shine upon you every day of your life—and beyond.

NOTES

1. *The Great Irish Famine: Remember Skibbereen*, Harvest Films Production for the Skibbereen Heritage Centre, 2009.
2. Ibid.
3. Colm Tóibín, *The Irish Famine* (London: Profile Books, 1998), 62.
4. Ibid., 63.
5. From the film *The Great Irish Famine: Remember Skibbereen*.
6. Ibid.
7. Ibid.
8. Tóibín, *The Irish Famine*, 65–66.

Ima, Give

A Choctaw Tribalography

LeAnne Howe

first heard about the Choctaw people giving money to the Irish from my mother, Christine Billy Poynor. I was in my early thirties when she told me the story. She'd been talking to my aunts, and I knew the three of them had been talking to their older brothers, Lonnie Billy and Schlicht Billy. That's how things were in those days. My mother would talk to my older aunts. My aunts would talk to their brothers who'd been talking to elder men around McAlester and other places in the Choctaw Nation. That's how the news bird traveled in those days, from one Choctaw to another Choctaw through the telephone lines. I didn't get the factual details of the 1847 Choctaw gift to the Irish, just the gist of what happened: our people took up a collection and sent money. The Irish were starving.

Over the years, our tribal newspaper *Biskinik* would report about the Choctaws' connection to the Irish Potato Famine, and later I would research the fuller story in library archives. The Choctaws heard of the terrible starvation in Ireland in the spring of 1847 in Skullyville, a town located one mile east of Spiro in the post-Removal Choctaw Nation. Skullyville was a gathering place where Choctaws collected government annuities, *and* news. It is likely that the Choctaw elders at Skullyville asked questions about why the Irish were starving. The answer was famine, and famine *is* weather. As climatologists know, weather and climate change are not just a twenty-first-century phenomenon. The earth's climate affects everything, everywhere, and our ability to grow food and sustain humankind. According to James Marusek's *A Chronological Listing of Early Weather Events*, "Famines can be thought of as a product of abnormal weather," including rainfall and other related consequences.[1] In Ireland in 1845–51, constant rainfall and damp conditions brought a unique kind of potato blight, another population killer, to Ireland.[2] Blight is caused by fungus, and fungi grow best in damp conditions. In the case of the Irish blight, it overwintered on infected plants and was spread by splashing rain, irrigation, insects, and implements such as digging sticks and wooden hoes. The disease was carried on potato tubers.

Marusek's report states, "There was a great famine in Ireland that was caused less by the weather, but by blight, and the heavy reliance on a single crop, the potato. In 1845, a pestilential blight of unexampled severity caused the whole potato crop to rot. At that time three-fourths of the population of the island was entirely dependent upon this staple for food. The resulting suffering can scarcely be imagined. In March and April 1847, 2,500 died weekly in the workhouses alone. Thousands of starving peasants poured into England, many dying of famine fever while on board of emigrant ships. The total death toll was between 200,000 and 300,000."

Similar weather-related histories of famine and flooding occurred among the Choctaws in the early French colonial period. Jean Baptiste Le Moyne, Sieur de Bienville reported often on hunger in New France and that often they had to rely on Indian corn supplied by the Choctaws and other Native tribes. In 1719, he reported on the destruction of the fledgling New Orleans colony by a fierce hurricane and flooding that destroyed buildings and livestock.

Today the Choctaw Nation of Oklahoma, located in Durant, Oklahoma, has a population of over 223,000 members. We carry many stories of great floods; some are likely twinned with biblical stories, but others suggest our vast history. As I have said in past scholarship, adding stories to one's tribal history is an act of tribal sovereignty. "Native stories, no matter what form they take (novel, poem, drama, memoir, film, history) seem to pull all the elements together of the storyteller's tribe, meaning the people, the land, multiple characters and all their manifestations and revelations, and connect these in past, present, and future milieu. (Present, and future milieu means a world that includes non-Indians)."[3] Tribalography, then, comes from the Native propensity for bringing things together, for making consensus, and for symbiotically connecting one thing to another. In this case, our stories connected us with the Irish Potato Famine in 1847. Choctaws may have recalled, in story, their own lived experiences over hundreds of years with extreme weather-related flooding in the Lower Mississippi Valley. Perhaps then it is the story itself that urged them to send money abroad to Ireland.

These many years later, I'm still amazed at the similarities our two nations faced: English colonization of lands, starvation, famine, great flooding, and loss in the Choctaws' case, loss of one-quarter of the population during Andrew Jackson's Removal. When gazed at through a lens of similarities, the Choctaws' Irish famine relief of 1847 is an act of tribal generosity linking Choctaw lifeways with Ireland's survival. Here I'm not suggesting Irish people survived because of the Choctaws' gift; rather I'm saying that buried deeply within the Choctaw body politic is a sense of giving shelter, food, and/or aid to our relatives, friends, and allies. *Ima*, giving, is a cultural lifeway and shows a Choctawan sense of prosperity in ancient times, as in the present. While the Choctaw aid to the French in the eighteenth century had a disastrous end, this too is also part of our tribalography.

Chi Niah Katima, How's Your Fat

To navigate the history of the Choctaw-Irish Gift Exchange, I highlight an old-timey Choctaw colloquialism, *chi niah katima* ("How's your fat"), conveyed in greetings among elder men. *Chi niah katima* in the twentieth century may have caused a great deal of joking by men on the size of their bellies.[4] However the expression has deeper cultural roots in the Choctaw historical past, e.g., the Trail of Tears, 1831–33, and even earlier in times of great upheaval in the eighteenth century. Times when the Choctaws themselves were hard pressed to survive.

While I mentioned the French and Bienville earlier in this essay, it's important to consider for a moment the state of the Lower Mississippi Valley some 320 years ago. The French arrived on our shores (and stayed) from 1682 to 1763. The Choctaws were one of the largest and most widespread confederacies throughout much of the Southeast. Our villages and towns stretched from Louisiana to Mississippi and much of Alabama. The Muscogee Creek confederacy spanned parts of Alabama, Georgia, and northern Florida. These boundaries were always shifting depending on the population and trade. Jean Baptiste Le Moyne, Sieur de Bienville recognized that to be knowledgeable and understood in the Southeast, the tribal language he needed to learn was Choctawan. The Choctaws also recognized how their alliance with the French could be beneficial, so they went so far as to build Jean Baptiste a small cabin at Chickasawhay to stay in when he came to visit. In 1707, Bienville was worried less about warfare among the tribes and more about the great hunger that the fledgling French colony was experiencing.

> I have supported this garrison for six months on the Indian corn which I had had bought at a low price from the Indians since I did not wish to send a brigantine to New Cruz, knowing that the fleet of Spanish galleons was there and that provisions there would be extraordinarily dear. . . . In times of famine one hears nothing by grumbling every day especially about a thousand little things that the soldiers need and lack such as blankets and coats.[5]

Bienville goes on to talk of famine and bad weather plaguing the French, and the slow development of their preferred crops, wheat and other grains. Yet the Choctaws, allies of the French in 1707, had enough surplus corn to give to the French in exchange for French trinkets. I say trinkets because in 1707, the French supplies were depleted and they had no spare guns or bullets to trade with the Indians. As corn is a sacred food to the Choctaws, they may have brought it to Bienville as a staple grain against starvation that they had blessed in ceremony, knowing that the trade goods they would receive would be meager until more supply ships from France arrived. In other words the saving of lives was also part of their charity.

In this way the Choctaws gave the gift of survival to the French. In return, the French would betray them. Considering that the French colony was always in danger of flooding (and starving), Bienville in his early correspondence writes regularly asking for more food and supplies to be sent from France, and a salary increase for himself. In these early letters he anguishes about the future of the French colony, and he writes about the Natives and their endurance in the Lower Mississippi Valley. We know, for instance, that the tribes regularly practiced reciprocity with their friends, families, and many other allies, including the adopted French kinsmen. I think Bienville's letters reveal something more interesting: that it is the French who are assimilating and adapting to the Choctaws, not the other way around. In a very long and wide-ranging letter on October 27, 1711, to the French government's secretary of state, Jerome Pontchartrain, Bienville writes that he must replicate the ways of the Indians (if the colony is to survive).

> It has been seven years since I received one *sou* of my salary which is very modest and which would not even be enough to receive the Indians who drop in to see me

every day, to whom I cannot refuse to give food because it is in that way that they regard those whom they go and see. Although we do not give them scrumptious fare the quantity costs a great deal.[6]

Bienville seems to know that the friendship between the Choctaws and the French will continue if both parties practice reciprocity. Corn, and protection by the Choctaw Confederacy, in exchange for French gifts seems rather paltry. In fact, too paltry, so much so that I suggest their treatment of the French constitutes not a gift in the minds of the Choctaws but something more akin to "foreign aid."

I ask you to imagine today that a foreigner, a Frenchman, comes to the state of Louisiana and asks to see the governor. The Frenchman says he's hungry and that he will trade his Swiss watch for some cornbread and beans. Sounds absurd, but in a way that's exactly what happened to the eighteenth-century Choctaws. The French had little to nothing to eat after their wheat flour became rancid. Time and again they had to trade for food. Beginning as early as 1699, the French, under the direction of d'Iberville and then later his brother, Bienville, began to treat with the Choctaw Confederacy as they settled in the Lower Mississippi Valley. It's clear from their correspondence that they needed food. French colonists, the majority of men and women, had no experience as farmers and were unable to feed themselves. Repeatedly in the early years they starved. Hurricanes also destroyed the new settlements and their food stores again in 1722 and 1723. But hurricanes are only a part of the weather-related disasters. New Orleans, a city that Bienville staked out as the capital for French Louisiana in 1718, was always going to be a site of weather-related diseases because the river floods. Three hundred years ago the rivers replenished the soils and nourished the lands for planting, but their devastation also wreaked havoc on the French colony. Since the Choctaws had adopted the French early on as their brothers, they brought them the gift of corn for sustenance. *Ima*, give. As suggested earlier, the Choctaws' continuing food aid to the French had self-interest at its heart. In order to survive the onslaught of English weaponry, they continued trading for badly needed weapons and ammunition to fight their cousins, the Chickasaws. The English were aiding the Chickasaws with guns. And here I want to be clear that the French were never in a position of "authority" over the Choctaw Confederacy, as their self-serving correspondence to the king of France suggests. That's political hogwash driven by a sense of superiority over those that fed them.

In 1718 Bienville's decision to place the capital of French Louisiana at the spot on the Mississippi River reflected his calculation of the river's economic promise for the city of New Orleans. Ari Kelman has stated in *A River and Its City: The Nature of Landscape in New Orleans* that "He [Bienville] saw only the Mississippi River system as the most magnificent system of watery roads, a tapestry of commercial empire woven from the strands of the river system's watercourses."[7] A year after its establishment, heavy spring rains and floods delayed work on the construction of the city. Bienville was forced to build a new fort in Biloxi instead. Leslie Harris, associate professor at Emory University, argues in her essay "Subaltern City, Subaltern Citizens: New Orleans, Urban Identity, and People of African Descent" that by 1722 there were 5,400 foreigners, or non-Indians, living in New Orleans, compared with 70,000 southeastern Natives. Times had changed. By 1723 the tribes in the Lower Mississippi Valley were warring with the colonial powers, the English and the French, and with each other. Bienville in his correspondence was convinced that his troops should go and wipe out the Natchez before they killed all the Frenchmen in the area. Yet further down in the same letter he comments again on hunger and disease.

> The things that are opposed to my proposal are the general sickness, the want of provisions since we are without bread and meat, and a very small number of troops, all great obstacles to such an enterprise, but the welfare of the colony, and the honor of the nation are too dear to me, not to surmount them.[8]

Throughout the 1722–23 period, one subject appears again and again in the French correspondence: the tribes are raiding each other's villages for food. Why? Answer: Hurricane, continued rainfall, and flooding, not warfare. That the Choctaws continued to help the French throughout this turbulent period is a stunning example of how they viewed their obligations to an adopted friend and ally. *Ima*, give whenever possible.

Memory Calendar

The Choctaws have collective memories about starvation, so much so that they named a month of the year, March-April, as *Hohchafo Chito*, "Big Famine." When Cyrus Byington began collecting Choctaw words for his dictionary, he found that the months of the year were divided into two series of six months, a summer series and a winter series, and they often reflect historical events. September 21 was one half of the year beginning with harvest.[9] March 21, the vernal equinox, is a time when food stores may be depleted, thus a hunger time. The month also signals a time for planting gardens and corn. The autumnal and vernal equinoxes can both be starting points for growing and harvesting. What we should note in *Hohchafo Chito* is that it identifies a time of year in our traditional Choctaw calendar when our people remembered starvation. The phrase *Chi niah katima*, "How's your fat," can then be thought of as a double entendre reflecting the Choctaws' long-ago collective memories. I suggest that Choctaws learned a variety of painful lessons in the eighteenth century: they could not stop the wave of immigrants into their homelands, and they could no longer give foreign aid to the French.

The Time of Naholla Is Upon Us

Starving is still anathema to the Choctaws, and for good reason. In 1831 Choctaws nearly starved to death walking on the Trail of Tears thanks to the president, Andrew Jackson, and his government's appetite for Native lands. "Indians must give" seems to have been a theme of Andrew Jackson's government. This is painfully ironic since Andrew Jackson Sr. and his mother, Elizabeth Hutchinson, as well as two brothers, Hugh and Robert, emigrated from Northern Ireland in the 1740s. They came to the Colonies to seek a better life. President Andrew Jackson, the son of Irish immigrants, would ensure that whites would indeed have more land, and potentially better lives, by driving American Indians from their eastern homelands.

Andrew Jackson called on southeastern Indians to give aid (food) and warriors to fight in the War of 1812 between Great Britain and the United States. Choctaws responded with food and warriors. As a reward for our solidarity with the fledgling American government, Jackson forced Choctaws to remove to the west, giving up their cornfields, potato patches, bean and tomato gardens, and our sacred sites— such as the Nanih Waiya, our mother mound. *Ima*, give. We gave and the Americans took; here's the short version: the terms of the Treaty of Dancing Rabbit Creek called for Choctaws to cede 11 million acres to the foreign government of America in exchange for 15 million acres in Indian Territory.[10] Sounds like a fair exchange, except there was very little water in Indian Territory. Later in the same decade all other southeastern tribes would follow the Choctaws on their own Trail of Tears. My ancestors were part of that removal from Mississippi. When they arrived in Indian Territory, they settled on land around Tannehill, just outside of McAlester, now in

Oklahoma, and they eked out a living. They lived, died, and were buried there near my grandmother's allotment land.

Choctaws Continue to Answer the Call

In 1995 the Irish began an ongoing reciprocal exchange with the Choctaw Nation. Since 2015 two new monuments have been created in Cork, Ireland, to honor the Choctaws' 1847 gift. In 2017 the Choctaw Nation of Oklahoma chief Gary Batton and Ireland's president Michael D. Higgins's government met in Cork to commemorate the long-standing friendship that began as a gift from the Choctaw people over 170 years ago.

As has been recounted in this volume, the Great Famine killed one million people in Ireland, while another million emigrated from there. The history of the famine in Ireland is one of the western world's great nineteenth-century tragedies.

In this environment of growing global connections, the call went out to the Choctaws in Skullyville reporting that the Irish people were starving to death. The newspaper accounts of the era say that many of the Choctaws cried when they heard the news. On March 23, shortly after the vernal equinox, the Choctaws took up a collection for famine relief in Skullyville in Indian Territory. According to the *Arkansas Intelligencer*, April 3, 1847, the Choctaws collected $710.00.[11]

At Chi Hullo Li, I Care for You

In 2018, once again the Choctaw Nation came to the aid of another nation; this time it was the Standing Rock Sioux Tribe in North Dakota. When Dakotas protested the Dakota Access Pipeline, thousands of Natives across the United States came to their rescue, as well as indigenous people from around the world. The Choctaw Nation of Oklahoma sent aid, and most importantly they sent tribal members to North Dakota. Choctaw citizen Cody Wilson and other tribal members bought firewood, sleeping bags, generators, propane heaters, tents, thousands of gallons of water, and other supplies in North Dakota stores to give to the Dakota people. The gift was to help conserve the "fat of the physical body"—the Standing Rock Sioux Tribe. Perhaps the Choctaws' colloquialism *Chi niah katima*, "How's your fat," is also a mode of resistance. To help the Irish in 1847 was an act of resistance against the English, and later Americans who sought to starve us to death during the Trail of Tears in 1830–31 *and* beyond. To help the Dakotas in 2018 was to resist corporate powers that threatened the Dakotas' water supply on Lake Oahe.

What I have tried to show in this brief account is that throughout the last three centuries, the Choctaw people have given aid to the poor, and even the wealthy.

Ima. Give. We are givers.

NOTES

1. https://wattsupwiththat.files.wordpress.com/2011/09/weather1.pdf.

2. https://www.history.com/news/after-168-years-potato-famine-mystery-solved.

3. LeAnne Howe, "The Story of America: A Tribalography," in *Clearing a Path: Theorizing the Past in Native American Studies*, ed. Nancy Shoemaker (New York: Routledge Press, 2001).

4. Poet Jim Barnes, Choctaw, tells this story about elderly Choctaw men patting one another on the belly and saying, "chi niah katima."

5. *Mississippi Provincial Archives, 1704–1743, French Dominion*, vol. 3 (Jackson: Press of the Mississippi Department of Archives and History, 1932), 112.

6. Ibid., 169.

7. Ari Kelman, *A River and Its City: The Nature of Landscape in New Orleans* (Berkeley: University of California Press, 2003), 4.

8. Ibid., August 1723, 361.

9. Cyrus Byington, *A Dictionary of the Choctaw Language*, ed. John R. Swanton and Henry S. Halbert, Smithsonian Institution, Bureau of American Ethnology, Bulletin 46 (Washington, DC: Government Printing Office, 1915).

10. The treaty called for the Choctaws to cede 11 million acres to the government in exchange for 15 million acres in Indian Territory. The Choctaws listened to the proposal. Seven elderly women heard the arguments on both sides and voted against removal. I suggest that these seven women represented the seven oldest towns in the Choctaw homelands, and their authority was thwarted by one Choctaw district chief, Greenwood LeFlore. He signed the removal treaty that the Americans said made the treaty legal.

11. As has been discussed by others in this volume, the amount is in question. Recent scholars have suggested that the amount was $170.00. It seems likely that the newspaper may have made a typo. But again, $710.00 was the number reported in the Arkansas newspaper.

Setting Out from Home with Louis Owens

Mixedblood Messages

Eamonn Wall

t is early evening in Enniscorthy, County Wexford. I have left my parents' house on the west side of the river, crossed the Slaney on the old bridge into a part of town called the Shannon, named after Ireland's longest river. Enniscorthy's founder in 510 AD was St. Senan, a monk from Scattery Island on the River Shannon, the monastery he founded on the east side of the Slaney being the town's original settlement. Though his monastery has long lain in ruin, the area around it has retained both its name and, thereby, its connection to Senan's area of origin. After crossing Templeshannon, I turn right and begin to ascend the steep hill that leads toward Vinegar Hill. At various points this bright summer evening, I pause to speak with people I know, taking advantage of these conversation breaks to catch my breath. Closer to the hilltop, I take two sharp left turns to walk on roads narrowing as they close in on their destination. Before the first of these turns, one will notice a small housing development created to accommodate families of settled Travelers. Though it is only 400 feet above sea level, Vinegar Hill commands the landscape of the surrounding countryside and is further enhanced by the role it played in the Irish struggle for independence from Great Britain. Here, the 1798 rebels, making a last heroic stand, were routed by a British force under General Lake. They fled for their lives—both rebels and their families—off into the lush countryside of Wexford on that fateful June day. Many of the Redcoats who engaged with the rebels that day had earlier seen service in the American War of Independence, where they may have fought alongside and against American Indians.

In addition to occupying a central place in the narrative of Irish history, Enniscorthy has been a cradle of, and a setting-out point for, many contemporary authors. Of living writers born and raised in the town and surroundings, Anthony Cronin, Colm Tóibín, George O'Brien, Barbara Tóibín, Gerard Whelan, Patrick Kehoe, Mogue Doyle, Paul O'Reilly, and Peter Murphy have published many volumes of prose and poetry that have received notice both at home and abroad. The recent success of *Brooklyn*, Colm Tóibín's novel, and the subsequent film version that was partially shot in the town has placed Enniscorthy squarely in the national and international limelight. Today, visitors to the town are encouraged to sign up for a "Brooklyn Movie Tour": "You don't have to travel to Hollywood to see the set of *Brooklyn* because it was filmed right here in Enniscorthy. This is what makes it all the more unique. It was filmed on the actual streets and in the places named in the book!" What Louis Owens has identified about Native American writers is equally valid for the writers who began their careers in Enniscorthy. "As writers, we tell stories, weaving what we have been told, what we have experienced and felt, and what we have read into a fabric of imagination, and I assume that most of us who have no fantasies of growing rich from words tell stories that are necessary for survival in one way or another, stories that we must tell and that come out of our larger selves."[1] The financial gift that the Choctaw made to the Irish during the Great Hunger has been widely honored and commented upon both in Ireland and within the Choctaw Nation. In addition to being a gesture born from an empathy that is heart-wringing in its generosity, the gift directs us to refocus and realign our notions of human migration and geography during this period. While people in Ireland died of starvation and disease or left for America, the Choctaw, as globally engaged as the Irish, watched and acted. For both, being subject to the whims and cruelties of great powers, to anticipate trouble and potential beyond their communities was necessary for survival. In this context, it makes complete sense that the Choctaw took an interest in what was occurring in Ireland. Being Irish, we are trained to think of America with a westward bias, to direct our thoughts from Ireland across the Atlantic; the Choctaw gift forces us to explore the movement from the opposite direction and asks us to consider how interdependent we humans are.

In various literary genres, the work of Enniscorthy's writers is notably narra-tive-driven and guided by a desire, as Owens points out, to tell stories directly while at the same time retaining the literary nuances and grace notes that underline good writing everywhere. As Patrick Kehoe reveals:

> Those of whom we think
> Are no longer with us, but they are yet here.
>
> When spring comes
> In a grape sky fit to burst with rain
>
> In the spill of light along the corrugated roof
> They rise with the dawn.
>
> On grain store walls in slanting lanes
> Where ivy cleaves, their exact voices call.[2]

As Kehoe illustrates, writing preserves the spirits of those whose bodies have departed—they can live on publicly in literary works and as spiritual presences of the natural and built landscapes of Enniscorthy. Irish writing, in common with the Native American work that Owens references, retains tangible connections to oral culture—linguistically, thematically, structurally, and in how authors imagine their audiences. What they write is simultaneously the product of kitchen and barn, classroom and library. Also, for all of their hard histories, Irish and Native American writers, more often than not, resort to humor. In both the Irish and American Indian literary worlds, rich traditions of sophisticated oral literacy long preceded the writing down of stories that would eventually be reshaped into literary forms. Irish and Native American writers speak/write with grafted tongues—the tongue of imperial masters violently appended to the mother tongue—as John Montague has illustrated in relation to Ireland:

> An Irish
> child weeps in school
> repeating its English.
> After each mistake
>
> The master
> gouges another mark

on the tally stick
hung about its neck.[3]

Native American and Irish literary traditions, both oral and written, emerged from the margins of, and often in opposition to, more refined European cultural orthodoxies and beliefs. From the nineteenth century to the present, writers from these often brutalized spaces—on the edge of Europe and in the Americas—would develop unique modes of literary expression in English that simultaneously belong both within and outside of British and American traditions. Our Irish and American Indian stories, as Owens so wisely indicates, "come out of our larger selves," and this larger self for each individual who adds his/her contribution to the Irish and Native American traditions includes not only the fruits of book learning but also what has been learned from family and place.[4] Each Irish and Native American literary tradition in the English language is possessed of a distinctive taste, or *blas* to use the Irish term, that is woven into the fabric of the poem, story, novel, and play. To enter an Irish or Native American home, where a special place is reserved for tradition, is to be welcomed into a harmonious place. We bring gifts to share; we laugh and sing; we honor our elders. Each human carries narratives fit for transmission. As well as being literary works, Irish and American Indian novels, short stories, poems, essays, and plays are also homes that we carry with us, and homes we admit strangers to. And, work written in "grafted tongues" take on airs of resistance; as Montague observes, "Yet even English in these airts / Took a lawless turn."[5] Of course, the sophisticated natures of Irish and Native American cultures are concealed by clever informality that can serve as a shield.

Writing in *Ploughshares* in 1994, James Welch recalled the arrival of an Irish poet in Missoula, Montana, to replace Richard Hugo while the American poet enjoyed a sabbatical in Italy:

> Twenty-five years ago a poet from Ireland came to the University of Montana. . . . I was one of the students that the Irish poet, Anthony Cronin, inherited, and he was quite pleased that I had an American Indian heritage and identified myself as an Indian. But he wondered how an Indian could have a name like Welch. That was an Irish name. I told him that I had two Irish grandfathers and one Blackfeet and one Gros Ventre grandmother. . . . One night about a week later, Tony hurried into Eddy's Club, a local writer/graduate student/hippie haunt and pulled out a slick chunk of paper and unfolded it before me. It was a map of Ireland and it took up

the whole table. He pointed to a spot along the southern coast and said, "That's where you're from! That's where the Welch tribe originated."[6]

Anthony Cronin, who passed away in 2016, was a distinguished Irish poet and novelist; the author of acclaimed biographies of Flann O'Brien and Samuel Beckett, and *Dead as Doornails*, the finest chronicle of literary Dublin during the 1950s and 1960s; and the guiding father of Aosdána, the state-sponsored organization founded to honor and support Irish artists across disciplines.[7] A generation or more removed from my own, Cronin, like me, grew up in Enniscorthy. His childhood family home on Slaney St. is less than two hundred yards from my own home on Barrack St. From my perch atop Vinegar Hill, I can pinpoint the locations of both of our family homes. As he located the hinterland of the Welches for a young writing student in a bar in Missoula, Cronin's fingers likely would have strayed across to County Wexford, as the area of Welch influence extended throughout the southeastern part of Ireland. Like many Irish families we consider to be quintessentially Irish, the Welches are of Anglo-Norman stock, arriving in Ireland as part of the Norman Invasion of 1169. So deeply did the Normans assimilate into Gaelic Ireland that it quickly became impossible to separate them from the Gaels they had displaced. My reading of this Missoula encounter between a well-established Irish author and the fledgling Native American writer, which is largely derived from the tone of Welch's prose, is that it was deeply enabling for Welch, for not only was his own heritage and background being accepted and honored by a senior writer but also the young writer's place of origin, complex history, and family ties were being absorbed into a larger cultural and literary narrative: James Welch was Native American but also partly of Irish descent. Also, this encounter reminds us of how over time people who arrive as friendly outsiders or unwelcome conquerors can, whether by strategy or accident, become embedded in communities distant from the place they started out from. It becomes perfectly natural to encounter Welches both in the Irish South-East and in Indian Territory in Montana. So entwined do people become within the fabric of the new families and locations that have absorbed them that, over time, they separate completely from their ancient places of origin, and from received allegiances. At the same time, as James Welch indicated to Anthony Cronin by tracing his own lineage, genealogy is not as simple as belonging. The people who belong to a place and who define it by virtue of long and intense attachments to its buildings and pathways are often individuals whose familial histories are complex. It is often motion rather than settlement that defines the histories of families.

Also, meeting with James Welch allowed Cronin to develop a deeper insight into Montana, where he was spending a short period as a visiting professor. A few years ago in New Mexico, while sharing lunch with a group of Native American writers and scholars at a conference, each woman present was pleased to claim some Irish heritage. Of course, I could not reciprocate by claiming to be Native American, nor did I try to, and this was my bona fides as a visitor who had come to listen and learn rather than lecture or preach.

In both Enniscorthy in particular and Ireland in general, writers have distinguished themselves, often fighting above their weight and winning against all odds. Who would have thought it possible in the dreadful days of mid-nineteenth-century Ireland that such literary masters would emerge from the physical, psychic, and economic catastrophe that was the Potato Famine: Yeats, Shaw, Joyce, Beckett, Boland, Mahon, Ní Dhomhnaill, Muldoon, McCann, to mention but a few (and to omit many other brilliant and worthy authors). A similar resurgence occurred within the Native American communities of North America, where such writers as D'Arcy McNickle, N. Scott Momaday—the first Native author to be awarded the Pulitzer Prize for fiction for his novel *House Made of Dawn* (1969)—Louise Erdrich, Leslie Marmon Silko, Vine Deloria Jr., Linda Hogan, Thomas King, Joy Harjo, James Welch, Sherman Alexie, and others have produced innovative and acclaimed work. Native American history, though it is not the same as Ireland's, can also be defined by exploitation, confiscation, genocide, disrespect for indigenous traditions, and bigotry. American Indian writers, like their Irish counterparts, have raised human experience to the level of art while always remaining true to their roots: in family, place, and orality. Neither is worthy just because of who they are or where they have come from; rather, because of the literary shapes they have used to frame stories—these being narratives of times and places observed richly.

Though we should be careful not to too closely align Irish and Native American national narratives, we can, nevertheless, draw parallels between both. Exploring Louis Owens's astonishing *Mixedblood Messages: Literature, Film, Family, Place* (1998), one will learn that the cultural and literary debates over form and language taking place among Indian writers are similar to those that have occurred in the Irish context from the Literary Revival of the late nineteenth century up until the present. From Owens and other Native American writers, one understands the degree to which they, like the Irish, are drawn to place. Owens (Choctaw-Cherokee-Irish) begins *John Steinbeck's Re-Vision of America*, his first book, with a fine-tuned and elegant evocation of the place we associate with Steinbeck:

Monterey County in northern California is Steinbeck country, a region dominated by the long sweep of the Salinas Valley with its subterranean river and opposing ranges of mountains—the rolling Gabilans to the east and the darker, rugged Santa Lucias to the west. To the east Steinbeck Country extends beyond the Gabilans into the Great Central Valley, and in the west it drops from the flanks of the Santa Lucias into the Pacific Ocean. From this intricately textured landscape came the settings, the themes, the symbols of Steinbeck's greatest fiction. In this part of California, Steinbeck found the resources necessary for a life's work; when he left this country, as critics have often noted, he left behind not only these resources but his greatest work as well.[8]

Of course this is a part of California that Owens also knew well from his own childhood, and this same material, landscape, and perspective is reprised in "Water Witch," the more personal essay that appears in *Mixedblood Messages*.[9] In America—from the first encounters between northern Europeans and Native peoples—the Irish would have been indistinguishable from others who had crossed the Atlantic. Anglo-Saxon and Celtic peoples, for all that we Irish might protest, are physically quite similar. Native Americans in the process of being invaded had neither opportunity nor inclination, I would guess, to meditate on the finer points of Celtic genetic history—that would come later. We can say that the Irish were no better or worse than other Europeans, coming as they did from all classes—from destitute survivors of famine and dispossession to former residents of Big Houses. It was often the case that the Irish dispossessed in their homeland and driven to America in turn dispossessed Native Americans. Desperate, poorly educated, and ill informed, many bought into the racialized, expansionist rhetoric that underlined expansion. Ironically, the Irish living in American cities were themselves victims of such ideologies—centered on notions of nativism. At the same time, as both Welch and Owens remind us, Irish people could also live peacefully and happily among Indian people, both being used to negotiation, accommodation, and trade. In *Days without End*, Sebastian Barry's sweeping novel of the American Frontier, the role played by the Irish in the Indian Wars is richly and unflinchingly described. In America, the Irish connected with places and peoples.[10]

Though Irish and the many Native American languages survive and are vital, collectively they are dwarfed by English. To engage with readers, Native American and Irish writers write in English mostly, as it is the language they have the greatest familiarity with, or into which they are willing to allow their work to be translated.

Seamus Heaney's exploration of the triumph of the Irish over English is one that connects Irish writing to its Native American equivalents. In an encounter in *Station Island*, Stephen Dedalus exhorts the poet:

> the feast of the Holy Tundish. "Who cares,"
> he jeered, "any more? The English language
> belongs to us. You are raking at dead fires,
>
> a waste of time for somebody your age.
> That subject people stuff is a cod's game,
> Infantile, like your peasant pilgrimage.[11]

Given their achievements, Native American writers can make the same claim regarding ownership of the English language. Louis Owens notes that "We humans have the ability to appropriate and liberate the other's discourse. Rather than merely reflecting back to him the master's own voice, we can, in an oft-quoted phrase, learn to make it bear the burden of our own experience. We can use the colonizer's language, as Momaday demonstrates so brilliantly in *The Way to Rainy Mountain*, to articulate our own words and find ourselves whole. This has been the project of Native American writers for a long time."[12] The Irish American writer Michael Stephens articulates this process thus: "Coming from an Irish background one has an obligation to use this language in two ways. The first is to write it better than any native speaker . . . and second, to subvert that language at every chance, knowing that the tradition you have inherited is one of experimentation."[13] Chinua Achebe's *Things Fall Apart* is underlined by a similar attitude, aesthetic, and approach to language. For his part, Achebe wrote, "I feel that the English language will be able to carry the weight of my African experience. But it will have to be a new English, still in full communion with its ancestral home but altered to suit its new African surroundings."[14] Though we cannot flatten and simplify Native American, Irish, Irish American, and Nigerian experience into some uniform one-size-fits-all manual, we are permitted to align literary works in shared acts of subversion: that is, writing English of a superior quality—an English underlined by innovative experiments with language and form. Renny Christopher describes Louis Owens "as a mixedblood Choctaw/Cherokee/Irish writer," an identity that Owens himself confirms and complicates in his own work.[15] From Irish, American Indian, and Nigerian literatures we learn that forcible cultural engagement signals dispossession. However, the dispossessed are always much smarter than they are given credit for, and the literature they give back in their grafted tongues—*Ulysses, House Made of Dawn, Things Fall Apart*—is pure dynamite.

From this mixed blood, an energetic, hybrid literary style emerges. My own sense has always been that such comparisons as I have outlined above provide clearer paths to understanding Native American writing than referencing Indian work in tandem with more generic American authors: there are reasons why Indians group themselves as nations in the manner of the Irish and the Nigerians. Ireland is also, at least to a degree, a mixedblood place where Celts, Danes, Normans, Flemish, Anglo-Saxons, and others have intermingled to form a nation. The Native American world, however, is quite unlike the Irish one in how tribal identity remains independent and has not been fully folded into a singular identity. The Native American world is more diverse and less monolithic than the Irish one. Furthermore, the Irish Literary Renaissance of the late nineteenth and early twentieth centuries was the creation of men and women—W. B. Yeats, Lady Augusta Gregory, John Millington Synge, for example—who had emerged from the conquering classes. As happened in Ireland, not all scholars/writers are prepared to embrace the mixedblood aesthetic. In *Mixedblood Messages*, Owens debates this issue with the great Lakota author Elizabeth Cook-Lynn, who sees in the mixedblood notion a certain diminution of cultural belonging and responsibility.[16] Owens reminds us that Cook-Lynn, an author I greatly admire, also takes "'real Indian writers Adrian Louis and Sherman Alexie to task in her essay . . . arguing that these two authors' works fail to 'suggest a responsibility of art as an ethical endeavor or the artist as responsible social critic.'"[17] The former argument, put into the Irish context, reprises beliefs held by Douglas Hyde and Daniel Corkery during the Literary Revival, while the latter was answered by Seamus Heaney when called upon during the Troubles to put his pen to the service of the IRA. Using Osip Mandelstam as a model, Heaney wrote that the Russian poet "served the people by serving their language" rather than employing poetry as a weapon of political propaganda.[18] Though I favor Cook-Lynn's argument in this debate, Owens's detailed approach to his subject matter, his wide scholarship, and range of sympathies revealed in the chapters that constitute *Mixedblood Messages* is breathtaking.

Recent commemorations of the 150th anniversary of the Irish Great Hunger have focused attention on the generosity displayed by the Choctaw Nation to the Irish during that calamity. As Christine Kinealy has pointed out, assistance to victims often came from "the poorest and most marginalized groups in society, such as the ex-slaves in the Caribbean, the Choctaw Nation in Oklahoma, as well as convicts and 'fallen women' in London." Kinealy provides a remarkable illustration from the U.S. *Gazette* from this period:

> Among the noble deeds of disinterested benevolence which the present famine has called forth, none can be more gratifying to enlightened men than the liberality of our red brethren in the Far West. . . . The unexpected contribution is the more acceptable that it comes from those upon whom the white man has but little claim. . . . Christianity has taught them that 'God hath made of one blood all nations of men to dwell upon the face of the earth.'"[19]

The Choctaw donated $170 and the Cherokee donated $245.25.[20] These gifts are parsed to promote Christian charitable values and actions; however, such claims are insulting to the humanity and good nature of those who made these donations. On all sides of his family, Louis Owens is connected to these gifts, being Choctaw/ Cherokee/Irish. His work, perhaps unintentionally, renews the contact between all three peoples. Anthony Cronin's gesture to James Welch is a more intentional act of renewal and friendship. During his 2018 St. Patrick's season visit to the United States, Irish prime minister Leo Varadkar visited Oklahoma to offer thanks to the Choctaw people for the generosity they had shown during the Famine. He said to the Choctaw people that "Your act of kinship and generosity almost two centuries ago is memorialized in our history books and is commemorated on many occasions. Your act of kindness never has been and never will be forgotten in Ireland."[21] Varadkar announced the creation of a scholarship fund to allow Choctaw students to study in Ireland. Choctaw chief Gary Batton replied that the Irish and the Choctaw "have a very similar history of tragedy, perseverance and strength," and called them "kindred spirits."[22] In addition to being Ireland's youngest ever prime minister (*Taoiseach*), Varadkar is also Ireland first *Taoiseach* who is gay, and he is the son of an Indian father and Irish mother—a mixedblood.

Very few people are on Vinegar Hill this evening: small, harmless bands of tourists; two young lovers seeking privacy; a small crowd of boys running and roaring aimlessly about. Sit beside me and you too will enjoy the view of orderly fields stretching all the way to the Backstairs Mountains, of a countryside lit by evening seeming to fall away from, then push back towards where I sit, like the waves of barley, below and to my left, moving in the breeze. On days such as this, there is about this aspect of mid-Wexford some warm hint of the sublime. The town below, somewhat larger than it had been when I grew up here in the 1950s and 1960s, has an orderly grace that pushes out from its older center of castle, churches, cathedral, and many fine stone houses built by Quakers in the aftermath of the 1798 Rebellion, to its newer edges where concrete gives way to grass, hedge, limb, and leaf. Like everywhere on earth, from the oldest settlement to the newest suburb, Enniscorthy has acquired its unique sense of place that has developed through its various built environments, its natural bounty, and through the stories of its people. In Irish, we favor the term *dinnseanchas,* or lore of place, that best captures the interaction of these forces. Along with what we learn at home, we are formed by the collision of these forces. The environment is a teacher.

Surveying the town, one takes note of the river and the roads that engage Enniscorthy with elsewhere. As a child, I desired no other life than one passed here among a group of people so closely bound together that they seemed indigenous to this place and nowhere else rather than persons belonging to a nation or affiliated to a wider world. It was not until the 1970s that the town, like many in Ireland, began to engage fully with the world beyond it. We might leave town to attend hurling matches at Croke Park or the Spring Show at the RDS in Dublin, but we returned quickly home. Our mindset was an ancient one that tied us to the environs that St. Senan had founded in the sixth century: we should not stray too far from our psychological allotment, that visible space between river and hills. Later on, like all children, I understood that these same roads and river were invitations to escape and adventure. Eventually, I packed up my suitcase and made my departure. Others, remaining at home, daily walking these ancient streets, have made imaginative travels throughout the world or have taken advantage of cheaper air travel to satisfy their wanderlust in brief, intense bursts. At the same time, even the old people I would meet as a child who had rarely been to Dublin or had never visited the West of Ireland were full of national and international news gleaned from newspapers, the radio, and from family and friends. Being in one place is no barrier to curiosity.

Twenty years ago, my family and I made a road trip from Omaha, Nebraska, to the Black Hills of South Dakota. Looking back, I can say that this road trip changed my life, though as is often the case recalling such experiences, I have a hard time explaining any of it. I was a young father in the company of my gorgeous bride and beautiful children making my first American road trip, driving into and through new places, exploring the American West for the first time, and I had a feeling of a kind of liberation. Throughout the Black Hills, I was able to absorb something of the sacredness of place; around each bend, more became visible—if not to the eye then perhaps in the heart and in the soul, those deep wells of knowledge coordinating my waking dream. On one level, I experienced a form of raw exposure and firm renewal there, though these were things I could not articulate. Other people, I became aware, have reacted to Ireland in this manner, this primal, almost ignorant, mode of reception. Subsequently, I read a great deal concerning Lakota history and beliefs, and what emerged, more than anything, was a deeper understanding of the history and beliefs of my own place—the town in County Wexford I had left behind—rather than a thorough knowledge of Lakota lore and history. In the Black Hills, I might identify but not understand. It was better to leave this work to the Lakota. Of Irish and Lakota history, I noted common themes of dispossession, treachery, genocide, appropriation, denial of rights and language, though I also understood that our histories are unique and incomparable in important ways. Many Irish played roles in the dispossession of the Lakota, and as a mere traveler who had spent little time in this place, I had no authority to generalize. There can hardly be a better articulation of this fraught process than the one provided by Elizabeth Cook-Lynn in answer to Willa Cather:

> Pages written by an eponymous white woman
> whose point was: "the history of every
> country begins in the heart of a man or woman."
> It is the immigrant story. Different from
> the indigenous one which says "the heart
> of any country begins in the heart
> of the Earth." My thoughts turn to the place
> of the rivers and the wind she thinks of
> now as vestigial, mere remnant, traces of a human past[23]

Of course, I recognized this famous quote from Cather's *My Ántonia*, one of my favorite novels. Cook-Lynn's riposte sent me back to my own place. The progress of Christianity in Ireland diminished pre-Christian belief while, at the same time, incorporating aspects of the ancient—holy wells, for example—into the new. Growing up in rural Ireland, I knew that we were deeply connected to the earth and to its built environments, and I knew that the River Slaney, as well as flowing through our town of Enniscorthy, also coursed through our veins. My visit to the Black Hills and my reading of Elizabeth Cook-Lynn's work served to reengage me more deeply with my own home place. My own heart I learned from this road trip to South Dakota had its beginning in the Earth. This is how travel changes one's life.

As children we knew little about Native Americans, though that did not prevent us from considering ourselves experts on American Indian history and manners. We spent many afternoons at matinees in the Astor Cinema on Weafer St., its proprietor the best man at my parents' wedding, where the fare was dominated by Hollywood Westerns. Yearly after Christmas—from St. Stephen's Day to when primary school resumed after the feast of the Epiphany—we attended double-headers, bringing to the cinema cap guns that we fired in great cacophony in rhythm with the action taking place onscreen. Given the paucity of available entertainment in 1960s Ireland and the habitually dire winter weather, this was the only show in town for boys. Our parents were happy to have us out of the house for a few hours. For the staff of the Astor Cinema—the long-suffering manager, Mr. George Pepper, in particular—the wild hollering and cap-gun firing must have been ear-splitting and nightmarish. I would like to think that we identified with the American Indians onscreen and saw in their predicament parallels to how we Irish had been treated by our own colonial masters; however, I doubt if we were sophisticated enough to reach such enlightened judgments. Writing about such eponymous heroes of Westerns, John Wayne in particular, Louis Owens has noted that "even before I learned that the 'Duke' began life as a Midwestern boy named Marion Michael Morrison, I suspected he was not real. For one thing, he seemed too big and inescapable, always there during my childhood, spurring his horse across all of our lives, looming large in doorways and blocking the light."[24] To decode these movies in the manner of Owens would have required abilities to see behind the deep veneers that Hollywood had created. Adults would not have been able to help us children either, because in those days films were not taken seriously as art forms, with the result that discussion surrounding them rarely rose beyond identification of film titles with film stars. Not once as a child can I recall a film director's name being mentioned. Films were as disposable as newspapers. Our local library, quite small in those days, had many Westerns available for rent. In the decades of censorship that followed Irish Independence, Westerns, favoring violence over sex, were seen as inhabiting the moral high ground.

Most of my life, I have lived at a great distance from this place where I was born and raised. Nevertheless, even when I am not here, Enniscorthy speaks to me, offers me comfort and advice—some of it cold, I should add—and reminds me of who I am, or who I might have become had I remained in the place of my birth. It is through connection with place that Irish identity is formed. Before leaving my family home on Barrack St. this evening to walk to Vinegar Hill, I had been reading a response written by George W. Hawkins, a mixed-heritage Choctaw leader, to the removal of his people from Mississippi to Oklahoma on the "Trail of Tears":

> We were hedged in by two evils, and chose that which we thought least. Yet we could not recognize the right that the state of Mississippi had assumed to legislate for us. Although the legislature of the state were qualified to make laws for their own citizens, that did not qualify them to become law makers to a people who were so dissimilar in manners and customs as the Choctaws are to the Mississippians. Admitting that they understood the people, could they remove that mountain of prejudice that has ever obstructed the streams of justice, and prevented their salutary influence from reaching my devoted countrymen? We as Choctaws rather chose to suffer and be free, than live under the degrading influence of laws, where our voice could not be heard in their formation. . . . Here is the land of our progenitors, and here are their bones; they left them as a sacred deposit, and we have been compelled to venerate its trust; it is dear to us yet we cannot stay, my people are dear to me, with them I must go. Could I stay and forget them and leave them to struggle alone, unaided, unfriended, and forgotten by our great father? I should then be unworthy the name of a Choctaw, and be a disgrace to my blood. I must go with them; my destiny is cast among the Choctaw people. If they suffer, so will I; if they prosper, then I will rejoice. Let me ask you to regard us with feelings of kindness.[25]

Observing the privations that the Choctaw suffered as they made their way out of Mississippi toward Oklahoma, Joseph Kerr, a farmer, wrote a letter of protest to the War Department:

> I live now on the side of, and within forty feet of, the road, and the only one by which the Choctaw Indians have passed, and must pass, that go by land. Their extreme poverty and consequent suffering in passing last fall, attracted my particular notice, and the Houston case explained to me in some measure the cause of their extreme suffering from hunger, while passing. . . . Here they received worse than a scanty supply, to do them eighty miles through an uninhabited country, fifty miles of which is an overflowed swamp, and in which distance are two large deep streams that must be crossed in a boat or on a raft, and one other nearly impassable in any way.

... And this was to be performed under the pressure of hunger by *old* women and young children, without any covering for their feet, legs, or body, except a cotton under-dress generally.... I have seen poverty amongst the northern Indians, but theirs is nothing compared to that of those of the south.[26]

These accounts provide examples of how the Choctaw were treated by the government, how and why they felt as they did about their home place, and the terrible ritual and suffering that was Removal. Nobody was better placed to understand the suffering that the Great Hunger induced than the Choctaw. Even though they had good reason to ignore that catastrophe in Ireland, they did not. Aid was sent.

It is only in recent years, after more than three decades living in the United States, that I have found opportunities to spend time in Mississippi. My son-in-law served as a combat engineer in the U.S. Army, was a veteran of Iraq and Afghanistan, and was based at Fort Polk, Louisiana. Often, we drive from St. Louis, Missouri, down through Mississippi, crossing into Louisiana from Vicksburg. At first, I thought of myself as a cultural traveler going through the Memphis of Elvis Presley and Dr. Martin Luther King and the Delta of Robert Johnson and Muddy Waters. On one of these trips, we took a short detour to Oxford to spend a couple of hours at the home of William Faulkner. Later, looking beyond the Rand McNally road atlas and finding deeper maps, I have learned that much of the modern state of Mississippi incorporates the ancient homelands of the Choctaw, the tribe who had been so generous with aid to the Irish, my own ancient people, during the Great Hunger in the mid-nineteenth century. Thinking of my son-in-law, I am reminded of the many memorials I witnessed in the cemetery in Pine Ridge to Lakota who had served honorably in the U.S. military, and reminded further how complex history is, how much we are defined by multiple senses of belonging, by love and marriage, the activities of our lives, and how and where we think and feel. Writing this essay, I have been able to draw on the library and support of my wife Drucilla Wall, whose father, Paul C. Mims, is the son of a Creek/Muskogee father from Alabama and a World War Two veteran who served in the U.S. Marine Corps. Authors as divergent as George W. Hawkins, Elizabeth Cook-Lynn, and Louis Owens reveal to us the degree to which American Indians live at the meeting points of place and blood. We Irish think and feel in like ways and weep when cut adrift from such anchors. Out of absence and loss, we have both crafted significant and resonant literatures that garner influence beyond our own communities. We have our own stories to tell, and sometimes, it is harder to convince those at home!

These days, I live and work in St. Louis, another river town, where the confluence of the Missouri and Mississippi occurs. From what I have been able to observe, it looks like the leaders of my home state have, over time, done everything possible to erase the Native American presence from Missouri. Like Elizabeth Cook-Lynn and Louis Owens before me, I work in a university. Even though I hold a privileged position that I deeply appreciate, I have often felt great unease at the pettiness and intolerance present within the academy. Instead of despairing, and given the difficulty of resisting as a "foreigner," I try to follow Owens's example by seeking always to connect respectfully with others, to observe where our rivers meet. I revisit, more than any other teaching aid, Cook-Lynn's "End of a Failed Metaphor," an essay in which she advocates for an ethical and respectful scholarship that brings together the earth, stories learned at home and in texts, and a sense of responsibility to people and origins.[27] Now, I have found another guide: Louis Owens's *Mixedblood Messages: Literature, Film, Family, Place*. Though a great many years have passed since the Great Hunger, Native American authors continue to provide sustenance for the Irish through their poems and stories, and we hope that we provide some good things in return. I look forward to hearing or reading about the experiences of the Choctaw students in Ireland.

NOTES

1. Louis Owens, *Mixedblood Messages: Literature, Film, Family, Place* (Norman: University of Oklahoma Press, 1998), 160.

2. Patrick Kehoe, *Its Words You Want* (Cliffs of Moher, Co. Clare, Ireland: Salmon Poetry, 2011), 83.

3. John Montague, "A Grafted Tongue," *Collected Poems* (Winston-Salem, NC: Wake Forest University Press, 1995), 37.

4. Owens, *Mixedblood Messages*, 160.

5. Montague, *Collected Poems*, 38.

6. James Welch, "Introduction," to Tribes: Stories and Poems Volume, ed. James Welch, *Ploughshares* 20, no. 1 (Spring 1994): 5–7, 5.

7. Anthony Cronin, *Dead as Doornails: Memoir* (Dublin: Lilliput, 2000).

8. Louis Owens, *John Steinbeck's Re-Vision of America* (Athens: University of Georgia Press, 1985), 3.

9. Owens, *Mixedblood Messages*, 184–89.

10. Sebastian Barry, *Days without End* (New York: Penguin, 2017), 93.

11. Seamus Heaney, *Station Island* (New York: FSG, 1985), 93.

12. Owens, *Mixedblood Messages*, xiii.

13. Michael Stephens, *Green Dreams: Essays under the Influence of the Irish* (Athens: University of Georgia Press, 1994), 78.

14. Nicholas Wroe, "Chinua Achebe: A Life in Writing," *Guardian*, December 13, 2010.

15. Renny Christopher, "Louis Owens's Representations of Working-Class Consciousness," in *Louis Owens: Literary Reflections on His Life and Work*, ed. Jacquelyn Kilpatrick (Norman: University of Oklahoma Press, 2004), 154–74, 154.

16. Owens, *Mixedblood Messages*, 150–55.

17. Ibid., 154.

18. Seamus Heaney, *Preoccupations: Selected Prose, 1968–1978* (New York: FSG, 1980), 218.

19. Christine Kinealy, *Charity and the Great Hunger in Ireland: The Kindness of Strangers* (London: Bloomsbury, 2013), 1, 105.

20. As mentioned elsewhere in this collection, and as noted by various sources, there are reports of two amounts. I am using the lower figure here, $170. I do so because this was the figure that I first came across and have seen mentioned quite often. Kinealy, *Charity and the Great Hunger in Ireland*, 104–5.

21. Justin Wintergerter, *Oklahoman*, March 13, 2018, http://newsok.com/article/5586811/irish-prime-minister-visits-the-choctaws-to-thank-them-for-170-donation-171-years-ago.

22. Ibid.

23. Elizabeth Cook-Lynn, *I Remember the Fallen Tree: New and Selected Poems* (Cheney: Eastern Washington University Press, 1998), 128.

24. Owens, *Mixedblood Messages*, 100.

25. George W. Hawkins, "A Choctaw Farewell, 1832," in *Indian Removal*, by David S. Heidler and Jeanne T. Heidler (New York: Norton, 2007), 162–64.

26. Joseph Kerr, "A White Samaritan on the Choctaw Trek, 1832," in *Indian Removal*, by David S. Heidler and Jeanne T. Heidler (New York: Norton, 2007), 165–67, 166.

27. Elizabeth Cook-Lynn, "End of a Failed Metaphor," *Why I Can't Read Wallace Stegner and Other Essays* (Madison: University of Wisconsin Press, 1996), 142–49.

Nakfi, Brother, as He Helps Sister Load the Cart

LeAnne Howe

Our leaving will be sung in every church pew like a hymn.

Famine pot found on Hooker farm in Tipperary, Ireland.

An tAmhrán Ocrach

Doireann Ní Ghríofa

Ní thig linn an seansaol
a fheiceáil ach trí pholl eochrach,
radharc cúng orthu siúd
a ghlaonn go ciúin
ón dtaobh eile
den doras.

The past can be seen only
through a keyhole we peer through,
to find this narrow, shadowed view
of those who wait there,
a murmuring heard
from the other side
of the door.

Poll eocrach
Poll ocrach

Poll dubh a shlog
Poll a sciob

Keyhole
Hole that hungered
Hole that swallowed
Hole that stole

Cuirim cluas leis
an bpoll eocrach.
Cuirim beola leis.
Glaoim orthu arís
le buíochas
a ghabháil leo

And so, I press an ear
to the keyhole.
I press lips to it.
I call again;
in gratitude,
I call to them.

I know they are there,
I can almost hear them speak
as they prepare to leave.

Reconciliation

Jacki Thompson Rand

T he history of Irish-Choctaw relations, forged in the intersection of colonialism, narrative making, and memory production, is one of irony and contradiction. My aim here is to examine a predominantly celebratory footnote to that history concerning the tribe's monetary donation as reported in nineteenth-century U.S. newspapers and maintained ever since through Irish oral history and commemoration. Subsequent Irish expressions of gratitude found in print and commemorative practice intimate a kind of political solidarity between two oppressed peoples upon whom colonial powers inflicted terrible traumas leading to land and population losses. Irish and U.S. accounts commonly include references and gestures to the Choctaw removal to Indian Territory in the 1830s to emphasize the tribe's selflessness and empathy for the Irish. Missing, however, are crucial elements of colonial ideologies, racial hierarchies, and destructive federal Indian policies that supported assimilation and removal. Irish accounts are striking for the absence of reference to their presence in the Southeast since the early eighteenth century places them in the center of the maelstrom that drove tribes out of the region. In the United States, the self-congratulatory view of the gift is an affirmative sign of Choctaw cultural advancement through assimilation. This narrative version of Indian redemption from an original state of savagery, an

"Soup Pot, Bodyke Burial Ground, County Clare."

effrontery to Christianity, ignores the Choctaws' pre-Removal reality as a prosperous, politically astute people. Instead, the gift became an opportunity for the nation to take credit for the Choctaws' philanthropic contribution as an outcome of the federal assimilation project that one ardent assimilationist would later defend as, paraphrasing, killing the Indian to save the man. The context of selective memory in which the gift is represented in nineteenth-century U.S. newspapers, and by twentieth-century Irish commentators, performs a certain kind of work in colonial narrative making.[1]

The romantic version of this historical event, perpetuated by newspaper stories, Irish accounts, and, now, the Choctaw government, overlooks a prior century of relations between Irish settlers and southeastern Indian occupants, much of it detrimental to the Indians. Early Removal architect Thomas Jefferson recognized the destructive impact of the settler presence on indigenous peoples through, for example, the alcohol trade that simultaneously enriched settlers like the Irish while it impoverished Indians. He justified removal as a way to separate American Indians from settlers, like the Irish, whose land greed and trade ambitions ultimately required that the Indians leave the homeland for their very survival. If we accept the empathic Choctaw interpretation, we must be willing to imagine that the Choctaw donors, too, had fallen into a state of historical amnesia about the Irish role in their expropriation. Or, is there some other explanation? For example, did the Choctaws opportunistically seize on the occasion of the gift to engage in their practiced arts of diplomacy in order to enhance their weakened position vis-à-vis a settler nation, and expansionist federal government, whose land greed was not yet sated? We cannot know at this point, but we can revisit the historical context in which Irish-Choctaw relations evolved and imagine that the accepted motivation behind the Choctaw donation—Choctaw empathy—is worthy of interrogation.

Indian Removal, also known as the Trail of Tears, was rooted in the historical forces of the prerevolutionary United States. Pressures from the settler population and shifting political relations forced Choctaws and many other tribes to surrender lands to the federal government, before they finally conceded to relocation. Removal was the culmination of an engineered diminution in Indian land status. The treaty, first introduced by King George III via the Proclamation of 1763 and carried on by the Americans, had replaced the private contract by which Indians, as recognized proprietors, sold lands to the early British newcomers in the seventeenth and early eighteenth centuries.[2] Contracts attest to the colonial belief that Indians owned their land without erasing coercive aspects of such transactions. The Crown's change in policy fueled a market in preemption rights, speculative land claims made in advance of treaties, and formalized land cessions that intensified speculator and settler pressure on Indian lands. Settler incursions into Indian lands and instigations of conflict and violence, carried out with impunity, invariably resulted in government intervention on the side of the settlers and in land cessions to restore the peace. Following the Revolution, the stage was set to formalize large-scale land expropriations through treaty. Thomas Jefferson's Indian civilization blueprint and controversial Louisiana Purchase provided both justification and space for the relocation of American Indians to the west.

The once-accepted idea that Indians owned their land eroded and ultimately gave way to the manufactured idea that American Indians had never possessed land title. Rather, as U.S. Supreme Court chief justice John Marshall's decision in *Johnson v. M'Intosh* (1823) asserted, American Indians had only a right to occupancy.[3] He later reversed himself in *Worcester v. Georgia*, but it was too late to stop Indian Removal.[4] President Andrew Jackson, son of Irish immigrants, states' rights sympathizer, and advocate for Georgia's decades-long effort to see the state rid of the

Cherokee people, had pushed the 1830 Indian Removal Act through Congress to pave the way for removal treaties with the southeastern tribes.[5] Jackson refused to reverse his plans even when the Supreme Court affirmed Indian land title, effectively nullifying the legal standing for removal. Meanwhile, settler incursions and growing populations in the Southeast solidified facts on the ground in favor of the colonizers' version of history. Settlers, including Irish immigrants, had possession of the land; their numbers were significant and increasing, and the state and federal governments were on their side. Indian Removal was forced upon the five tribes.

The Treaty of Dancing Rabbit Creek authorized the Choctaws' relocation from Mississippi to Indian Territory. The suffering they endured in 1831–33 has been well documented in Grant Foreman's early work *Indian Removal: The Emigration of the Five Civilized Tribes of Indians*, Arthur H. DeRosier's *The Removal of the Choctaw Indians*, and Anthony F. C. Wallace's *The Long, Bitter Trail: Andrew Jackson and the Indians*. The Department of War oversaw the operation during which the dispossessed were exposed to cruel winter conditions and suffered starvation as a result of insufficient resources. The Indians, lacking blankets, winter clothing, shoes, and shelter, first gathered in open stockades, then traveled unprotected from the elements. Walking through unsettled environments, some died as they became trapped in wetlands, unable to escape as winter set in. One of the Choctaw groups encountered cholera at Memphis, where severe rains delayed their departure, leaving many to perish because the organizers had failed to arrange medical care for the weeks-long relocation. This was just one example, one legal scholar argues, of removal as a massive failure of administrative, bureaucratic, and legal systems.

Those failures created pressures on organizers to economize and maintain persistent frugality. Given the unprecedented scale of the cruel governmental effort, combined with harsh weather and the undeveloped environment through which the Choctaws walked, thousands of deaths and untold human suffering occurred, much of it unnecessary. Choctaw women died in childbirth. Choctaw elders perished from the difficult travel. The suffering did not end with the Choctaws' arrival in Indian Territory, where they rebuilt an already stratified society. Those who had prospered under Mushulatubbee's and David Folsom's economic reforms in Mississippi and had capital improvements were better positioned to start anew, making farms, raising cattle, and building horse herds, as they had been compensated for their losses. But Choctaws who had persisted in the older subsistence practices of raising gardens, hunting, and fishing received no compensation for their losses. They encountered severe difficulties in Indian Territory after months of delay and a long walking journey interrupted their seasonal growing and gathering cycles. In sum, Indian Removal was a radical policy that dramatically upended the lives of American Indian peoples.

Indian Removal, a traumatic chapter in American Indian history for the five largest southeastern tribes, as well as smaller tribes in the region, is directly linked to the growth of aggressive settler populations and land greed. We can see it in examples of Irish immigrants who prospered as traders and used their foothold in the United States to sponsor prospective Irish émigrés. George Galphin was one such Irishman who immigrated to the Southeast in the eighteenth century.[6] He was the eldest son of an Ulster family of linen weavers in that "impersonal and colonized economy." The Galphin family lived on small rented farms where they grew flax and subsistence gardens to supplement meager incomes from weaving. Self-sufficiency, modest living, and rare comfort purchases earned them the moniker "truly industrious poor." As the oldest son at the time of his father's death, Galphin assumed the position of patriarch and all his father's responsibilities at a young age. When his younger siblings spent their days working on the subsistence gardens, cleaning, spinning, and weaving linen, Galphin oversaw the flaxseed crop and managed linen sales. The linen economy enriched some, but not lowly linen families like the Galphins whose labor produced just enough for rent. The Galphins' vulnerability left them unable to absorb ups and downs in the linen market. Crop failures between 1717 and 1730 led to devastation as linen prices fell and credit dried up. Landlords raised rents, evicted families, and sold lands, leading to a subsistence crisis, and forcing families like the Galphins to take desperate measures.

George, as head of the family, took steps to emigrate to the Colonies and enter into the deerskin trade. Being "too poor to pay the fare in advance," he was most likely a contract laborer. He was one of many Irish immigrants escaping previous crop failures who arrived in the Southeast to overcome their losses and make their fortunes in the early eighteenth century. Protestants from Northern Ireland, Wales, and the Anglo-Scottish border country entered the Colonies along the Atlantic Seaboard, and through New Orleans after the Napoleonic Wars ended. New Orleans was unwelcoming to them. During the famine period, anti-Catholic prejudice prevented them from finding even the most menial employment. Seeking economic and religious freedom in significant numbers, the Irish received generous land grants from the governors of Pennsylvania, Virginia, and the Carolinas along the Appalachian frontier. After landing in Charleston, Galphin acquired land in 1740 with the help of his employers, Archibald McGillivray and William Sludders, both earlier immigrants, and set out to become established in the Indian trade. McGillivray had started his business on the Savannah River near Augusta, a growing trade center conveniently linked by waterway to Savannah.[7] Galphin moved to present-day Louisville, Georgia, and established the settlement of Queensborough on some 50,000 acres from which he traded with the Creeks and Choctaws. He later expanded his successful businesses into Florida.

The immigrants played a major role in building the southeastern Indian trade, with significant consequences for the Creek, Choctaw, Seminole, and Chickasaw Indians. They engaged in unregulated trade, integrated themselves into the economy, and married into American Indian kinship networks. Just as the French penetrated the St. Lawrence River Valley and Great Lakes region via intermarriage, in time becoming dominant in the beaver pelt trade, Irish and Scottish immigrants prospered in the deerskin trade. This history challenges the common representation of the Irish in America as urban immigrants struggling in the face of anti-Catholic prejudice. The colonial governments welcomed the Irish and other immigrants as a buffer from the so-called hostile Indian tribes in the Southeast. The Irish in the Southeast transformed into colonizers who were primarily concerned with enriching themselves at the Indians' expense, gaining political influence, and appropriating Indian land. Simply put, the Irish, like the oppressive British landlords who had once impoverished their families and forced them to scatter across the globe, became agents in American Indian dispossession and removal.

Galphin, like many others, including American founders and presidents, engaged in the practice of obtaining Indian land by nefarious means typical of colonial relations. Land acquisition was central to realizing the American dream in the settler imagination.[8] He, along with other immigrants, settled among the southeastern tribes and exerted pressure on Indian lands through conflict, debt creation, and sometimes violence. In exchange for manufactured goods, blankets, and rum, the Indians traded corn, captive slaves, and deerskins. Galphin took advantage of Indians, he boasted, by plying them with alcohol during their transactions, which always left them in arrears to the trade store. This practice ensured that the next season's hides would come to Galphin. The Irish, like many other ethnic groups, made fortunes from the Indians who drank away their gains and grew crippling account balances. The Indians' indebtedness to traders such as Galphin made them, *and their lands*, vulnerable to dishonest white men. The immigrants allowed the

Indians to trade on debt until paying it off became prohibitive, especially as the deerskin business went into decline in the second half of the eighteenth century. This opened the door to bigger stakes trading. Indians were forced to settle debts with land cessions, also foreseen by Thomas Jefferson.

The later federal version of this scheme was called the "factory system," established by Congress in 1795 at the behest of George Washington, who promised to protect the Indians from exploitative traders like Galphin.[9] Instead, government stores mimicked the practices of settlers like Galphin, allowing American Indians to trade on account, to run up insurmountable debt, and to clear the debt with land cessions to the United States. Thomas Jefferson, who well understood that American Indians were disadvantaged in trade, encouraged Indian debt. Numerous treaties came about to allow Indians to retire debt with traders like Galphin who were usually present at treaty negotiations and first in line to receive proceeds from the sale. He, like his friends, encouraged Irish immigration to the Southeast including the settlement at Queensborough. The colonies were good to Galphin. He sided with the Continental Congress during the Revolution and, likely because he had developed close relations with the southeastern tribes through trade activities, was appointed Indian commissioner to the South and given responsibility for neutralizing the Indians in the Revolution.

Galphin built a fortune and gained influence by taking advantage of people just as the landlords had prospered on the backs of his impoverished family and others in the eighteenth century. In the nineteenth century, the Irish experienced loss and hardship during the Famine. Protestant landlords owned some 50 percent of the land in Ireland at this time. Tenant farmers, controlled by roughly 750 landowner families, rarely faced eviction. But when the blight appeared, the resulting agricultural devastation created a tenancy crisis. Evictions rose exponentially to some 90,000 between 1847 and 1850. The only option for many Irish was to emigrate. Five million Irish, both rural poor and members of the commercial farming class, made their way to the United States in the nineteenth century. Irish immigration peaked in the 1840s, just before the height of the Famine in 1848. Between 1845 and 1855, 1.5 million came to the United States, 340,000 to Canada, and 200,000–300,000 to Great Britain. The Irish, like many immigrants then and now, faced enormous challenges in their quest to make the Americas their home. They had their fair share of suffering and discrimination in the Southeast. They also caused great environmental damage and inflicted suffering on indigenous peoples.[10] It was the great harm that the Choctaws experienced from removal that gave the story of the gift an intense poignancy to readers and later storytellers. The romantic version of the gift, however, relies on a narrow bandwidth of Removal history that is striking.

————————

Over the years, both the Irish in Ireland, and Choctaws in Oklahoma have actively cultivated practices in public history. Both peoples use the commemorative walk as a way to preserve the memory of significant historic events and to encourage knowledge production across generations. It was a commemorative walk that drew the Irish and Choctaws together after a century and a half passed following the Irish Potato Famine. In 1992, the Oklahoma Choctaws held the inaugural commemoration of the Choctaw removal, hosting a Trail of Tears walk in southeastern Oklahoma, which is now an annual event. Choctaws and non-Natives retraced the last twenty miles of the Trail of Tears, shared a communal lunch, and listened to family stories about the ancestors who experienced removal, a historical chapter that remained intact for over a century and a half. Over time, Indian Removal had transformed into a condensed symbol of U.S. oppression, settler violence, suffering, and resilience. The commemorative walk had taken on significant cultural power in the face of many losses, such as Choctaw fluency resulting from separating children from parents for boarding-school placement. (We're witnessing a similar tactic being used in 2018 by the federal government to separate immigrant mothers and their children.) The commemorative walk marked the beginning of the Choctaw efforts to strengthen language, revitalize stickball traditions, capture Choctaw stories, and revive material culture production. Christian churches had successfully replaced traditional dances; however, today the Choctaws are reviving.

Coincidentally, four years before the Choctaw event in 1992, the Irish held the first Famine Walk in County Mayo to commemorate the 1849 "Doolough Tragedy," when weak and starving Irish had gathered for an inspection by authorities representing the British Crown as required to secure relief. Following instructions to meet the inspectors eleven miles away, hundreds undertook the walk only to be turned away again at the distribution site. Some of the Irish died trying to make their way home, never having secured the promised relief. The Famine Walk in Ireland, which retraces their steps, is now an annual event. Like the Choctaw Trail of Tears, the Famine Walk serves as a symbol of a condensed memory of colonialism, suffering, and endurance. The Famine Walk also signifies the scattering of Irish to the four corners of the world, an event that separated families and depopulated Ireland.

In both instances, commemorative walks serve many purposes. The walk itself is a symbolic re-creation of a significant event by covering the same ground of the ancestors whose lives the walk remembers and honors. The walk maintains connection to the ancestors' lives and suffering. It reinforces memory, and therefore preserves history and heritage, a common outcome associated with memory work. The victims, marginal in life and largely invisible in history, are ensured a place in the community's memory. Through careful planning, common meals, presence of food, prayer, and speeches, the descendent community expresses gratitude for the victims' sacrifice. Such activities reinforce community ties, assert the event's historical significance, and transfer knowledge to the next generations. Commemorative practices offer comfort, but they also contain an element of political work in that they push back against sanitized national narratives that overlook the losses sustained as a result of nation-building and of colonial oppression. Commemorative work asserts the historical perspective of the colonized subjects and that which they deem to be significant. It fills an existing absence or silence with the presence of the oppressed and marginalized.

In the early 1990s there was a series of exchanges between the Choctaws and Irish that centered on the commemorative walks each had established in relation to their histories under colonialism. In 1990 the Irish invited a delegation of Choctaw officials to participate in the annual walk in County Mayo, organized by Don Mullan, director of Action, a nonprofit philanthropic organization.[11] Mullen then took a group of Irish activists to the United States, to walk the Trail of Tears from Oklahoma to Mississippi as part of a larger project titled "The Great Famine" to commemorate the 150th anniversary of the Great Hunger. Mullen picked up the global theme of the famine-fueled emigration, linking the two commemorative walks to a philanthropic effort in support of starving Somalis.[12] The walkers began in Broken Bow, deep in the Choctaw counties of southeastern Oklahoma. Walking nineteen miles a day, they reached the reservations of the Mississippi Band of Choctaw Indians, where tribal representatives escorted them to Nanih Waiya, the Choctaw mother mound in Neshoba County. In an interview with the press, a Choctaw spokesperson explained the itinerary that had been planned for the hikers. He added that Choctaws also wanted to learn more about the gift their ancestors gave to the starving Irish, indicating that the history of the gift was not well known in the community. Mullan met Gary White Deer, a Choctaw/Chickasaw man from around Ada, Oklahoma, who came to play an important role in the revitalization of the memory and in bridge-building between the Irish and Choctaws. The two men became friends and maintained communication. Mullan invited White Deer to Ireland to join the walk in County Mayo. He has remained in Ireland ever since.

Accounts of this meeting suggest that indeed the Choctaws had not retained a collective memory of the gift, but were eager to learn about it from the Irish visitors. The absence of memory makes a striking comparison to the Irish memory of the gift. In contrast, the Irish people have acknowledged the Choctaw gift in popular publications and in memorials. One memorial near Battery Park in Manhattan, New York, attests to the significance of the Choctaw gift in the Irish memory of the Famine. There the Irish Hunger Memorial garden includes a Famine-era stone cottage from County Mayo. The stone base includes an etching that notes the donation by "the Children of the Forest, our Red Brethren of the Choctaw Nation." Accounts of the famine in Irish popular publications commonly include a reference to the Choctaw famine gift with somber tones of deep gratitude and acknowledgment of the Choctaws' own difficult history.

Since the reunion in the early 1990s, the Irish and Choctaws have traveled across the Atlantic many times to maintain the newly redrawn ties of friendship and shared history. In 1995, Mary Robinson, the first woman president of Ireland, traveled to Oklahoma and met with tribal leaders to thank the Choctaws for the Irish Famine gift. The Choctaws made Robinson an honorary chief and signed onto a new organization for world famine relief. The Irish commissioned a painting by White Deer of a Choctaw woman holding an Irish child, with an Irish woman embracing a "Third World" baby as part of the 150th anniversary commemoration. Since the anniversary, Irish and Choctaws have continued to visit one another and to collaborate on projects, including a children's book and a film. Missing, however, are references to Irish complicity in colonization in the Southeast, land expropriation, and exploitation of indigenous traders.

The historical context of the gift complicates a simplified explanation of Native generosity that does not appear in Choctaw memory. History tells us that Indian Territory was not kind to the victims of Removal. The Choctaws struggled throughout the nineteenth century to keep their land and to protect the tribe's political sovereignty. That fight continued through the Civil War, followed by successful resistance to the General Allotment Act, and defeat in the face of the 1898 Curtis Act, which amended the Dawes Act to allow the breakup of the governments and lands of the "Five Civilized Tribes," including the Choctaws. Allotment resulted in the loss of some 15 million acres in Indian Territory by the end of the nineteenth century. The Homestead Act made it possible for poor immigrants to receive 160 acres of public land for a filing fee and five years' continuous residence. (In 1992, director Ron Howard made a romanticized film version of the Homestead Act, titled *Far and Away*. The film stars Tom Cruise and Nicole Kidman play two plucky Irish characters expecting to find a better life in the New World. The two come to America, where Shannon expects to claim a piece of land for herself in the ongoing Land Rush deals. Watch it and you'll have some idea of how grating it is to southeastern Natives.) By 1900, the Choctaw government had been dismantled, the Choctaw territory greatly reduced, and the people, many impoverished, were at the mercy of settlers and the United States government. Therefore I suggest the Choctaw gift was a memory that never had the chance to take hold in the imaginations of average Choctaws, who spent the remainder of the nineteenth century resisting U.S. land grabs and greedy settlers. The tribe, like most others, entered the twentieth century with their governments nearly destroyed by an aggressive and powerful Bureau of Indian Affairs.

Meanwhile, the Choctaw donation had been preserved in the Irish assertion of self-determination and accounting of atrocities endured under colonialism. The gift that saved Irish lives, coming from a colonized and abused people, became a celebratory sign of solidarity and resistance. The bonds have since been renewed through shared commemorative work and exchanges from the level of community projects to the highest reaches of government. Overlooked is the sad reality of what, in the final analysis, it cost the Choctaws, and that is the pressure of more Irish countrymen turned new colonizers/settlers seeking Choctaw lands. Perhaps the irreconcilable contradictions in this layered history is what made it impossible for the Choctaws to retain a memory of the gift in the way the Irish have so carefully preserved it. The difficulty of this history is made clear in its absence from today's commemorations.

The Choctaw people's donation was among the earliest instances of global philanthropy and affirmed the "noble savage" to mainstream papers around the United States.[13] Timing and striking similarity in experience between the Indians and Irish drew public attention to Choctaw philanthropy. A stratified Choctaw society included large landholders who possessed slaves and poor Choctaws who engaged in subsistence living. To newspaper consumers, the tragic narrative of Indian Removal followed by the inspiring donation, which in all likelihood may have been by wealthier Choctaws, made for a powerful story. Choctaws were credited for their generosity toward others who suffered as they had. The price to the Choctaws had been high, but advancing the civilization project made it worthwhile. But the Choctaws' experiences with immigrants, including those from Ireland, raises questions about the nature of empathy as motivation behind the Choctaw donation. With removal recently endured, following on decades of pressure on their lands rising from intrusive settlers, why would they feel a kinship with the very people who helped lead to their removal? At least one scholar reads the donation as an ambiguous gesture that allowed the Choctaws to seize an opportunity to speak, albeit indirectly, about the destructive consequences of the Removal policy, about the exercise of hegemonic power by the United States over American Indians, and about the Choctaws' insistence on their own sovereignty. If so, the message has changed during the revival of Irish-Choctaw contact and the ensuing construction of the memory of the gift.

Perhaps here is an opportunity to resist avoiding a difficult and challenging history. While colonized peoples in many locations persist, and fail, in bringing about some kind of historical peacemaking through reconciliation projects with reluctant colonial governments, here the Choctaws and the Irish *peoples* have an opportunity to experiment with the idea of reconciliation in a purposeful way. But it requires a full acknowledgment of the historical Choctaw-Irish relationship as a beginning. On the occasion of the 2017 installation of a steel memorial by Alex Pentek in the shape of a bowl made out of feathers, a Choctaw delegation traveled to Ireland in June 2017 for the dedication of the sculpture and to commemorate the 1847 gift. *Kindred Spirits* serves as a gift in that it is a formal visual pledge that the Choctaw gift will remain in Irish oral and written history. But it is clear that this moment of friendship, as sincere as it is, rests on a contradiction and on a silence. I am reminded of Mauss's canonical work about which Mary Douglas wrote in her introduction, "A gift that does nothing to enhance solidarity is a contradiction."[14] In this moment when we stop to memorialize the Choctaw gift to the Irish, let us pledge to correct the oversight and clear the path of contradiction. As survivors of colonialism, we, the Choctaw and Irish peoples, are strong enough to reckon with memory in an inclusive and responsible way, taking measure of the difficult and uncomfortable aspects of our shared experiences, with integrity. Let us affirm our commitment to social justice, to anticolonialism, and to liberation.

NOTES

1. Anelise Hanson Shrout, "A 'Voice of Benevolence from the Western Wilderness': The Politics of Native Philanthropy in the Trans-Mississippi West," *Journal of the Early*

Republic 35 (Winter 2015): 562.

2. Stuart Banner, *How the Indians Lost Their Land: Law and Power on the Frontier* (Cambridge, MA: Belknap, Harvard University Press, 2005), 85–95.

3. Walter R. Echo-Hawk, *In the Courts of the Conqueror: The 10 Worst Indian Law Cases Ever Decided* (Golden, CO: Fulcrum Press, 2010), 75–76.

4. Banner, *How the Indians Lost Their Land*, 220–21.

5. Jackson's parents left Carrickfergus, County Antrim, just months before his birth. James E. Doan, "How the Irish and Scots Became Indians: Colonial Traders and Agents in the Southeastern Tribes," *New Hibernia Review* 3, no. 3 (Autumn 1999): 9–19. In some modern accounts of the Choctaw gift, Jackson's Irishness is recognized as an irony rather than opening a door to further historical contextualization.

6. Bryan C. Rindfleisch, "Family, Linen, and Immigration in Ulster, 1700–1740: The Galphin Family in Two Worlds," *New Hibernia Review* 20, no. 4 (Winter 2016).

7. Amos J. Wright, *The McGillivray and McIntosh Traders: On the Old Southwest Frontier, 1716–1815* (Montgomery, AL: NewSouth Books, 2007), 77–78.

8. Padraig Kirwan, "Translatlantic Irishness: Irish and American Frontiers in Patrick McCabe's *The Butcher Boy*," *Comparative Literature* 63, no. 1 (2011): 11. Kirwan critically discusses the image of the Irish as the quintessential embodiment of the "American Dream" in this article on the representation of Irishness.

9. Robert J. Miller, "The Federal Factory System," *Encyclopedia of United States Indian Policy and Law* (Washington, DC: Congressional Quarterly Press, Sage Publications, March 8, 2009).

10. Patrick Brennan, "Getting Out of the Crescent City: Irish Immigration and the Yellow Fever Epidemic of 1853," *Louisiana History: Journal of the Louisiana Historical Association* 52, no. 2 (Spring 2011): 189–205.

11. Robin Barovick, "The Choctaw Tribe and the Irish Famine," Irish America, https://irishamerica.com/2018/03/the-choctaw-tribe-and-the-irish-famine/.

12. Dylan Foley, "Irish Retrace the 'Trail of Tears' for Somalia," *Earth Island Journal* 8, no. 1 (Winter 1992): 27.

13. Anelise H. Shrout, "'Benevolence from the Western Wilderness': American Indians, the Irish Famine and Transnational Philanthropy," a chapter from "Distressing News from Ireland: The Famine, the News and International Philanthropy" (PhD diss., New York University, 2013).

14. Marcel Mauss, *The Gift: The Form and Reason for Exchange in Archaic Societies*, intro. Mary Douglas (New York: W.W. Norton & Co., 2000).

Famine Irish Catholics, Their "Eloquent Indian" Priest, and the "Chinese Question"

Peter D. O'Neill

The invitation to Choctaw leaders to the unveiling of the *Kindred Spirits* sculpture in Midleton, County Cork, in June 2017, is the latest in a series of public acknowledgments of Ireland's indebtedness to the Choctaw people. The sculpture commemorates the 1847 Choctaw gift of monies for Irish Famine relief. That a people so devastated by the U.S. government's genocidal policies could find the resources and energy to help another oppressed people several thousand miles away, speaks volumes about Choctaw generosity, and the fundamental human urge to help other humans in need. Yet to focus solely on this act of solidarity and empathy does disservice to the memory of those indigenous peoples whose humanity was denied by white supremacist America. So, while the essays in this volume concern the 1847 Choctaw gift, I want to broaden the conversation to take into account the brutality of the white supremacist U.S. racial state, which Irish Famine immigrants not only found refuge in, but also helped bolster.

My story, then, is a sister narrative to Choctaw-Irish famine relief accounts, one that takes place in the Wild West and is told through a Native American pastor, his Irish Catholic flock, and their Chinese neighbors in San Francisco. This peculiar nineteenth-century California triangle exemplifies the sordid nature of the U.S. racial state, a form of governmentality in which race constitutes the primary factor in determining eligibility for citizenship. Like the concept of race itself, this triangular relationship is volatile: when two of its sides stake claims for ideal American citizenship and bond as one under the equally unstable category called "whiteness," a new racial triangle forms. Establishing a new, single side—a new white alliance—are the pastor and flock. The Chinese remain the second side, while a third side emerges, consisting of the California Native American people whom white settlers slur as "Diggers." Here is the story of that re-formation.

Whiteness and Colonial Discourse

One of the earliest examples of European colonial discourse contains the following passage: "They are a wild and inhospitable people. They live on beasts only and live like beasts. They have not progressed at all from the primitive habits of pastoral living." The writer excoriates the Natives for their apparent inability to tend to a land so ripe for cultivation. "For given only to leisure, and devoted only to laziness, they think that the greatest pleasure is not to work, and the greatest wealth is to enjoy liberty. This people is . . . a barbarous people, literally barbarous." The writer then situates "barbarity" as modernity's binary opposite. "Judged according to modern ideas, they are uncultivated. . . . All their habits are habits of barbarians." The only solution, he concludes, is to liberate these people from their lands. From the late fifteenth century onwards, such justificatory reasoning flowed frequently from the quills of Spanish, Portuguese, and English scribes employed to explicate a rationale for the colonial conquest of the Americas. These lines, however, are from a treatise called *Topographia Hiberniae*, written circa 1187 by one Giraldus Cambrensis, or Gerald of Wales, who accompanied the army of Prince John, son of King Henry II, on England's first major military expedition to Ireland.[1] For centuries, *Topographia Hiberniae* was a standard reference book for all English historiography on Ireland.

The writings of Giraldus Cambrensis will sound familiar to anyone acquainted with the founding documents of English North America. Undoubtedly the early colonialists in Virginia and elsewhere were well acquainted with his works, for it is he who provided them the template for colonial justificatory discourse. As scholars like Ronald Takaki and Nicholas Canny have shown, other links exist between the Irish and American conquests. For example, many of the same personnel who crossed the Atlantic to subdue Native Americans first learned their techniques in Ireland.[2] The conquest of North America saw the racial dimensions of colonialism intensify. Notions of white supremacy—manifested in the extermination of indigenous peoples and in the kidnapping, transatlantic transportation, and enslavement of Africans—created the conditions for American economic growth.

Irish America and the Foundations of the U.S. Racial State

Over the past two centuries, a number of Irish nationalists have expressed a certain affinity with the indigenous peoples of North America while remaining muted, or downright hostile, with regard to expressions of solidarity with enslaved African Americans. The nationalist icon John Mitchel, for example, supported the American institution of slavery vociferously, even boasting of a desire to own his own slave plantation.[3] Irish nationalist affinity with America's indigenous peoples, however, remained limited to self-serving analogy. As Mary L. Mullen maintains, by employing analogies between Irish and indigenous peoples, Irish nationalists "assert the reality of Irish colonial history through depictions of unreal American Indians. In the process, they question settlement in Ireland while legitimating and participating in the settlement of America."[4]

It is perhaps facile to condemn the nineteenth-century transatlantic Irish migrants for not expressing solidarity with the oppressed peoples of the United States, especially having been victims of a dehumanizing colonial power themselves. However, many of the Irish migrants during the Great Hunger (1845–52) had little choice but to leave Ireland or perish. Upon arrival at American ports, most, impoverished and traumatized, no doubt felt compelled to accept the credo of their new home and seek the loftiest perch they could reach in the U.S. racial hierarchy. These Famine Irish were, in general, too weak or too poor for frontier homesteading, so mid-nineteenth-century Irish encounters with race in America took place, for the most part, in urban contact zones where few Native Americans were to be found.[5] This is not to claim for the Famine Irish innocence regarding either the theft of Native American lands or the erasure of Native American cultures. Indeed, Irish Americans, as settler colonialists, participated in the erasure of indigenous peoples by extending the structures of the U.S. racial state. "Irish people," Mullen writes, "sometimes quite actively participated in these settler colonial formations, in such ways as fighting in the Indian wars, settling on Indian land, or encouraging American expansion. But even descriptions of how the Irish flourish in America naturalize these formations because they work to claim the land."[6]

The Atlantic crossing of Dillon O'Brien serves as a timely reminder that not every Famine Irish migrant lived in urban America, nor did every migrant come from the subaltern class. Once prosperous in his native Ireland, he emigrated after the Famine left him landless. Within a decade, O'Brien—and the narrator of his 1866 novel, *The Dalys of Dalystown*—could be found on an Apostle Island in the U.S. Great Lakes, teaching at a "Government Indian School."[7] It was an occupation that underscored both the swift entry of the Irish into the ranks of what then was called "free white labor" and the continued subjection of Native peoples to governmentally imposed dependency.[8] If his experiences among the Chippewa led to a greater understanding of the plight of indigenous peoples, he did not show it in his subsequent writings, both fictional and nonfictional.

After six years in the Apostle Islands, O'Brien and family moved south to Minneapolis/St. Paul in 1873, to become editor of the Catholic weekly *The Northwest Chronicle*. He managed to complete three more works of fiction, including *Dead Broke: A Western Tale* (1873), which features an indigenous character named "Indian Dick," who bears the brunt of the narrator's racist humor and gross stereotyping. In Minnesota O'Brien teamed up with Kilkenny-born Fr. John Ireland, the future first Catholic archbishop of St. Paul, to promote Irish Catholic colonization. In 1876, they established the Catholic Colonization Bureau of St. Paul, with O'Brien as its administrator. This bureau was to act as agent for frontier landowners, the St. Paul & Pacific Railroad Company. By adding railroad land to the Minnesota indigenous people's land that had been confiscated and made available to white settlers for a nominal sum through the Homestead Act of 1862, O'Brien and Ireland expressed lofty ambitions to colonize over 150,000 acres with Irish Catholic colonizers. Although they failed to attract significant numbers of the poorer Irish from Eastern Seaboard city slums, between 1876 and 1880, the two men did succeed in establishing a total of ten colonies in Minnesota, and the bureau contracted for an impressive total of 380,000 acres.[9]

O'Brien and Ireland were not alone in promoting Irish colonization. James P. Shannon's *Catholic Colonization on the Western Frontier* (1957) records a number of other similar efforts, including the establishment of the Irish Catholic Colonization Association of the United States, or ICCA. O'Brien and Ireland attended the inaugural convention in Chicago, on St. Patrick's Day, 1879, organized by Chicago businessman William J. Onahan and Bishop John Lancaster Spalding. The ICCA managed to set up an Irish colony in Nebraska and also provided financial support for one of O'Brien's Minnesota colonies. But again success was limited. In general, the Irish of America's Eastern Seaboard were just too poor and too weak for this strenuous and risky undertaking. For them, the more communal, urban living, despite all its attendant misery, felt a better option than the solitary life in the prairie.

The most common facilitator of encounters between the Irish and Native Americans, however, was the U.S. Army. Although it is difficult to get an accurate figure, an estimated five thousand Irish-born soldiers fought for the U.S. Army in the so-called Mexican War, 1846–48. [10] Irish recruitment continued at a brisk pace over the next decade as more Famine Irish refugees arrived at Eastern Seaboard ports. By the outbreak of the Civil War, one Union Army unit alone, the famous Irish Brigade, consisted of approximately seven thousand Irishmen. [11] That said, Irish military engagement with Native Americans occurred not so much in the Mexican War or in the Civil War as in the period of so-called "western expansion"—that is, the deluge of death and destruction unleashed from the fluffy, celestial clouds of Manifest Destiny, a subject to which we will return shortly.

In *Racial Formation in the United States*, Michael Omi and Howard Winant contend that "the state is inherently racial . . . the preeminent site of racial conflict."[12] David Goldberg takes this argument further in *The Racial State*: race, he maintains, "is integral to the emergence, development and transformations (conceptually, philosophically, materially) of the modern nation-state. Race marks and orders the modern nation-state, and so state projects, more or less from its point of conceptual and institutional emergence."[13] The state carries out this racial marking and ordering mainly through state legal apparatuses. Thus, for example, the founding legal document of the United States, the 1776 American Declaration of Independence, slurs Natives as "merciless Indian Savages" fit for destruction, while subsequent racist laws in the southern states denied the humanity of the African Americans through the legal institutionalization of slavery. Fear fueled—and continues to fuel—white supremacist ideology and politics. In the early days of the Republic, perceived threats to the stability of the U.S. state, especially threats posed by "outsider agitators," culminated in the establishment of the Alien and Sedition Acts of 1798.[14] The fledgling state fretted about existential threats from both within and without.

At its most basic, the internal threat to the nineteenth-century U.S. racial state was a brutal numbers game. White Anglo-Saxon Protestants were in the minority of the population in the South, while to the west, the sheer numbers of indigenous peoples and Mexicans threatened white American hegemony. The ruling elite knew that draconian laws and military power alone could not ensure the racial status quo.

Besides, a growing capitalist economy demanded a willing population, comprising both workers to build the economic infrastructure and consumers to buy what the economy produced. Even though sections of the U.S. elite expressed fears of cultural contamination, particularly from Catholics and other non-WASP migrants, the most powerful of the capitalist class recognized that European immigration, irrespective of these migrants' religious affiliation, offered the most pragmatic way to secure the foundations of the racial state. In addition, these migrants helped fuel state expansion, thereby driving the economy forward. Significantly, the Alien and Sedition Acts contained the first U.S. immigration law, the 1790 Naturalization Act, which decreed "That any alien, being a free white person, who shall have resided within the limits and under the jurisdiction of the United States for the term of two years, may be admitted to become a citizen thereof."[15] Though amended several times over the next couple of decades or so, the act cleared the way for the massive influx of Irish migrants that soon would follow.

In the thirty years following the conclusion of the Napoleonic Wars in 1815, an estimated 800,000 to 1 million Irish people sailed to North America, roughly twice the figure for the preceding two hundred years.[16] That figure swelled in the next decade—1845 to 1855, a decade known in Ireland as the Great Hunger or Great Famine—when almost 1.5 million Irish made the crossing to the United States.[17] A total of 2.1 million persons are estimated to have fled Ireland in that period, while between 1.1 million and 1.5 million more died from starvation or famine-related diseases. In a mere ten years, the Irish population of around 8.5 million in 1845 had been cut almost in half.[18]

Despite the sheer scale of the catastrophe, the Famine, until quite recently, has generated a peculiar and pervasive amnesia in Ireland.[19] How my own family survived the Great Hunger, for example, is a story that has never been told to me, or my siblings. In fact, knowledge of my ancestors, on either side of my family, does not extend past my grandparents, all of whom were born in the latter stages of the nineteenth century. My O'Neill and Kerlin Famine-era antecedents seem to have fallen off the face of the earth. Yet, in my hometown of Derry, and especially in its hinterland, the immediate effects of nineteenth-century Europe's greatest demographic disaster must have been painfully evident. Breandán Mac Suibhne's *The End of Outrage: Post-Famine Adjustments in Rural Ireland* (2017) centers on a part of that hinterland, in neighboring County Donegal. He skillfully excavates some uncomfortable truths about Famine survival that lurk beneath the surface of the blue tar roads of "progress" that cover the county like a spider's web. In the process, Mac Suibhne reveals an ethical demimonde animated by unsavory and self-serving operators. Yet Famine survival does not fit easily into a Manichaean worldview. About his cast of survivors, Mac Suibhne observes, "if there is no cartoon villain here, there is no hero."[20] The lesson to be learned here is maybe this: what our ancestors did or did not do is not as important as what we do now.

Much has been written about the causes of the catastrophe, but recent scholarship leaves little doubt about it.[21] The so-called "Famine" was a man-made disaster, orchestrated by a British government determined to rid the land of its people. If this sounds like the story of the American Indians at the hands of the colonizing British, and later American cavalry, the two histories share similarities. Concerning Ireland, Christine Kinealy writes: "The Irish poor did not starve because there was an inadequate supply of food within the country." She continues, "they starved because political, commercial and individual greed was given priority over the saving of lives in one part of the United Kingdom."[22] Years before the catastrophe, the political economist Thomas Malthus decreed the subaltern Irish a "redundant population" superfluous to the needs of the British colonial state in Ireland. Malthus urged that "to give the full effect to the natural resources of the country a great part of the population should be swept of its people."[23]

Irish persons who managed to sweep themselves, if you will—first to escape colonial Ireland, then to survive an often-brutal transatlantic crossing, and finally to land in the United States—saw their relationship to the state alter instantaneously. Instead of being superfluous to state needs, the Famine Irish became essential matériel for a state eager to boost its number of white citizenry. The anti-Catholicism of significant sections of the WASP elite, not to mention rampant poverty and disease in the urban slums of the Eastern Seaboard, did pose hindrances to Irish Famine immigrant assimilation. However, as I have discussed elsewhere, U.S. state apparatuses—for example, the Democratic Party, the Roman Catholic Church, local police and fire services, and state militias—facilitated the entry of Irish immigrants into the white settler colonial project. In short, legal and political needs prevailed over cultural and religious objections.[24] Such political and legal maneuvering paved the way for the construction of the Irish side of San Francisco's racial triangle, the focus of my study.

Western Expansion/Manifest Destiny

Malthus's insistence in imperial Britain that Ireland "should be swept of its people to give the full effect to the natural resources of the country" finds resonance in tenets of the American doctrine of Manifest Destiny. This doctrine—a postulation that U.S. state expansion and removal of indigenous peoples should occur by whatever means necessary—was an invention of an Irish American, John L. O'Sullivan, a journalist and editor whose father once prepared for the Catholic priesthood in his native Ireland.[25] As did Malthus with respect to Britain, O'Sullivan *fils* believed that U.S. state expansion was not only self-evident but also divinely inspired. Furthering this belief was a key moment in U.S. history, the 1848 discovery of gold in the Sierra Mountains of California. The ensuing Gold Rush gave promise for continental hegemony, a principal goal of Manifest Destiny. But prospects for untold wealth stoked rivalries that descended quickly into ethnicity-based differentiations. In no time, the Gold Rush became a focal point of militant nativism, and also served to change the dynamics of the Irish American encounter with race dramatically.[26] In 1850, legislators in the brand-new State of California reacted with patriotic vigor to the racial tension in the Sierras by imposing a tax on all "foreign-born" miners. Although the legislature intended the tax to harm miners from China, Mexico, and South America, the tax affected miners of Irish, English, German, and Canadian birth, too. The latter group objected violently to being lumped in with "non-white" miners, and in short order, California rewrote the law to exempt any "free white person."[27] Thus, by excluding Mexicans, South Americans, and Chinese persons as "non-white," Sierra gold confirmed Irish whiteness. Nevertheless, with a few notable exceptions, gold did not bestow on the Irish miner the moniker "wealthy"; as a result, great numbers of disillusioned and disgruntled Irish soon moved to stake their futures in the nearby city of San Francisco.[28]

Irish men, women, and children eager for a fresh start flocked to San Francisco from elsewhere as well—from as far away as Australia, and from Eastern cities such as New York, Philadelphia, Boston, and New Orleans.[29] In the 1850s and 1860s, most did not arrive directly from Ireland, but undertook arduous overland treks or months-long sea journeys from eastern U.S. cities where they had managed to save the funds necessary for the move. Although old anti-Irish prejudices accompanied them, many Irish tended to fare well in this western urban center that, unlike cities in the East, lacked an entrenched elite.[30] "Stabilized and experienced," Timothy Sarbaugh writes, "the Irish—numerous, urbanized immigrant families—competed well in an early San Francisco that was dominated by young and single males without urban experience."[31]

Protestant Brahmins long had considered California a battleground in the fight against the spread of Catholicism in America. But Roman Catholicism was both too well-established in the Golden State and pivotal to the establishment of California, a polity that Alexander Saxton labels the "White Republic."[32] In the early days of California, Anglo-American settlers grasped the need for white solidarity in the face of the sheer numbers of non-white persons. Thus they allied themselves first with the Spanish-speaking *Californios*, whose Christianity set them apart from other non-whites, particularly Native Americans, and later on with the Chinese as well. It did not hurt that in California's early days the Catholic Church hierarchy comprised bourgeois Iberians like Joseph Alemany, the first archbishop of San Francisco, whose erudition impressed his equally bourgeois Protestant neighbors.

Thus, upon arrival in San Francisco, in contrast to places like Boston, the Catholic Irish found a ready-built Church structure within which to nurture their faith and advance their material well-being. The Irish soon provided a steady stream of priests and nuns, not to mention stipend-paying parishioners. The wealthiest among the Irish—the Irish Four Silver Kings: John Mackay, James Flood, James Fair, and William O'Brien; Hibernia Bank founders John Sullivan, Richard Tobin, and Myles Sweeney; and the Donahue brothers, owners of iron foundries—gave generously to build Catholic churches, convents, and schools.[33] In no time, the sheer number of Irish wielded tremendous political power. Census figures show significant increases both in the total number of Irish and in the percentage of Irish in relation to all San Franciscans: the Irish contingent grew from 5,600 persons, or 15.5 percent, in 1852, to 30.5 percent of the population, or 45,875 persons, by 1870, the year following the completion of the transcontinental railroad (see table 1). That coast-to-coast innovation made travel to California much faster and more economical than sailing around Cape Horn, so that the following decade witnessed an influx of Irish people that would make "the group the largest of any in San Francisco."[34]

Religion has always played a central role in the contested interstices between state and culture in the U.S. racial state. As I argue in *Famine Irish and the American Racial State*, the nineteenth-century Irish Catholic immigrant, while qualified for white American citizenship, a legal category, had to earn his or her claim to white American nationality, a category that fell within the realm of the cultural imaginary.[35] Many WASP Americans regarded Catholicism as inimical to the ideals of American democracy, viewing it as ruled by an "alien" pope—himself the head of a foreign government, the Papal States—and bolstered by thoroughly anti-democratic Church structures. Despite the popular view that the struggle of the Catholic Church to prove its allegiance to the sovereignty of the United States occurred mainly in the cultural battlefields of the East Coast, nowhere was the nativist anti-Catholic viewpoint challenged more than in the State of California. This was true especially during the U.S. Civil War and its aftermath, Reconstruction. As Joshua Paddison suggests: "Reconstruction was a multiracial and multiregional process of national imagining. It ended not with the removal of federal troops from the South in 1877 but in a knitting together of North, South, and West around a newly robust white Christian identity during the course of the following decade."[36] Paddison sees California, a site often overlooked by historians of Reconstruction, as especially crucial to the construction of the "white Christian identity" that was forged out of the dehumanization and the figurative and literal erasure of Chinese migrants and California Indians. Both of the latter groups provided opportunities for Irish claims on American nationality; that said, in the contact zone of San Francisco, it was what popular culture then called the "Heathen Chinee" that offered greater opportunity for the Irish, and thus two sides of San Francisco's racial triangle formed, the Irish on one side and the Chinese on the other. This observation invites the positing of a simple binary between the Irish and the Chinese, without mention of Native Americans. It would be too simplistic, however. The perversity of racial hierarchization often challenges the construction of simple binaries, and this is especially true in the triangular San Francisco story that follows. A Catholic priest dubbed the "eloquent Indian" completes this particular racial geometric formation.

Eloquent Indian

The life of James Chrysostom Bouchard, SJ, "the first American Indian ordained to the Roman Catholic priesthood in the United States of America," in many ways epitomizes the convoluted nature of the nineteenth-century U.S. racial state in formation. The priest's very name, with its multiple variations, reflects the ever-shifting and contradictory terrain of American national identity: accounts refer to him as Beshor, Bucheur, Buchard, or Bouchard, all in addition to the name given him at the time of his birth in 1823. According to John Bernard McGloin, whose 1949 book *Eloquent Indian: The Life of James Bouchard, California Jesuit* remains the only full-length biography of this extraordinary pioneer. Father Bouchard was "born in a wigwam and named Watomika––the 'Swift-Footed One'––by his Delaware elders."[37] McGloin gleaned much information from an 1854 autobiographical essay that Father Bouchard penned, using the third person, as a gift to his Jesuit superior, Father Pierre-Jean De Smet. In 1989, *American Indian Quarterly* reprinted this autobiography along with Jay Miller's helpful introduction.[38] The work consists of three parts, with the first two concerning the priest's family history and his adventures among the "Delawares." Named by the British after the river that in turn was named after Lord Delaware (1577–1617), one of Virginia's English governors, the Delaware tribe's actual name is Lenni Lenape. The third part of the autobiography gives a somewhat dubious account of this tribe's religious practices. According to Miller, "The manuscript has far more literary than ethnographic interest; much of the information about Indian practices is generalized and some of it spurious. Nevertheless, it is one of the earliest autobiographies by someone acknowledged (during his own lifetime) to be a Native American."[39]

The following summarizes Bouchard's account of his origins.[40] His grandfather, a Frenchman named Bucheur, migrated to the Texas wilderness from Auvergne with his wife and young child, Louis. A second child, Marie-Elizabeth, was born there. After white men kill a Comanche hunting party, Comanche warriors seek revenge; unable to catch the responsible culprits, the warriors instead kill the parents of Marie-Elizabeth, then seven, and her brother. The Comanches adopt and raise the two orphans as their own. McGloin estimates Marie-Elizabeth's age as fifteen when she is betrothed to a Lenni Lenape chief, Kristalwa, or "He Who Walks the Mountain Path."[41] Marie-Elizabeth is given the name Monotawan, or "White Fawn," and eventually gives birth to the autobiography's author, Watomika, in Muskagola, in the Delaware Reserve, near Leavenworth, Kansas.

Raised in the spiritual and material traditions of the Lenni Lenape, Watomika, "the idol of his parents," is adept at hunting, brave in battle, and thoroughly inculcated in the religious practices of the Great Spirit. Yet sometime in his early teens, a Presbyterian minister, Mr. Williamson, persuades Watomika to accompany him and two other Lenni Lenapes to "Marietta College, Ohio, for the purpose of being instructed in the human Sciences and Christianity (for Watomika and his companions were still pagans)."[42] When his two companions decide to return home, Watomika stays behind, determined to learn more about Christianity. His autobiography does not detail his turn away from Presbyterianism, though it refers to previous correspondence he had with Father De Smet on the subject. De Smet recalled what he knew of Watomika's conversion to Catholicism in an 1855 letter to the Brussels-based Jesuit journal *Précis Historiques*. Apparently Watomika's hours of meditation and frequent fasting did not endear him to the Calvinists at Marietta College.

Despite seeds of doubt about his adopted religion, the young Lenni Lenape is unwavering in his desire to become a Presbyterian minister. Eventually successful in this quest, he is sent as a preacher to St. Louis. Passing a Catholic church during a stroll one day, his curiosity gets the better of him and he enters the chapel to find a catechism class in progress. It impresses him so much that he quits the Presbyterians and enrolls to become a Jesuit. At the time of writing his letter to the *Précis Historiques*, De Smet was able to report that "Watomika, a child of the forest, a worthy descendant of a powerful American race.... will soon receive Holy Orders."[43]

As Miller observes, "We know a great deal about Watomika's life after the period covered in his autobiography because he stepped firmly into the world of written documents."[44] It is recorded, for example, that he took a version of his mother's surname, Beshor, and was baptized as "James" on May 23, 1847. He chose the name "Chrysostom," in honor of Saint John Chrysostom, a renowned orator, at his confirmation. Following his ordination, he was assigned to Missouri and then to a series of locations––Kansas, Chicago, and Frederick, Maryland––before being sent to California, where he would make his name as one of the best-known orators of the American West.[45]

Father Bouchard and the Anti-Chinese Movement

By the 1870s, the Irish had risen to a dominant position within the political power structures of San Francisco—and with that power came resentment, particularly from nativist Protestants and fiercely anti-Catholic satirical magazines like the *Jolly Giant* and the *Wasp*. Such publications lampooned both Catholicism and the many Irish immigrants who packed Sunday Masses throughout the city. Coarse, simianized Irish men and beefy, masculinized Irish women adorned these magazines' pages with some frequency. As a result, while San Francisco's Irish Catholics could point with pride to their material and political successes, they still smarted from the sting of nativist ridicule that questioned their suitability for American citizenship. The Catholic Church not only offered spiritual guidance, but also provided a safe place for the Irish to gather in ethnic solidarity. The demand for priests who could relate to their needs and experiences thus became critical.

One of the San Francisco Catholic churches most popular among the Irish during the 1860s was St. Ignatius. The Italian Jesuits who founded the church realized soon enough that their English-speaking congregation struggled to understand their heavy accents, so that the arrival in 1861 of the American-born Father Bouchard seemed a divine intervention. Even better news for the Italians was that Bouchard happened to be a gifted practitioner of the rococo style of public speaking so admired in nineteenth-century San Francisco, a city where a talented sermonizer was treated as the equivalent of one of today's minor rock stars. Word of Bouchard's mellifluous oratory quickly spread, and soon he became one of California's most celebrated Catholic clergymen. Massive crowds turned up to hear him, so that at its height, St. Ignatius catered every Sunday to an estimated eight thousand Mass-goers. "Stirring oratory drew standing-room-only crowds of Protestants as well as Catholics eager to hear sermons of great length, which were reprinted in the city's newspapers."[46] Bouchard's fellow Jesuits were thrilled, as were his parishioners. "For three decades," writes Gerald McKevitt, "California audiences listened in open-mouth amazement to the eloquent Indian, who, according to contemporaries, charmed 'by the sound of his silvery voice, by the power of his nervous eloquence.' People were, an Italian priest said, 'wild to have a preacher like him'"[47] Indeed, the clamor to hear Bouchard speak extended far beyond San Francisco. "He became," as McGloin puts it, "the beloved evangelist of Mother Lode and Comstock Lode mining camps, a distinguished orator of the Golden City, and preacher in cathedrals and country churches of the Far West."[48]

The Irish were attracted to Father Bouchard for reasons beyond his flowery oratory. To begin with, since his sermons drew audience members from all religious denominations, the priest offered the Irish respectability by association—he was someone his Irish congregants could be proud of, someone whose Americanness made them feel American themselves. Bouchard also could articulate their grievances effectively and stand up for them in the public sphere, and for this reason he became an effective counter to nativist attack. When, from the 1860s onwards, the biggest grievance of San Francisco's Irish Catholics became the presence of the Chinese, Father Bouchard did not hesitate to take up the anti-Chinese cause.

The 1870 U.S. Census put the number of Irish in San Francisco at almost 46,000 persons, or around 30 percent of the total population, while the total for the Chinese amounted to about 12,000, or 8 percent (see table 1).

Despite this distinct statistical advantage, the Irish feared and loathed the Chinese. The Irish fear stemmed from the fact that they were being compared to

TABLE 1. Irish and Chinese Population in Late Nineteenth-Century San Francisco

YEAR	TOTAL POPULATION	IRISH (NUMBER)	IRISH (PERCENTAGE)	CHINESE (NUMBER)	CHINESE (PERCENTAGE)
1852	36,154	5,600	15.5	3,500	9.7
1860	56,082	9,363	16.5	2,719	4.8
1870	149,473	45,875	30.6	12,030	8.0
1880	233,959	78,421	33.5	21,790	9.3

Source: Peter D. O'Neill, *Famine Irish and the American Racial State* (New York: Routledge, 2017), 190.

the Chinese in nativist press, and the comparison was far from flattering. Thus, the Irish loathed the Chinese—and the loathing opened up a path that led to the sought-after cultural acceptability, to a place within the comforting embrace of American nationality.[49] It is little wonder that they would lead the way in the anti-Chinese movement in 1870s San Francisco, aided and abetted by the "eloquent Indian."

Another probable reason why Bouchard received the love of the San Francisco Irish was the fact that he felt at ease in their company, and they in his. Among his closest California friends were Irish-born men such as Eugene O'Connell, the first Roman Catholic bishop of Grass Valley–Nevada City, and Patrick Manogue, a Virginia City priest who eventually became the first bishop of Sacramento; and Irish-born women such as Mother Teresa Comerford and Mother Xavier Daly, both of whom belonged to the Sisters of the Presentation of the Blessed Virgin, an order founded in Cork in 1775, a county at the very heart of the Famine when the Choctaw sent monies in 1847.[50] Bouchard first preached at the Presentation Convent in October 1861, not long after he arrived in the city, and he maintained a close bond with the institution for the rest of his life.[51] In fact, it was while raising funds on behalf of the convent that the reverend father gave his most infamous speech, one that would prove an inspiration to organizers of the Workingmen's Party of California (WPC).[52] Furthermore, it would help solidify the tremulous structures of San Francisco's racial triangle.

Chinaman or White Man, Which?

In San Francisco on February 25, 1873, St. Francis of Assisi Church, the largest in the diocese, was packed to the gills for a charity event. The organizers hoped to raise funds for the schools attached to the Presentation Convent, which owed the city a considerable amount of back taxes. Fearful for their future, the Irish nuns of the Presentation had asked their friend and benefactor, Father Bouchard, to give one of his famous public lectures in the hope of attracting a large and generous crowd. The priest obliged Mother Comerford and her charges, giving his talk a title he knew would guarantee the nuns a packed house: "Chinaman or White Man, Which?"

Promoting the event was the *Monitor*, one of two Catholic publications in the city. An editorial stated: "The subject is an interesting one, and the well-known ability of the lecturer is a warrant that it will be well-handled. . . . If you want to be entertained, instructed, and pleased, go (Tickets, one dollar)."[53] Go they certainly did. The other Catholic paper, the *San Francisco Catholic Guardian*, noted that there was "neither sitting nor standing room left. Every space where a man could get was occupied." Mother Comerford reported with obvious delight that approximately $3,000 was raised, more than enough to cover the debt.[54]

By all accounts the Jesuit did not disappoint his overflowing audience. The following brief extracts are from a transcript of the speech recorded in the *Catholic Guardian*. Bouchard began his assault by proclaiming that the Chinese were taking jobs away from white people, and then he declared them unsuitable for American citizenship. The Chinese were "people of low intellect," Bouchard asserted, " . . . who are an idolatrous, vicious, corrupt and pusillanimous race that we are inviting to become residents among us. . . . These are a people whom, perhaps, we pay for coming to fill the purlieus of our cities with vice, with disease and death." By the end of the speech he was in full venomous flow. "It is the white race that we want. The white man, the head of all his kind in bone and muscle, in pluck and endurance, in intellect, a head and shoulder above all the other races; a man even in the natural order, more or less governed by sentiments of honor and the obligations of honesty and, in addition, more or less under the influence of a conscience trained under the influence of the principle of Christianity and controlled by Christian morality in his every day life."[55]

Bouchard finished his speech in a way that ensured that his Irish audience went home satisfied, their whiteness confirmed once again. "Allowing the Chinese to enter the USA," he intoned, "must drive away, or prevent from coming, a class of immigrants that would be a credit to the country, a benefit to the country, and would help to make this the greatest and grandest nation on the face of the earth."[56] Through the vilification of the Chinese, Father Bouchard had conjured their polar opposite, Irish immigrants, who were members of "the white race that we want." The nominative plural "we" in the previous sentence unifies Americanness and whiteness, the "eloquent Indian" and the Irish immigrant, to the exclusion of the racial other.

The nativist Protestant press soon responded, with the Presbyterians leading the charge. "Father Burchard a Romish priest of the Society of Jesuits, lately delivered an address before the Irish portion of our population, aimed against the Chinese," observed the March 6 edition of the San Francisco Presbyterian Church's weekly publication, *The Occident*, misspelling the Catholic priest's name. The *Occident* item continued: "The whole speech was calculated to arouse the indignation of the classes engaged in manual labor against the Chinese. We well recollect that when Irish laborers were introduced into America to dig canals, the same outcry was made. But the effect was to elevate these laborers in comforts and intelligence. We believe similar results will attend the introduction of the Chinese."[57] The Methodists joined the condemnation eight days later, in the form of a speech by the Reverend Otis Gibson. Later published as a thirty-page pamphlet, Gibson's speech excoriates "Buchard," the Jesuits, and Romanism, and puts forward a defense that contrasts paternalism for the Chinese with bile for the Catholic Irish. Gibson patently sees the Irish as a bigger threat to America than the Chinese. "Little by little," he maintains, "by fair means and by foul means, the memory of our own immortal Washington, and the principles which his name represents, are pushed aside, and the name of St. Patrick, and the institutions which that name suggests, are brought to the front. . . . St. Patrick is all very well, but for Americans I think Washington should be first, St. Patrick afterwards."[58] Gibson continues: "To the questions 'Chinaman or White man, which?' I understand Father Buchard to answer, the white man alone." He then points to a prominent anti-Chinese politician of the time, stating: "Hon. Frank Pixley answers, neither white nor Chinaman. America belongs to the Indian—the red man." Then Gibson offers his own view: "But according to the genius and spirit of our government and our national history, I stand here to answer thus: *The doors of our country are open equally for both. We have room for all. Ours is 'the land of the brave, and the home of the free.'*"[59] Gibson thus ends his screed by supposedly considering two answers to the original question posed by Bouchard. But in actual fact he considers only one. He ignores completely the claims of the "red man," choosing instead to refer to America as a land of the immigrant, whether of transpacific or transatlantic variety. In doing so, Gibson performs a rhetorical trick in his use of the concept of American "freedom"—a trick that would be repeated ad nauseam right up to the present day. As Lisa Lowe points out, "The affirmation of the desire for freedom is so inhabited by the forgetting of its condition of possibility that every narrative articulation of freedom is haunted by its burial, by the violence of forgetting."[60] American "freedom" can only be considered through the effacement of the indigenous peoples, not to mention the denial of African American humanity.

Diggers! California's Indigenous Peoples

Among those who have examined Father Bouchard's "Chinamen or White Men, Which?" speech is Paddison, who declares, using his own preferred spelling of the priest's name, "Buchard's former identity as a Delaware Indian further complicates the meaning of the speech."[61] That is an understatement. One can only imagine how Gibson would have responded if he had known that his Jesuit nemesis's birth name was not James Bouchard, but Watomika. The same might be asked of Bouchard's audience of Irish Catholic San Franciscans. How would they have responded to such information? Only a few of his fellow priests and closest confidants knew about Bouchard's background. His "physiognomy, education, and status as a Jesuit priest," Paddison points out, "afforded him the option of living as white, which he exercised to the point of appointing himself as protector of whiteness himself."[62] This protector-of-whiteness role cemented his relationship with his Irish Catholic devotees. By standing up for them with such oratorical flare, Bouchard offered the Irish respectability. His assertion of their whiteness made them feel American—as much as it did Bouchard himself. This is key, for when we add the indigenous peoples of California to this racial geometry, a new triangle emerges. The Chinese remain on one side, but the other two sides change. The California Indians form a new side, while a third side materializes consisting of the Lenni Lenape priest and his Irish Catholic flock, united in their mutually professed whiteness, and opposition to the other two sides of the triangle.

Paddison detects "a minor tradition of Indians in California objecting to the presence of the Chinese, just as Chinese community leaders tried to elevate themselves above Indians; this tradition dates from the 1850s, when conflicts between the two groups were common in mining areas." He gives a few examples of the animosity that existed between the two groups, citing, for example, the Nisenan Indian leader Weimah, who balked at being moved to a reservation on these grounds: "'The Indians are better than the Chinese, and you allow them to remain among you,' he reportedly said. 'Remove the Chinese first—then we will go.'" The priest thus may have been part of a tradition that enacted within Native Americans' feelings of superiority over the Chinese, but that would account for only a partial explanation of his position.[63]

"Denouncing the Chinese in the name of promoting the 'white race,'" Paddison argues, "was part of Buchards's [*sic*] process of distancing himself from his own past."[64] Perhaps. But while Bouchard did not advertise his Indian ancestry, he did not bury it, either. As his autobiographical writings show, he was, in fact, quite proud of his Native American past. Given his belief in the racial hierarchy of the U.S. racial state, however, it seems more than likely that he placed the Lenni Lenape, the tribe into which he was born on America's Great Plains, on a quite different level from California's indigenous peoples. It is crucial to remember that Bouchard was an Indian in California, not a Californian Indian. This distinction highlights another minor tradition of which Bouchard was surely part—the tradition by which people from eastern tribes looked down upon those from Californian tribes.[65] The latter were known by the derogatory name "Diggers." The term supposedly referred to the hunter-gatherer existence of most of California's indigenous peoples; however, the term's homophonous resemblance to a slur aimed at blacks no doubt was a source of endless amusement among the white settlers who coined it.

Bouchard's anti-Chinese sentiments can be understood as symptomatic of the hegemonic reach of racial state ideology. The same may be said about Bouchard's silence regarding both his Lenni Lenape origins and the mass murder of California's indigenous. As noted earlier, McGloin claimed that Bouchard "became the beloved evangelist of Mother Lode and Comstoke Lode mining camps."[66] Yet as recent works by Brendan Lindsay and Benjamin Madley demonstrate, around the same time that Bouchard was evangelizing in the Sierra foothills, miners from these very same localities formed vigilante groups responsible for some of the worst atrocities against indigenous peoples ever recorded.[67] To date, no writings or speeches by Bouchard condemning such actions have been uncovered. It is unlikely that a record of such writings or speeches exists, though. Bouchard, like many of his fellow Easterners, would have been at pains to distance himself from the lowly "Diggers."

The tradition of people from eastern indigenous tribes relegating California's indigenous peoples to inferior status has significant roots. One of the earliest examples of this bias may be found in the bestselling thriller *The Life and Adventures of Joaquin Murieta*. Its author, Yellow Bird, was better known by his Anglo name of John Rollin Ridge, the son of a wealthy and politically powerful Cherokee lawyer who signed the New Echota Treaty of 1835. That treaty agreed to the removal of the Cherokee from their ancestral lands in Georgia to the "Indian Territory" in Oklahoma, an eviction that would lead to the catastrophic "Trail of Tears."[68] Members of the rival Cherokee faction assassinated the father, and twelve-year-old John witnessed the fatal knife attack.[69]

Ridge and Bouchard shared other similarities besides their eastern tribal origins. Like Bouchard, Ridge's mother was white. Both men were able to pass as white themselves, and both benefited from a good education and a sharp intellect. Their reasons for moving to California, however, could not have been more different. Ridge murdered a rival from the same faction that had assassinated his father, and then fled west to escape reprisal.[70] He arrived in California in 1850, as the Gold Rush and the concomitant mass murder of California's Native tribes were well underway.

Turning from gold mining to writing, Ridge published *The Life and Adventures of Joaquin Murieta* in 1854. John Carlos Rowe describes the novel as being "organized around the myth of progressive individualism, a crucial part of the dominant cultural values in the United States in the 1850s."[71] The novel is also notable for its portrayal of sickening violence against Chinese miners, whose humanity is questioned throughout the narrative. According to Rowe, Ridge appears to use the Chinese "as subjects of the gang's worst violence, as if to indulge white readers' fantasies of punishing the alien Chinese."[72] He portrays the Chinese as lazy and primitive and mocks their customs and traditions, and by doing so, he emphasizes his own cultural sophistication, his own whiteness. By extension, when Father Bouchard professes his own whiteness and the whiteness of his Irish flock from the pulpit, he distances himself not only from the Chinese, but also, like his compatriot Ridge, from California's Native peoples.

The story of the "eloquent Indian" priest, his racist alliance with his Irish flock against the Chinese in nineteenth-century San Francisco, and by extension, the indigenous peoples of California, illustrates perfectly the inconsistencies, the fissures, the contradictions inherent in American racial politics. A product of the nineteenth-century American racial state in which success was measured according to one's place on the rungs of the racial ladder, this faulty triangular relationship reveals the instability of racial categories. It also illustrates the fluidity of racial identity in the nineteenth century. And though a tale from our Wild West past, increasingly it resonates in our alarming and precarious present.

As someone whose recent scholarship centers upon the nineteenth-century American racial state, I find the story of the Choctaw gift to the Irish in 1847 a heartwarming and hopeful contrast to the ugliness of that period. This is truly one of the great acts of solidarity to emerge from the Atlantic world. However, like our Wild West tale, it is as much a story of the present, and of the future, as it is of the past. Since its reemergence into Irish public consciousness in the 1990s, valiant efforts have been made to maintain Irish-Choctaw ties. The *Kindred Spirits* event mentioned at the beginning of this chapter is one; this very essay collection is another. Hopefully, more acts of solidarity are to come, and it is crucial that they do. Recent events have shown that neither white supremacy nor the ultranationalism that feeds on it are going away any time soon. They are clear and present dangers to us all. Only acts of solidarity such as those described in this volume can defeat these racist cancers, but to succeed, we must be fully aware of the nature of the disease that confronts us. As we go forward, then, let us not forget the uglier truths that history teaches us. Let us remember those stories, whether from Ireland or America, that make us uncomfortable, as well as those that offer us hope.

NOTES

1. These lines are quoted from an excerpt of *Topographia Hiberniae* found in Deane 1:239. See Giraldus Cambrensis, "Topographia Hiberniae" (An excerpt), in *The Field Day Anthology of Irish Writing*, ed. Seamus Deane (Derry: Field Day, 1991), 1:238–40.

2. See for example Nicolas P. Canny, "The Ideology of English Colonization: From Ireland to America," *William and Mary Quarterly*, 3rd series, vol. 30, no. 4 (October 1973): 573–98; Ronald Takaki, *A Different Mirror: A History of Multicultural America* (New York: Little, Brown & Co., 1993).

3. See Peter D. O'Neill, "Memory and John Mitchel's Appropriation of the Slave Narrative," *Atlantic Studies: Global Currents* 11, no. 3 (Fall 2014): 321–43.

4. Mary L. Mullen, "How the Irish Became Settlers: Metaphors of Indigeneity and the Erasure of Indigenous Peoples," *New Hibernia Review/Iris Éireannach Nua* 20, no. 3 (Fómhar/Autumn 2016): 81–96, 84.

5. For a sustained analysis of the U.S. racial state and the position to the Famine Irish within

it, see Peter D. O'Neill, *Famine Irish and the American Racial State* (New York: Routledge, 2017).

6. Ibid., 84.

7. Charles Fanning, *The Irish Voice in America: 250 Years of Irish-American Fiction*, 2nd ed. (Lexington: University Press of Kentucky, 2000), 88–89.

8. For a fascinating comparative study of nineteenth-century state educational policies in the U.S. and Ireland aimed at suppressing indigenous language, religion, and politics, see Michael C. Coleman, *American Indians, the Irish, and Government Schooling: A Comparative Study* (Lincoln: University of Nebraska Press, 2007).

9. Marvin R. O'Connell, *John Ireland and the American Catholic Church* (St. Paul: Minnesota Historical Society Press, 1988), 144.

10. Susannah J. Ural, *The Harp and the Eagle: Irish-American Volunteers and the Union Army, 1861–1865* (New York: New York University Press, 2006), 37.

11. Thomas J. Craughwell, *The Greatest Brigade: How the Irish Brigade Cleared the Way to Victory in the American Civil War* (New York: Crestline, 2011), 11.

12. Michael Omi and Howard Winant, *Racial Formation in the United States: From the 1960s to the 1990s*, 2nd ed. (New York: Routledge, 1994), 82.

13. David Theo Goldberg, *The Racial State* (Oxford: Blackwell, 2002), 4.

14. John Carlos Rowe, *Literary Culture and U.S. Imperialism: From the Revolution to World War II* (New York: Oxford University Press, 2000), 16, 26.

15. For a useful analysis of the act, see Joanne B. Freeman, "Explaining the Unexplainable: The Cultural Context of the Sedition Act," in *The Democratic Experiment: New Directions in American Political History* (Princeton, NJ: Princeton University Press, 2003), 20–49.

16. Kerby A. Miller, *Emigrants and Exiles: Ireland and the Irish Exodus to North America* (New York: Oxford University Press, 1988).

17. Ibid., 291.

18. Kevin Kenny, *The American Irish: A History* (New York: Pearson, 2000), 89.

19. For an excellent account of how the Famine is remembered in nineteenth-century Irish and Irish diasporic fiction, see Marguérite Corporaal, *Relocated Memories: The Great Famine in Irish and Diasporic Fiction, 1846–1870* (Syracuse, NY: Syracuse University Press, 2017).

20. Breandán Mac Suibhne, *The End of Outrage: Post-Famine Adjustments in Rural Ireland* (Oxford: Oxford University Press, 2017), 18.

21. See monographs by Christine Kinealy, *The Great Irish Famine: Impact, Ideology and Rebellion* (Basingstoke, UK: Palgrave Macmillan, 2002); David Nally, *Human Encumbrances: Political Violence and the Great Irish Famine* (Notre Dame, IN: University

of Notre Dame Press, 2011); Enda Delaney, *The Curse of Reason: The Great Irish Famine* (Dublin: Gill & Macmillan, 2012); Ciarán Ó Murchada, *The Great Famine: Ireland's Agony* (London: Continuum, 2011); and John Kelly, *The Graves Are Walking: The Great Famine and the Saga of the Irish People* (New York: Henry Holt, 2012); as well as *Atlas of the Great Irish Famine*, a compendium of essays edited by John Crowley, Willie Smyth, and Mike Murphy (New York: New York University Press, 2012).

22. Crowley, Smyth, and Murphy, eds., *Atlas of the Great Irish Famine*, 90–91.

23. Quoted in Joel Mokyr, *Why Ireland Starved: A Quantitative and Analytical History of the Irish Economy, 1800–1850* (London: Allen & Unwin, 1983), 38.

24. For a thorough analysis of the role of the state in the Americanization of the Irish, see O'Neill, *Famine Irish*.

25. In 1839 O'Sullivan wrote of Manifest Destiny: "In its magnificent domain of space and time, the nation of many nations is *destined to manifest* to mankind the excellence of divine principles; to establish on earth the noblest temple ever dedicated to the worship of the Most High—the Sacred and the True." John L. O'Sullivan [unsigned editorial], "The Great Nation of Futurity," *United States Democratic Review* 6, no. 23 (November 1839): 426–30, 427 [my emphasis], http://digital.library.cornell.edu. Also see Robert Sampson, *John L. O'Sullivan and His Times* (Kent, OH: Kent State University Press, 2003), 1–3.

26. Takaki, *Different Mirror*.

27. Jean Pfaelzer, *Driven Out: The Forgotten War against Chinese Americans* (New York: Random House, 2007), 22.

28. J. M. Guinn, D. E. Appleton, and J. Sweet Robinson, "Songs from a California Songster," *Annual Publication of the Historical Society of Southern California* 7, nos. 2–3 (1907–8): 207–15, 213.

29. For more on Irish migrants to California from Australia during the Gold Rush era, see Malcolm Campbell, "Ireland's Furthest Shores: Irish Immigrant Settlement in Nineteenth-Century California and Eastern Australia," *Pacific Historical Review* 71, no. 1 (February 2002): 59–90.

30. See Kevin Starr, *Americans and the California Dream, 1850–1915* (Oxford: Oxford University Press, 1996), 94.

31. Timothy Sarbaugh, "Exiles of Confidence: The Irish-American Community of San Francisco, 1880 to 1920," in *From Paddy to Studs: Irish-American Communities in the Turn of the Century Era, 1880 to 1920*, ed. Timothy J. Meagher (Westport, CT: Greenwood Press, 1986), 161–79, 163. See also James P. Walsh, "The Irish in Early San Francisco," in *The San Francisco Irish*, ed. James P. Walsh (San Francisco: Irish Literary and Historical Society, 1978), 9–25.

32. Starr, *Americans and the California Dream*, 93. This term was coined by Alexander Saxton to describe the establishment of the State of California. See *The Rise and Fall of the White Republic: Class Politics and Mass Culture in Nineteenth Century America* (1990; London: Verso, 2003).

33. See R. A. Burchell, *The San Francisco Irish, 1848–1880* (Berkeley: University of California Press, 1980), 9–11.

34. Ibid., 4.

35. See O'Neill, *Famine Irish*, "Introduction." For more on the nineteenth-century U.S. cultural imaginary, see ibid., chap. 5.

36. Joshua Paddison, *American Heathens: Religion, Race, and Reconstruction in California* (Berkeley: University of California Press, 2012), 5.

37. John Bernard McGloin, *Eloquent Indian: The Life of James Bouchard, California Jesuit* (Stanford, CA: Stanford University Press, 1949), 35, 51 n. 21.

38. Bouchard's accounts may be found in several other sources, including Pierre-Jean De Smet, *Western Missions and Missionaries: A Series of Letters* (New York: J. B. Kirker, 1863).

39. Jay Miller, "The Early Years of Watomika (James Bouchard): Delaware and Jesuit," *American Indian Quarterly* 13, no. 2 (Spring 1989): 165–88, 165.

40. See James Chrysostom Bouchard, "Biographical Sketch Watomika," *American Indian Quarterly* 13, no. 2 (Spring 1989): 172–75. See also McGloin, *Eloquent Indian*, chap. 4.

41. McGloin, *Eloquent Indian*, 40.

42. Ibid., 175, 184.

43. De Smet, *Western Missions and Missionaries*, 218–20.

44. Miller, "The Early Years of Watomika (James Bouchard)," 166.

45. Ibid., 180, 166.

46. Gerald S. J. McKevitt, *Brokers of Culture: Italian Jesuits in the American West, 1848–1919* (Stanford, CA: Stanford University Press, 2007), 245.

47. Ibid.

48. McGloin, *Eloquent Indian*, 35.

49. See O'Neill, *Famine Irish*, chaps. 5 and 6.

50. McGloin, *Eloquent Indian*, 197, 292–93.

51. Ibid., 105.

52. The WPC came to power in 1877 following a series of anti-Chinese meetings held in the sandlots beside San Francisco City Hall. Research has shown that a high percentage of party membership was either Irish-born or of Irish descent. The same was true for most of the party leaders, including the infamous demagogue Cork-born Denis Kearney, the party's most nationally recognized leader. A skilled orator, Kearney made a habit of

ending all of his speeches with the words "The Chinese Must Go!" For more on the Irish involvement in the WPC, see Neal Larry Shumsky, *The Evolution of Political Protest and the Workingmen's Party of California* (Columbus: Ohio State University Press, 1991). See also Burchell, *The San Francisco Irish*; Alexander Saxton, *The Indispensable Enemy: Labor and the Anti-Chinese Movement in California* (Berkeley: University of California Press, 1971).

53. Quoted in McGloin, *Eloquent Indian*, 177 (original punctuation).
54. Ibid., 178.
55. Quoted in McGloin, *Eloquent Indian*, 179–80.
56. Ibid., 180.
57. Ibid., 180.
58. Otis Gibson, *"Chinaman or White Man, Which?": Reply to Father Buchard* (San Francisco: Alta California Printing Press, 1873), 16.
59. Ibid., 30 (original italics and punctuation).
60. Lisa Lowe, "The Intimacies of Four Continents," in *Haunted by Empire: Geographies of Intimacy in North American History*, ed. Ann Laura Stoler (Durham, NC: Duke University Press, 2006), 191–212, 206.
61. Paddison, *American Heathens*, 86.
62. Ibid., 87.
63. Ibid., 87.
64. Ibid., 86–87.
65. See Rowe, *Literary Culture and U.S. Imperialism*, 114–15.
66. McGloin, *Eloquent Indian*, 35.
67. See Brendan C. Lindsay, *Murder State: California's Native American Genocide, 1846–1873* (Lincoln: University of Nebraska Press, 2012); and Benjamin Madley, *An American Genocide: The United States and the California Indian Catastrophe* (New Haven, CT: Yale University Press, 2016).
68. Rowe, *Literary Culture and U.S. Imperialism*, 101.
69. Although the California tribes were targets of Ridge's utter disdain in *Joaquin*, Alanna Hickey notes that his poetry and journalism "frequently addressed the plight of the 'Digger' Indians." Alanna Hickey, "'Let Paler Nations Vaunt Themselves': John Rollin Ridge's 'Official Verse' and Racial Citizenship in Gold Rush California," *Studies in American Indian Literatures* 27, no. 4 (Winter 2015): 66–100, 67.
70. Ibid., 102.
71. Rowe, *Literary Culture and U.S. Imperialism*, 98. Mark Rifkin disagrees with Rowe's assessment "that Ridge's endorsement of capitalism is the equivalent to a desire for assimilation to the U.S." See Rifkin, "'For the Wrongs of Our Poor Bleeding Country':

Sensation, Class, and Empire in Ridge's *Joaquín Murieta*," *Arizona Quarterly* 65, no. 2 (Summer 2009): 43. In Rifkin's view, the novel can be interpreted "as part of an elitist critique of U.S. expansion" (44).

72. Rowe, *Literary Culture and U.S. Imperialism*, 114.

Listen: Still, the Echo

Doireann Ní Ghríofa

Of Loss. Sing again
Of how, in our hunger, our land
produced food in abundance.
Sing, now, of how it was denied to us,
how it moved, instead, over waves
to English mouths.

Inis dúinn go bplúchann ocras focail, nach gcothaíonn ocras ach tost.

Tell us once more
how hunger suckles only silence,
how hunger fills a mouth,
until only silence comes out.

Sa tréimhse úd, bhí Teanga ar cheann de na príomhearraí a tógadh uainn
le hiompar thar lear.

Sing. Tell us again. Remind us

how many tonnes of grain they chose to export,
how much beef, how much pork. Tell us
how among their biggest exports
from our land was Tongue.
Stand up. Sing. Tell us.

Postcards from Moundville

Phillip Carroll Morgan

Should I call all my Indian friends,
start a Movement to fill
this archaeological park campground
year round with Indians?

Or should I keep it all for myself,
like the Euroamericans,
become an expert,
pitch little canvas tents,
dig up and play with choice pieces of it
whenever I want?

In the shade
of a massive oak tree
I sit and write
having pitched my tent
in this ancient Mississippian
city of our foremothers,

Tamaha Minko Tushka Lusa,
the City of the Black Warrior King.

Within the plaza formed by an oval-shaped
two-mile cluster of platform mound earthworks
stands the umbrella oak six feet in diameter,
twenty in circumference, eighty tall,
immense branches a foot thick
extending sixty feet horizontally
from her trunk. She gathers me
like a hawk her tierce
under outstretched wings.

I am the Irishman returned to Ireland
generations after the Famine.
I am the Syrian refugee returned to Damascus
to rebuild his shattered home.
I am the Mayan woman
returned to the Guatemalan highlands

after decades of fighting.
I am Choctaw, returned to the ancient city
and capital of my ancestors, the Imoklasha,
on the Black Warrior River.
I am every man and every woman
who has been expelled or exiled
from their home
and returned.

Contributors

Doireann Ní Ghríofa writes both prose and poetry, in both Irish and English. Her books explore birth, death, desire, and domesticity. Awards for her writing include a Lannan Literary Fellowship (USA, 2018), a Seamus Heaney Fellowship (Queen's University, 2018), the Ostana Prize (Italy, 2018), and the Rooney Prize for Irish Literature (Trinity College, 2016), among others. Doireann's artistic practice encompasses cross-disciplinary collaborations, fusing poetry with film, dance, music, and visual art, and she has been invited to perform her work internationally, most recently in Scotland, Paris, Italy, and New Zealand. Her work has been commissioned by the Poetry Society (Britain), Poetry Ireland, the Embassy of Ireland in Britain, and the Department of Foreign Affairs, and she was recently elected to Aosdána.

LeAnne Howe, born and raised in Oklahoma, is an enrolled citizen of the Choctaw Nation. Some of her awards include the Western Literature Association's 2015 Distinguished Achievement Award for her body of work, the inaugural 2014 MLA Prize for Studies in Native American Literatures, a 2012 United States Artists Ford Fellowship, and a 2010 Fulbright Scholarship to Jordan. She received the American Book Award in 2002 for her first novel, *Shell Shaker*. Her most recent book, *Savage Conversations* (2019), is the story of Mary Todd Lincoln and a "Savage Indian" spirit that she invented who tortures her nightly. The book is based on Mary's letters and reports from her doctors. Scholar Philip J. Deloria writes, "[The book] explodes with the stench and guilt and insanity that undergirds the American story." LeAnne is co-producing a new documentary, *Searching for Sequoyah*, with Ojibwe filmmaker James M. Fortier. The film is set in the United States and Mexico and aired in 2021. Howe is the Eidson Distinguished Professor of American Literature in English at the University of Georgia.

Christine Kinealy completed her PhD at Trinity College in Ireland and has worked in educational and research institutes in Ireland, England, and more recently in the United States. In September 2013, Kinealy was appointed the founding director of Ireland's Great Hunger Institute at Quinnipiac University in Connecticut. She has published extensively on modern Ireland, with a focus on the Great Hunger. Her publications include *This Great Calamity: The Irish Famine, 1845–52*, and *Charity and the Great Hunger in Ireland: The Kindness of Strangers*. Her latest research has focused on the abolition movement in Ireland, leading to the recently published *Frederick Douglass and Ireland: In His Own Words*. In 2017, Kinealy won an Emmy for her contribution to the documentary *Ireland's Great Hunger and the Irish Diaspora*.

Padraig Kirwan is senior lecturer in the Department of English and Comparative Literature, Goldsmiths, University of London. His first book was *Sovereign Stories: Aesthetics, Autonomy and Contemporary Native American Writing* (2013). He coedited *Affecting Irishness* (2009). He has published essays in *Novel, Comparative Literature, the Journal of American Studies*, and the *Times Higher Education* magazine. Padraig is currently writing a monograph titled *Unsettling Irishness: American Culture and Contemporary Irish Fiction*. In 2018 he co-organized the thirty-eighth meeting of the American Indian Workshop at Goldsmiths with Stirrup (University of Kent).

Phillip Carroll Morgan is a Choctaw/Chickasaw poet, a painter, a songwriter, biographer, historian, literary critic, and novelist. Four of the six books he has authored or coauthored since 2006 have won regional, national, or international awards. White Dog Press published in 2014 his novel *Anompolichi the Wordmaster*, a story set in 1399 in the pre-American Southeast. White Dog plans to publish in 2020 the sequel novel, *Anompolichi the Riverines*. The University of Nebraska Press published in 2016 his essay critiquing Choctaw intellectual James L. McDonald's 1831 manuscripts in *A Listening Wind: Native Literature from the Southeast*. Morgan lives with his family in the Chickasaw Nation near Blanchard, Oklahoma, and pursues the business of agroforestry on Morgan's Mulberry Grove Farm, his father's Indian allotment farm, under deed to the Morgan family for 114 years, since 1906, the year before Oklahoma statehood.

Peter D. O'Neill is an associate professor in the Comparative Literature Department at the University of Georgia, where he has served as a research fellow at UGA's Will-son Center for Humanities and Arts and as a Lilly Teaching Fellow. With David Lloyd, he coedited the essay collection *The Black and Green Atlantic: Crosscurrents of the African and Irish Diasporas* (2009), while a paperback edition of his award-winning book *Famine Irish and the American Racial State* was published in 2019. Currently, he is working on two projects: one is a cultural history of white nationalism and Irish America; the other, a biography of Irish American writer Dillon O'Brien.

Jacki Thompson Rand, citizen of the Choctaw Nation of Oklahoma, is an associate professor of history at the University of Iowa. She coordinates the Native American and Indigenous Studies Program. Rand is using her latest sabbatical to complete a manuscript that examines a tribe's self-determinative evolution in the second half of the twentieth century, asking questions about the consideration of women's conditions and issues during the turn to tribal government reorganization. She is also working on "Indigenous Midwest," an enduring digital project on the post-Removal indigenous presence in an overlooked region.

Tim Tingle is a member of the Choctaw Nation of Oklahoma. He's a world-traveling storyteller and the author of twenty books. Tingle's first children's book, *Crossing Bok Chitto*, was an Editor's Choice in the *New York Times* and won numerous state and national awards. *Walking the Choctaw Road* is a collection of tribal stories covering almost two centuries, including the "Trail of Tears" story that inspired Tingle's *How I Became a Ghost* series. Told in the voice of a ten-year-old Choctaw boy who dies on the Trail, the series shares many unspoken truths regarding the death and suffering on the Trail. Following an appearance at the 2013 Cape Clear Storytelling Festival, Tingle toured Ireland seeking information on the Famine. Through interviews and research, Tingle discovered alarming similarities between the Choctaw Trail of Tears and the Irish Famine, and is honored to share these findings in this important collection of essays.

Eamonn Wall is a professor of international studies and English at the University of Missouri-St. Louis. His books include *From Oven Lane to Sun Prairie: In Search of Irish America* (2019) and *Writing the Irish West: Ecologies and Traditions* (2011). *Junction City: New and Selected Poems, 1990–2015* was published in 2015. He is a past president of the American Conference for Irish Studies and currently serves as a vice president of Irish American Writers & Artists, Inc.

Permissions

Cover image includes a photograph of a famine pot taken at the National Famine Museum at Strokestown Park © 2019 Eunan Sweeney.

Photograph of the Choctaw delegation at Aras an Uachtaráin was provided by Deirdre Nally and courtesy of Aras an Uachtaráin.

Photograph of Alex Pentek's sculpture 'Kindred Spirits' was taken by Gavin Sheridan © Gavin Sheridan (@gavinsblog).

Pictures of Famine pots courtesy of Eleanor Hooker, Mark McGowan and John McManus.

Original poetry by Doireann Ní Ghríofa is published here with the permission of the author.

"Choctaw Corn Soup." Courtesy of Choctaw author Ian Thompson.

Index